At the Hinge of History

The University of Georgia Press   Athens and London

AT THE HINGE OF HISTORY

A Reporter's Story

JOSEPH C. HARSCH

Published by the
University of Georgia Press
Athens, Georgia 30602
© 1993 by Joseph C. Harsch
All rights reserved

Designed by Richard Hendel
Set in Bembo and Gill types
by Tseng Information Systems, Inc.
Printed and bound by Braun-Brumfield

The paper in this book meets
the guidelines for permanence and
durability of the Committee on
Production Guidelines for Book
Longevity of the Council on
Library Resources.

Printed in the United States
of America

Frontispiece: JCH in front of the
palace where U.S.-Chinese talks
started, Warsaw, 1967. Photo by
Judith Friedberg.

Library of Congress
Cataloging in Publication Data
Harsch, Joseph C. (Joseph Close), 1905–
At the hinge of history : a reporter's story /
Joseph C. Harsch.
    p.   cm.
Includes bibliographical references and index.
ISBN 0-8203-1515-X (alk. paper)
1. Harsch, Joseph C. (Joseph Close), 1905–
2. Journalists—United States—20th
century—Biography.   3. Television
broadcasting of news—United States.
4. Reporters and reporting—United States.
5. World War, 1939–1945.   I. Title.
PN4874.H37A3   1993
070'.92—dc20
[B]   92-28625

British Library Cataloging in Publication Data
available

97 96 95 94 93   C   5   4   3   2   1

To

Helene Morse Tidd

Amelia Belle Young

Edna Raemer

Contents

Foreword
Joseph Fromm

Among those of us who have devoted our careers to international journalism, Joe Harsch occupies a unique position. No other American journalist has covered so much history-in-the-making or performed the task with greater analytical acumen, intelligence, and vision.

As becomes a great reporter, he has managed to be at the right place at the right time for sixty years. From the rise of Japanese militarism and European fascism in the 1930s to the collapse of the Soviet empire, the disintegration of the Soviet Union, and the demise of world communism in the 1990s, Harsch has been at ringside to chronicle the seminal events.

In 1931, as a young reporter for the *Christian Science Monitor* in Washington covering the Hoover administration, he reported on the milestone event that opened the floodgates to Japanese imperialism—the refusal of President Hoover to join Britain in a military demonstration to challenge Japan's invasion of Manchuria. Four years later, in 1935, Harsch was on hand for the inevitable sequel—the Japanese walkout from the London Naval Conference, which marked a reversal of alliances for Tokyo and the collapse of the post–World War I international system. Hitler's repudiation of the military constraints of the Versailles treaty and his invasion of the Rhineland, the first step in his conquest of Europe, quickly followed.

Harsch was again there in London on September 3, 1939, when Prime Minister Neville Chamberlain declared war on Germany following Hitler's invasion of Poland. And he ended up shortly thereafter in Berlin, the first correspondent to cover both sides in World War II. He was there, too, at Pearl Harbor when the Japanese struck on December 7, 1941. His presence was a matter of sheer luck. He was on his way to Moscow for the *Christian Science Monitor* by way of Japan and China and had stopped in Honolulu to spend a few days on holiday with his wife, Anne, before a long separation. As the only experienced war correspondent on the scene, he gained an extraordinary insight into the unpreparedness of

American military forces for war. Twenty-four hours before the attack he was assured by Adm. Husband E. Kimmell in an interview that a Japanese war against the United States was not in the cards. And even as the bombs were falling on Pearl Harbor, Harsch was having breakfast in a beachside hotel dining room crowded with naval officers in their dress whites, preparing for a quiet Sunday and totally oblivious to the danger.

In the post–World War II era, both as a radio and television commentator and as a columnist for the *Christian Science Monitor*, Harsch continued his role as a scholarly chronicler of history-in-the-making. From bases in Washington, Europe, and eventually Boston, he reported on the formulation of an American strategy to contain Soviet imperialism and communism and to rehabilitate war-ravaged Western Europe and Japan, and on the success of that strategy in a forty-year confrontation with Moscow—a success that ultimately culminated in the retreat of the Soviets from their East European empire and the utter failure of the Communist experiment in the late 1980s and early 1990s.

Being at the right place at the right time over a sixty-year career is by no means the only or, indeed, the most important quality that accounts for Joe Harsch's unique status in international reporting. Even more important is a special skill that he brings to his work in this era of breathless and often superficial "parachute journalism." That skill is his constant striving not simply to report and analyze the news intelligently, but to put today's events into historic perspective. He prepared himself for the role as a young man by his concentration on the study of history at Williams College and during a two-year stint at Cambridge University. And he remains today an avid student of history.

This preoccupation with the sweep of history is reflected in his prophetic analysis of a number of the watershed events of the past half century. In March 1941, as he weighed Hitler's expansionist rampage in the context of Germany's historic ambitions toward the East, he warned of a German attack on the Soviet Union, which came three months later and surprised the world. In 1949, after a reporting trip through Eastern Europe, he wrote a book entitled *The Curtain Isn't Iron*, which demonstrated that the iron curtain could be breached and provided the backdrop for its collapse forty years later. And in the 1950s, impressed by a long history of Chinese-Russian rivalry, he predicted an inevitable break between China and the Soviet Union some ten years before the actual rupture occurred.

Harsch's professional style is as unusual as his historical approach to the news. In his quest for information and insights, he employs good-natured shock tactics, what one of his editors described with the French expression *pour épater les bourgeois* (to shock the conventional). I experienced this regularly during the years that Harsch phoned me and a few other professional friends from Boston on Sunday afternoons to discuss ideas for his columns in the week ahead. He usually opened the conversation by posing a slightly outrageous question about an event in the news to provoke instantly a lively and uninhibited exchange. His purpose was to jolt us out of our mental ruts of conventional thinking in order to help him test unconventional ideas. He employs the same unorthodox tactic in dealing with political luminaries. In the years that we worked together in London, I recall our meetings with the leading figures in British politics—Prime Minister Harold Macmillan, Prime Minister Harold Wilson, and Labor party leader Hugh Gaitskill to name a few—in which Harsch got their full attention, and respect, immediately with one of his slightly outrageous and exceedingly perceptive questions.

To concentrate exclusively on Joe Harsch's journalistic career would present a distorted picture. Those of us who have known him for many years as a colleague as well as a friend value his human qualities no less than his impressive professional achievements. Whether delivering a running commentary during a tour of a castle outside Avignon or dining in a London club or plotting a press club coup, he displays an unfaltering zest for life and a sense of fun. The intensity of his interest and energy is undiminished after sixty years and more of labor in the vineyards of international journalism.

At his eightieth birthday celebration, I found Harsch with one arm heavily swathed in bandages. He laughingly informed me that a few hours earlier he had fallen from a tree while trimming a branch with a chain saw. In his eighty-fifth year we celebrated by spending the day sailing in Narragansett Bay in his twenty-two-foot sloop under his command. Joe Harsch may not have discovered the Fountain of Youth, but he certainly has found a reasonable facsimile.

Few journalists have contributed so much to their profession—or to the pleasure of their friends and colleagues.

Preface

It has been noted, correctly, that Julius Caesar would be able to adjust fairly easily to the world of George Washington but that the two of them would have a difficult time fitting into the world of George Bush and Mikhail Gorbachev.

The world is constantly changing. The pace of change has been remarkably fast of late. Seldom, if ever, has it changed as much in one century as during this present one. I was born into this century of unusual change near its beginning, on May 25, 1905. I am writing this in sight of its conclusion. It seems appropriate at this time to review the main events through which I have lived, in which I have frequently had a part, and many of which I have helped to chronicle as a journalist. My hope is that by so doing I will be able to help to identify and to explain for the benefit of the next generation two enormous world wars, the second stemming inevitably out of the first and followed by a power rivalry which lasted for forty years involving two vicious local wars (Korea and Vietnam) and numerous lesser civil wars (Angola, Ethiopia, El Salvador, Nicaragua), all this accompanied by radical transformation of the surroundings of daily human life.

Jules Verne, writing a century ago, was a man of vivid imagination. He conceived of submarines and airships. But most of the things which are common in our routine lives today—radio, television, traffic jams, microwave ovens—were unconceived, hence inconceivable, even to a Jules Verne.

Let me begin with something of the flavor of daily life in midwest America (Toledo, Ohio) at the beginning of this century. My early memory is filled with horses. Our milk arrived every morning behind a horse. The iceman's wagon was pulled by a horse. The groceries were delivered behind a horse. True, steam power had taken over important functions. It pulled trains. It powered steam shovels and steam threshing machines.

But the steam shovel emptied its earth into horse-drawn wagons, the thresher emptied its grain into "box wagons" pulled by horses, and the buses which took passengers from the railway depot to their hotels were drawn by horses. The horse was still the prime provider of energy. And, incidentally, the horse pulled wheels in summer, but sleds in winter. With the first lasting snow, wagons and carriages shed their wheels and took on runners. Streets were cleared of snow by the spring thaw, not by plows. We shoveled our sidewalks in Toledo, Ohio, but the streets kept their snow and the wagons kept their runners right through the winter.

Next, let us consider the world of the great-power states within which this simpler, slower, horse-drawn life existed.

When the twentieth century opened, Britain was the greatest single power. Britannia's warships did indeed "rule the waves." Western Europe was the power center of the earth. Ethiopia was the only independent country in Africa. Japan, Thailand, and Tibet were the only independent countries in Asia. The rest of Africa and Asia belonged to one or another European empire—more to the British than to any other one. Much of the Americas were nominally independent, but not even the United States thought of itself in those days as one of the "great powers." Germany, Austria-Hungary, France, and Russia were the great land powers. True, in 1905 Japan dealt a sharp local defeat to the Russians at sea in the Tsushima strait and on land in Manchuria, but Japan was still a second-level power.

Between then and now there have been two tremendous wars called world wars, which in fact were largely fought in Europe between European powers, with the net effect of destroying Europe as the center of the world and clearing the way for a brief era during which history was dominated by the United States and a Russia that by then was calling itself the Soviet Union. That era in turn has now given way to a new situation in which Japan is the richest financial power, able to provide more economic aid to others than can the United States, and in which Western Europe is coalescing into a new economic entity that may well mature into the dominant world power, regaining for the heirs of the ancient Roman Empire the dominant position they have held through much of history.

But that lies ahead. As of today, we are at the end of an era that began a hundred years ago with Britain bestriding the earth. To understand what has happened during the intervening years there is one essential set of facts to keep in mind. Industrial power is the foundation of military power. In 1875 the United Kingdom of Great Britain and Northern Ireland produced 7.1 million tons of steel. This was nearly half of the total world production of steel. It built the ships and the guns that were the sinews of the vast British Empire. British steel production continued to grow. By 1900 it had reached 100 million tons. But by 1900 U.S. steel production had reached 115 million tons. Both Germany and France passed Britain in steel production in 1921. The Soviet Union went ahead in 1931 and Japan in 1954. Between 1875 and 1954 Britain slipped from being the world's first industrial power, by a wide margin of superiority, to being only the sixth.

When I was born in 1905 and the pace of daily life was still set by the horse, Britain was still seen as the supreme power. My mother recalled that when Queen Victoria died, in 1901, the main street of Bellevue, Ohio, where she lived then, was draped in black from end to end in mourning for Britain's queen-empress. That happened on Fifth Avenue in New York as well.

It was a different world.

Acknowledgments

My journalistic career has been supported by a happy succession of assistants, three of whom are dedicatees of this book. They had one thing in common. They all emerged from American liberal arts colleges (the first two from Washburn College in Topeka, Kansas, the third from Emerson College in Boston) able to think clearly, fairly, and without prejudice. They did much of my research, edited my copy, saved me hours of reading. Above all, they made me think through my news judgments fairly and objectively. My experience with the three has given me the highest respect for the education system that shaped their minds. Insofar as this book has merit, it is justly dedicated to them in appreciation of their able assistance through a writing career of sixty years. It could not have been done without their help. Officially they were listed as assistants. *Collaborator* more accurately describes their roles.

As I conclude this work, I remember with appreciation the many others who encouraged and supported me in my career. First mention goes to Charles Gratke, the foreign editor of the *Christian Science Monitor* when I arrived there in 1929. He had faith that I could learn to be a reporter when others had doubts. His encouragement and confidence cleared the path for me. Later, Raymond Gram Swing taught me about news broadcasting—including the importance of writing one line fewer per minute when talking from overseas. He along with Walter Lippmann helped me think through the intricacies of wartime and postwar policies and politics and to find my way through the corridors of power in Washington. Along those corridors I had the happy experience of getting to know and learn from and exchange ideas with Bromley Smith, whom I first knew when he worked at the State Department as Dean Acheson's personal public affairs officer and then when he moved over to run the "war room" at the White House for Lyndon Johnson. Robert R. Bowie first became a wise friend and counselor when he was running the Center for International Studies at Harvard. I have benefitted ever since from the clarity of his thinking about world affairs. What knowledge I have gleaned about military affairs I owe greatly to Admiral Stansfield Turner, another wise friend and counselor whom I met when he was NATO commander in the Mediterranean. Later he was president of the Naval War College and, later still, Director of Central Intelligence. Among journalistic colleagues I have particularly happy memories of collaboration with Frederic W. Collins of the *Providence Journal* and, from London days and since, with my wise and witty friend Joseph Fromm, who has written the foreword to this book. He was formerly foreign editor of *U.S. News and World Report* and, more recently, Washington representative of the International Institute for Strategic Studies. He has the unique distinction of being the only American to serve in India during World War II as an officer in His Britannic Majesty's Regiment of Ghurkas. Our frequent, sometimes daily, telephone exchanges have always been both mental stimulus and delight.

I served under several fine editors at the *Christian Science Monitor*, beginning with Willis J. Abbott, who gave me my first job there, and later, Erwin D. Canham, a world-respected teacher and practitioner of highest quality journalism, who was followed by John Hughes, who made me chief editorial writer. Of particular importance to this book are Katherine Fanning, who insisted that it be written, and David Anable, managing editor, who made valuable suggestions about the content and insisted on a chapter about the George Polk case. Without the encouragement and support of these two people, this book might never have been finished. The same can be said of the author and former publisher Clarkson Potter, who first persuaded me that this book was worth writing and then persistently prodded and encouraged me to keep going. I am also most grateful to the excellent people at the *Christian Science Monitor* Library for many years of helpfulness and to Ronald Swerczek of the National Archives, Raymond Teichman at the Franklin D. Roosevelt Library at Hyde Park, and Harold L. Miller, research archivist of the State Historical Society of Wisconsin, for finding and sending me copies of documents important to this work. And finally, a special word of warmest thanks to Sally Bourg for efficient secretarial support during my final Washington days and even more for her continued friendship and for bringing us from time to time the latest news from Washington to our island in Narragansett Bay.

At the Hinge of History

Cub Reporter

My career in American journalism began officially on the first day of October in 1929, but in fact it started twenty years earlier. Like most children I liked to turn book pages just to look at the pictures long before I could read the words. My earliest favorite was a history book left over from my mother's high school days. My earliest graphic memory is of a drawing in that book showing men climbing aboard a sailing ship and setting it on fire. It roused my curiosity. I wanted to know why they were doing it.

The ship was the British revenue cutter *Gaspee*. She was boarded and burned in 1772 in Narragansett Bay by merchants from Providence, Rhode Island, who objected to paying English customs duties. This was the first act of violence of the American Revolution. Finding out why some men wanted to burn that ship was my first exercise in seeking the explanation of an historic event.

I have been curious about the whys and wherefores of public events ever since. I read history both for pleasure and for knowledge. Recently I was reading the lives of Napoleon's marshals. I interspersed the writing of this chapter with rereading the story of that seventh earl of Cardigan who led the Light Brigade into the Russian guns at the battle of Balaclava. No fiction could be more exciting than that remarkable story of a Victorian English earl of large inherited wealth who prided himself on his horsemanship, his horses, and his splendidly trained regiment, the Eleventh Hussars, and who led them in a useless charge while knowing that the order must have been a mistake, as indeed it was. The British commander-in-chief at the battle, Lord Raglan, gazed in horror as his light cavalry wasted itself and its usefulness to him in a charge launched by a misunderstood order. Had the order been precise and in writing the charge would not have been aimed at the wrong target.

And anyway, why was a British army in the Crimea in 1854 fighting against the Russians? If the question holds interest for you, then you have the makings of a journalist.

There are several tools needed for a career in journalism. A knowledge of economics is more important now than ever. This book is being written as the countries of Western Europe are getting ready for perhaps the biggest change in their collective lives since the breakup of the Roman Empire some sixteen hundred years ago. The economic unification of Western Europe will (if it is in fact achieved) produce the wealthiest, most productive, and most powerful economy in the world. It will outclass both the American and the Soviet economies in all elements of economic power except geography. If the new community chooses to do so, it will be able to become the world's first military power. To grasp the meaning behind the news of the future will require a sure understanding of economics. Perhaps someday it will be at least as important as a grasp of history. But history is fundamental to an understanding of, and an intelligent writing about, today's events.

For example, in 1989 the Soviet Union loosened its grip on Central Europe and began pulling its troops back out of East Germany. Suddenly the reunification of Germany, an avowed goal of the Western countries since the signing of the NATO alliance in 1949, became possible. But when the prospect suddenly emerged as the Berlin Wall came down, it was greeted with extreme uneasiness in both Paris and London, and even in Washington. In London Prime Minister Margaret Thatcher summoned a special meeting of German experts to hear all the arguments against the reconstitution of a single greater German state. Any historian can tick off the reasons for a sudden reluctance in the rest of Western Europe and in the United States to accept what all had long professed to want.

Since the breakup of the Roman Empire, Europe has instinctively resisted any one country's becoming larger than the others. Whenever one threatened to dominate the whole, the others have formed a coalition against it. They joined against the Spaniards, whose bid for dominance ended in 1588 with the wreckage of the Great Armada along the western coast of Ireland. They joined against the imperial Hapsburgs in the Thirty Years' War (1618–48), against the France of Louis XIV during the second half of that same century, and a hundred years later against the same France when led by Napoléon Bonaparte. Twice in this century the smaller Europeans coalesced against German bids for dominance of the continent in World Wars I and II. The strength and vitality of Europe has sprung from its pluralism in culture and politics. No one country was ever allowed for long to grow bigger than the others.

Stalin's arbitrary division of Germany in 1945 suited the other Europeans. They were relieved of the fear of German power that had troubled them from the modern unification of the northern German states by Bismarck at the end of the Franco-Prussian War in 1870. From 1870 to 1945 Europe feared a Germany of super-European size. The West Germany that emerged in 1945 was a state of normal European size—roughly similar in size, population, and economic wealth to Britain, France, or Italy. Then, suddenly, in 1989 Moscow loosened its grip and permitted the revival of a new greater Germany that would equal in economic strength the combined economies of France and Britain. Did Europe truly want to have another super-Germany?

In 1989 Britain, France, and Italy would have preferred a continuation of a divided Germany, but by 1989 it was too late. All of them, with the United States, had so deeply committed themselves to the goal of reunification that they could not suddenly back away from it without offending both East and West Germans, most of whose people did want a revived greater Germany.

Fascination with history led me to do my honors in history at my American college, Williams. There Richard Newhall turned me to the Middle Ages. I read Froissart and wrote my thesis on the Hundred Years War (1340–1430). That whetted a desire to see the scenes of its battles and to learn more history. I was mentally headed for a medieval university, preferably Cambridge.

There was a splendid institution in those days called the Student Third Class Association. It germinated out of the fertile brain of a Yale man named Stan Robins. He booked the entire third-class accommodations of ships of the Holland America Line on the Atlantic run. He offered free passage to the college bands of a half dozen colleges. He put a band aboard each ship that headed out of New York with his student recruits aboard. By the hundreds we who largely came out of the Midwest and went east to college became an annual migration to Europe.

The accommodations were primitive. The inner decks of those third-class sections of the Dutch ships were floored in red cement. The bunks were in triple iron tiers. We ate off tin plates. But we were all from Eastern colleges. We had a band for dancing on the outside deck at night. We had a ball for the six days and nights of the trip. And when we got to Europe we learned a lot of things, among them the fact that students from older European universities had dashing items of apparel. Germans and Scandinavians wore splendid caps. The English had blazers.

I spent a holiday with a family that included a recent graduate from Cambridge, Nicholas Monserrat. He sported a rich assortment of blazers in bold colors with fascinating emblems on the pockets. I made a mental resolve that someday I would come home with a set of blazers from Cambridge. It was definitely to be Cambridge because in those days, as is still true, Cambridge led Oxford in history and because Rhodes scholars all went to Oxford. I was not up to Rhodes level on my academic record. I did not want to be a non–Rhodes scholar at Oxford. Another facet of this came out when my father went with me for a preliminary interview with the master of my prospective college at Cambridge, Corpus Christi. Father asked how many Americans were at Cambridge. Sir Will Spens, the master, understood the purport of the question and gave what to him was the correct and factual answer. He said, "We give thanks here daily to Cecil Rhodes because his scholarships keep most of the Americans at Oxford." It reassured father, and myself, that at Cambridge I would not be associating mostly with Americans. There were two other Americans at Corpus during my two years there: Harold James Coolidge and Franklin Williams. Coolidge was an anthropologist interested mainly in gorillas, and Williams was a scholar aiming at academic honors. I joined the ranks of the "hearties" who went rowing in "eights" on the Cam (lower reaches) on weekday afternoons, and punting on the Cam (upper reaches) on weekends—with a "lady," and tea with honey in the orchard at Grantchester where the clock still stood at "ten to three" as in Rupert Brooke's poem about that lovely bit of pastoral tranquillity that Grantchester still is—or was the last time I was there. May God grant that it be ever protected from the spoilers. The rest of the time was spent reading history and writing a weekly essay that, weekly, was torn verbally to shreds by Kenneth Pickthorn, who a year or two earlier had done the same to Edward Weeks, to Weeks's enormous literary advantage. It was the groundwork for his long tenure as editor of the *Atlantic Monthly* magazine. It was the groundwork for my own eventual ability to appreciate the virtues of the simple declarative sentence, the importance of accuracy about facts, and the equal importance of drawing a logical conclusion from facts.

I had two glorious years at Cambridge, alternately sweating or freezing in the Corpus first boat, showing off to a female audience my skill with a punt pole (the important thing is to be able to hoist the pole out of the water without wetting one's white flannels—always worn for punting), surviving Pickthorn's weekly sarcasm when an essay reached an unproven conclusion or my choice of words failed to convey my meaning, and accepting and enjoying, unconsciously, a life-style that no longer exists. It was "the good life." I had a set of rooms in the new court of Corpus, on the ground floor of the first entry, around to the left from the main gate. There was first a dark space with a cupboard for such minimum essentials as butter, jam, and biscuits. That opened into a sitting room with well-worn, unmatching furniture left over from previous occupants, and an open fireplace. It had a stone mullioned window on the courtyard and a door opposite into the bedroom. In the morning a college servant, named Pillsworth, came in early, laid and lighted a fire, picked out my clothes for the day (his choice), hung them on a rack in front of the fire, went to the college kitchens, brought back my breakfast (again his selection), and laid it on a table facing the fire. Then he woke me.

It seemed perfectly natural then to be so waited upon. The cost was modest. No one at Corpus in my day lived, or behaved, as extravagantly as did Brideshead in Evelyn Waugh's great novel. My own allowance was modest, but I could afford the extra two pounds per week that it cost me to have the special service of Pillsworth, who was always available to help if I chose to have a small lunch party or a few friends in for tea, which I did frequently—and with a careless disregard for English social distinctions. Years later a former fellow student commended me for having acted as a melting pot. He said that my room was the first place in which he ever found himself sharing food and conversation with "a person from a council school." In those days "council school" and "public school" did not mix.

Both Richard Newhall at Williams and Kenneth Pickthorn at Corpus were veterans of World War I. Both had been wounded with lasting damage. Newhall carried his left arm in a sling the rest of his life. Pickthorn was said to be in constant pain. To the two I owe much, including a layer of resistance to the political radicalism that was widely accepted in student circles at the time. Pickthorn was the Conservative party member of Parliament from Cambridge University. He was a true conservative. His primary political argument was that socialists believe in the perfectability of man while conservatives assume the contrary, that is, that man is imperfect and must be treated as such. In other words, the millenium is not achievable by social legislation, man responds to carrot and goad, man without the carrot of profit or the goad of unemployment ceases to be productive, socialism must fail because it outlaws both carrot and goad.

Like most of my student generation I was intrigued by the doctrines of socialism, but not converted. The teachers I most admired and respected (Newhall and Pickthorn) pointed in the contrary direction. Besides, my student days were finished before the great stock market crash of October 1929. I "came down" from Cambridge and was back in Toledo, Ohio, before that happened. It is a footnote to history that the four notorious English traitors—Guy Burgess, Donald Maclean, Kim Philby, and Anthony Blount—all came to Cambridge after the October market crash. Their cynicism and ultimate treason was nourished in the general economic collapse of the West, which brought with it unemployment and human misery.

But before that happened I had swanned around Toledo in my own set of Cambridge blazers until my father reminded me that there was a working world outside and what was I proposing to do next? He said he thought that Cambridge had probably spoiled me for a job in business and that I had better think about either teaching or journalism.

Fortunately for me I had called on Willis Abbot, the editor of the *Christian Science Monitor*, before going to Cambridge. I had told him that my father was giving me two years of postgraduate study after Williams and asked him whether I could to best advantage spend it at an American school of journalism or at Cambridge. "Cambridge by all means," he said; "I can always make a journalist out of an educated and intelligent man. I cannot necessarily make an intelligent or educated man out of a journalist." So, after those two happy years at Cambridge I could go back to Mr. Abbot and ask for a job. And since we all still thought we were living in Herbert Hoover's era of endless prosperity, a job was waiting for me. So begins my story of how I entered the life of an apprentice journalist with Herbert Hoover in the White House, endless prosperity supposedly in place, and a complacent British Empire presiding over a supposedly settled world.

I was the last recruit hired by the *Monitor* for some time. The bottom dropped out from under the New York stock market and from under just about everything else two weeks later. The Great Depression had begun. The *Monitor* did not hire more reporters, but did not fire anyone either. And it was a long time before there were any raises. I started at a salary of fifty dollars a week. My first raise came nine years later when I was appointed to be the *Monitor*'s war correspondent in Berlin. But in October 1929 I had a job and was one of the fortunate for that reason. Back home in Toledo a third of the work force was soon on the street and one out of every three shop windows downtown was soon empty.

My salary of fifty dollars a week sounds like very little today, but it may interest some economist that it was sufficient to feed, house, and clothe myself and also buy, on the installment plan of course, a Model A Ford roadster, green in color with a smart tan cloth top. This was considered to be an acceptable conveyance by debutantes of the era both in Boston, where I started, and in Washington, to which I was soon posted.

An incidental further footnote of possible interest to clothiers is that in Boston, although the stock market had crashed, I dressed in white tie and tails and wore a collapsible opera hat to take a young lady to the opera. A morning coat, alias a cutaway, was also required wearing at the weddings of my Williams College classmates. I had come back from England with a full set of such formal finery.

Lull Before the Storm

In looking back over my first years in journalism beginning in October 1929, I am amazed at how long it took people around me, and in government, to recognize the disastrous state of the American economy and the foreign dangers looming ahead. The bottom dropped out from under the stock market on October 24, 1929, twenty-four days into my journalistic career, and the Japanese invaded Manchuria on September 18, 1931. But well after the Black Thursday on Wall Street in 1929 and even after the Manchukuo Incident of less than two years later in Asia I and most of my fellow reporters in Boston and later in Washington were kept busy with the trivia of news. My first full year as a reporter on the local news desk of the *Monitor* was spent reporting such less-than-earthshaking events as the pulling down of an old post office, the arrival at Logan Airport of Amelia Earhart, and a report on the relationship between alcoholism and insanity. My managing editor, Paul Deland, wanted me to prove that alcoholism was the major cause of insanity in the United States. I wrote to all the major institutions dealing with the mentally disturbed. The information that came back failed to support Deland's thesis, but he stuck to it nonetheless and rewrote my lead to conform to his wishes. He was more concerned with defending prohibition, which was then coming under attack because of the crime and vast, illegal wealth that it generated, than he was interested in the rising tide of unemployment spreading through the industrial cities of the Midwest. I learned accidentally but could not get it printed that the Anti-Saloon League, the principal lobby in defense of prohibition, enjoyed a steady flow of funds from the bootlegging industry that throve on the illicit traffic in alcohol. The fact that the traffickers in illegal fluids were prime beneficiaries of prohibition made as little dent on the moralists and politicians then as similar facts about today's worse traffic in illegal drugs does on today's moralists and politicians. My news editor at the *Monitor* in those days believed fervently in prohibition and equally in Herbert Hoover's assurances about the state of the economy. Hoover told us that "prosperity is just around the corner." His spokesmen interpreted the downward slide of the stock market as a "technical correction."

I was sent to Washington in July 1931. The stock market was still declining. Yet I soon found myself joining in a daily ritual. Along with most other newspaper offices of that time, the *Monitor* office was in the National Press Building. From that building at about nine o'clock in the morning a migration occurred. It was led by J. Fred Essary of the *Baltimore Sun*, a man of portly elegance, carrying a walking stick and wearing a soft brown felt hat and, when weather required, a reversible Burberry coat. Perhaps thirty or forty reporters came out of the Press Building and turned left down Fourteenth Street. At unhurried pace, by small groups of four or five we would go first to the Department of Commerce, where we sought out the press room and scanned the morning crop of news releases. I found many a story that way—about a new lighthouse, or measures to protect a fishery, or an optimistic forecast of rising exports of something to somewhere. From there the migration moved to the Department of the Interior, where I could always find something about Indian affairs. A pair of reformist Quakers named Rhodes and Scattergood had taken over Indian affairs for Mr. Hoover. A new effort was being made to treat the American Indians less callously than had long been the custom.

From the Interior the migration would head for the State Department where Henry L. Stimson answered questions that had been submitted in writing in advance the day before. The subject seemed frequently to be about Latin America or about progress of the treaty to outlaw war, which his predecessor, Frank B. Kellogg, had launched. Occasionally I would drop in on General John J. Pershing, who headed the American Battle Monuments Commission from an elegant office (on the west side of the same corridor as the office of the secretary of state) from which he kept an eye on the performance of his successor as army chief of staff, at that time General Douglas MacArthur, whose office was diagonally across the corridor. I also dropped in on him a few times. Both were accessible to a cub reporter. I remember particularly the clipped white mustache of General Pershing and the firm diction of General MacArthur, but nothing of what we discussed. It could not have been of major importance in that pre–Hitler lull in world affairs. None of it made for exciting news copy. And finally, from State (which then occupied part, not all, of what is now called the Executive Office Building) to the White House across the street.

President Hoover received us in a small office on the west side of the building (the oval office came later) and, again, answered questions that had been submitted in writing.

The pace was slow. The news was scarce. There was no lively awareness of spreading unemployment or a rising tide of bankruptcies. Such unpleasantnesses were creeping into the news from the big cities. On the farms crop prices were declining. One heard about occasional farm foreclosures. Yet in Washington it seemed remote. Most people there worked for the federal government or, like reporters, were there because the government was there. Most newspapers were owned and run by Republicans, hence inclined to play down unpleasant economic news. Through 1930 and even into 1931 there was that daily pilgrimage from the Press Building, around the circuit from Commerce and Interior to State and White House, with an occasional "expert" stopping off at the Treasury on the way back to the Press Building. Washington was slow to feel and react to the spreading infection of the Great Depression.

It was just as slow in recognizing and reacting to the first warning of those events overseas that, unchecked, led into World War II. On September 18, 1931, Japanese armies based in Korea, at that time a Japanese possession, crossed the frontier into China and seized Mukden, the capital of the province of Manchuria. This was the first major act of imperialistic aggression by force of arms after World War I. Others watched to see whether the Japanese would get away with it unchallenged.

Henry L. Stimson was secretary of state in Hoover's cabinet. In his youth he had been one of Teddy Roosevelt's Rough Riders. Later he was secretary of war in the Taft cabinet. He believed in an assertive America. He saw in the Japanese invasion of China a danger to American interests in the Far East and a possible example to others. He sent a message to his opposite number in London, Sir John Simon, proposing a joint Anglo-American naval demonstration in the Pacific. There was a flurry of excitement. Might the United States and Britain jointly challenge Japanese expansion?

At that time *The Times* of London had a remarkable correspondent in Washington, Wilmot Lewis. A former Shakespearean actor, he had presence and a deep and commanding voice. He was recognized as the doyen of the Washington press corps. Newly arrived neophyte reporters made a courtesy call on him. I had made mine soon after arrival. I can still hear ringing in my ears the measured solemnity of his injunction, "Never forget, young man, that many a good story is ruined by ververifica- tion." The Japanese invasion of Manchuria tested his doctrine and found it wanting. He was on good personal terms with President Hoover. He went to the White House. He asked Hoover about the Stimson proposal to Simon. He told me that Mr. Hoover confirmed the possibility of a joint naval maneuver but added that he had instructed that in the opera- tion no American warship would go west of the Hawaiian Islands. Lewis at once reported to the British Embassy what Hoover had said. That was the end of the matter. Simon had no intention of getting into a tooth- less operation. A joint Anglo-American naval maneuver in Asian waters, near Japan, might have had some cautionary influence in Tokyo. But an exercise nailed to the Hawaiian Islands would be another way of say- ing "go ahead, we are doing nothing about it." Stimson was left with nothing to do but declare American neutrality and nonrecognition of the conquest of Manchuria.

That slowness was due partly to the remoteness of Washington from the main centers of both foreign and domestic distress. At home the smokestack cities of the Midwest were the first to suffer, but television did not exist to show those in Washington the silent factories, empty retail shops, and lines of hungry men, women, and children waiting for a free meal at a church or a Salvation Army meeting hall. Radio existed, but it was still largely a purveyor of music. News on radio came in the form of a news reader reading a series of news briefs collected from the Associated Press wire. There were no investigative reporters ferret- ing out unpleasant news or misbehavior in high places, and certainly no editorialization based on the news briefs.

As for Manchuria, or Manchukuo as the Japanese then called it, the distance was mentally as far away as Mars. A few prescient souls warned of the danger of allowing Japan to destabilize the status quo that had emerged from World War I. But to the average American and certainly to the average member of Congress in the early 1930s Manchuria might as well have been on another planet. Washington found it difficult to believe that Japan's invasion of China made any serious difference to the United States.

The Trance Is Shattered

And then, in May 1932, one group of Americans decided to take their distress to Washington. Many a World War I veteran was by that time in the ranks of the unemployed. In 1924 Congress had voted them a bonus, but to be paid off in 1945. Men whose mortgages were being foreclosed in 1932 or whose wages were insufficient to feed all their children wondered why they should have to wait until 1945 to collect their bonus. They decided to ask for it at once. They came to Washington, some on the train, some by hitching rides, some by just walking. There were twelve thousand in all. Some set up a shack city on the far side of the Anacostia River. Some moved into abandoned or partly demolished buildings along Pennsylvania Avenue at the foot of Capitol Hill in a tri-angle area that is now partly covered by the new wing of the Smithsonian and partly by park. They lobbied their legislators by day. They wandered the town asking for handouts in the evenings. Their condition was at best unsanitary and a contrast to the ordered elegance of the rest of Washing-ton. When the police tried to evict them from the abandoned buildings, there was shooting. One bonus marcher was killed. The White House decided that they had to be moved away. The cavalry was summoned from Fort Myer across the river. I found myself behind a line of mounted men armed with sabers facing a motley throng of bonus marchers. It was dark. There were flares. An order was given. The cavalry moved ahead in line, sabers at the slope, at a walk. Most of the marchers gave way and fell back. In front of me one stood his ground. A saber flashed in a swing-ing arc and grazed the cheek of the marcher. Blood flowed. The marcher backed away holding a hand to his bleeding ear. The action moved to the camp across the Anacostia River. I was standing near Gen. Douglas MacArthur, in full regimentals. He summoned a sergeant and gave him an order. I watched as the sergeant collected a squad and started down the row of makeshift huts. They wadded newspapers into a corner and set them alight. The row of huts was soon blazing, and the troops were pushing the marchers back out of Washington on the road to Baltimore.

Congress refused to grant the bonus that year, but the country remembered that President Hoover had called out the troops against the veterans. The marchers were driven out of Washington, and the places where they had camped were cleaned up and turned into parks. But the memory became one of the reasons why on election day that November the American electorate gave Roosevelt 22.8 million votes against 15.8 million for Herbert Hoover. It is unwise for any politician seeking re-election, or continuation in office, to call out the troops against his own people, particularly when those people are the veterans of the last previous war. It was a fatal political mistake on Mr. Hoover's part, but it gave me a chance to see cavalry in action. It was probably the last time blood was ever drawn by a saber wielded by an American cavalryman. There still were horse-mounted regiments in the U.S. Army as late as the Louisiana maneuvers in summer 1939, but by the time those regiments went to Europe in 1942 they had been remounted into tanks.

The bonus march in spring 1932 was the event that first shocked official Washington into something like awareness of mass distress and a rising mass demand for more remedial action in Washington. It was not the first time the Democrats began to see the political opportunities opening up for them in the wake of the stock market crash and the rapid descent into economic depression. The Democrats captured Congress in the midterm election of 1930 and reorganized the House. John Garner of Texas became Speaker. Almost immediately he began asking various offices, bureaus, and departments of government for their dream lists of new buildings and projects. Into his office there rolled a mighty list of new post offices, new dams, new customs houses, new barracks for the army, and new ships for the navy. Speaker Garner dumped it all together into the biggest public works program ever so far conceived or proposed. The arguments for and against began to make news. I myself graduated from the "downtown beat" with its round of trips to the departments of Commerce and Interior. I forgot about Indian affairs and lighthouses and began to learn about applied politics on the Hill. I was assigned to the House and began writing about unemployment and the arguments between Garner and the Republican leader, former Speaker Nicholas Longworth. I watched them denouncing each other's policies on the floor of the House and was then startled one day to see them walk off the floor, arms over each other's shoulders, to a small private hideaway for the Speaker just across the hall from the House lobby. I learned that this is where they went "to strike a blow for liberty," a phrase which translated into a shot of bourbon whiskey. They were enemies, or at least lively opponents, on the floor and each did his duty well for his party, but they were cronies in private and the fact that Prohibition was still the law of the land did not interfere with their personal habits.

Garner's great catchall public works bill was a forerunner of bigger and more imaginative projects to come later. He himself gained enough public attention and approval from his bill to become a major contender for the Democratic party's presidential nomination in 1932. In fact, he was the runner-up against Roosevelt, and the Roosevelt nomination was sewn up only after flamboyant California publisher and tycoon William Randolph Hearst (whose ranch-palace at St. Simeon is well worth a stop-over for any tourist) was persuaded by Joseph P. Kennedy to withdraw from the Garner candidacy. California's delegation switched to Roosevelt and thus paved the way for one of the most remarkable presidencies in American history. Also the role of Joe Kennedy in Roosevelt's nomination was the first important move made by a Kennedy of that family in national politics and led eventually to the presidency of his son, John F. Kennedy.

Many have wondered in retrospect how much popular unrest would have developed in the United States had Hoover been reelected in 1932 and had he persisted in policies which amounted to repression of protest. Was there a potential for real trouble? Democrats liked to say in later years that Roosevelt's New Deal policies headed off a revolution. Perhaps. Conditions were bad and getting worse. In my home town of Toledo, Ohio, every third shop front downtown was empty and one-third of the work force was unemployed and living on charity. The Salvation Army was a true salvation to the unemployed. My own parents had a live-in cook-maid. They let her go because they could no longer afford to pay her salary, little though it was. She came back a month later asking to be allowed to work just for room and board. She was. People argued over whether factory workers in the cities were worse off than farmers whose farms were foreclosed and who then started walking from Oklahoma to California. Farmer marches were brewing. Another year of Hoover-style response to public need would almost certainly have seen more marches on Washington of unemployed factory workers and dispossessed farmers as well as veterans.

The escape valve for the rising resentment of 1932 was in the two-party system. The depression had broken loose under Herbert Hoover. He did what he could to mitigate it, but it took a repudiation of his party at the polls to make drastic reforms and drastic remedies possible. There is no substitute yet devised by political man for a genuine two-party system that allows a dissatisfied populace to change its rulers, a lesson the leaders of the Communist world began to discover in the remarkable year of 1989 when, at least in Europe, the time had run out on using soldiery to suppress public resentment. Even the Chinese will probably, sooner or later, have to reform themselves and permit political pluralism. A change of party releases pent-up resentments. It may not change conditions immediately, but it releases political pressure and usually heads off violent revolution. Whatever else the New Deal did, plus or minus, it gave the underprivileged and the unemployed and the miserable a new sense of renewed opportunity. If there was any real danger of revolution in fall 1932 it evaporated from the moment Roosevelt was elected. The Roosevelt victory may or may not have averted an actual revolutionary situation, but it wiped out immediately the possibility of such a thing. The country settled back to see what Franklin Delano Roosevelt could do.

The Interregnum

Historian Samuel Eliot Morison in his admirable *History of the American People* calls the time that elapsed between Roosevelt's first election and his first inauguration an "embarrassing gap." A gap it was. In 1932, for the last time, there was a four-month interregnum between election day on November 8 and inauguration on the following March 4. Since then presidents have been inaugurated on January 20, leaving a gap of only two months. That four-month gap between Roosevelt's first election and first inauguration was a wonderful chance for him to organize his team for running the country, and for us of the Washington press corps to get acquainted with him and his ways. It was embarrassing for unfortunate Mr. Hoover, who had to preside over a continuing economic debacle without being able to do anything about it. He tried to persuade Roosevelt to join him in an international conference to stabilize currencies. Roosevelt wisely avoided taking any action before he held responsibility and power. Instead he went off to Warm Springs, Georgia, where he could polish his plans and projects in a familiar and quiet place. Warm Springs had originally been a summer resort in the Appalachian highlands for people from the hot coastal plain. By 1932 it had been converted into a sanitarium for victims of polio. The warm water from the springs fed into a big swimming pool where damaged limbs could be exercised more easily than on land, and almost indefinitely. Roosevelt had been going there regularly since his attack of polio in 1921. He was at home there. He knew everyone, and they knew him. He went there immediately after his election accompanied by Mrs. Roosevelt and his daughter Anna. Other members of the family came and went. He settled in to rest and recuperate in the pool and in the rooms by it where the physiotherapists did their work, and to plan for his presidency in circumstances he could control. It was no embarrassment for him. It was an almost ideal place in which to prepare for the vast task ahead of him in Washington.

I have many memories of the days at Warm Springs, one perhaps more vivid than the others. It was Thanksgiving Day. The president-elect was standing at the head of the table in the dining room at the Georgia Warm Springs Foundation. He looked around for Mrs. Roosevelt. She was not to be seen. His eye fell on me. "Harsch," he said, "would you find Mrs. Roosevelt and ask her to come to table. Tell her I am ready to sit down."

I worked my way through the crowd to the next room, where Mrs. Roosevelt was in deep conversation with a bevy of admirers. I said, "Mrs. Roosevelt, the president asked me to tell you that he is ready to sit down, and would you please come to table." She replied, sharply, "Tell him I'll come when I'm ready."

Years later I learned about Lucy Mercer and some of the reasons behind the sharpness in Mrs. Roosevelt's voice. At that moment, in 1932, I only knew that I could not go back to Mr. Roosevelt, standing in his painful leg braces and balancing on his crutches, and tell him that his wife was not going to respond to his summons on the instant. He was the newly elected, but not yet inaugurated, president of the United States. He was also, in her eyes (as we learned much later), a husband who had mis-behaved and was still being punished. She was certainly not pampering him. I backed out of sight of both.

The fact that he asked me, a newspaper reporter, to take the message to his wife is typical of the informality that surrounded the presidency in the Roosevelt II era. There was a Secret Service detail at the Warm Springs Foundation, but the president-elect did not move (as a successor does now) surrounded always by a swarm of aides and guards. At Warm Springs on that Thanksgiving Day he was one patient among others. The dining room was full of his fellow patients, their doctors, nurses, and physiotherapists, and the reporters who had been sent there with the president-elect to cover him during the interregnum. He came to know all of us, and we him, well during those four months. There were only fourteen of us. We lived in simple turn-of-the-century shingled cottages near the one he used, just down the street. We saw him twice a day—in the morning for the benefit of the afternoon papers and in the afternoon for the next morning's. There was no television at all and not even a reporter for radio at Warm Springs in 1932. Weather permitting he received us on a little porch just big enough for our group. It was fitted with a round, weathered wooden table surrounded by wooden benches—unpainted.

An example of the way he made news at those twice daily meetings was a morning when we arrived to find the table loaded with books about Russia. Obviously, the first question was whether he was thinking of recognizing Russia. The closest friend the Soviet Union had in Washington in those days was Sen. William Borah of Idaho, the senior Republican on the Senate Foreign Relations Committee. He believed we should recognize Russia. He developed personal relations with the Soviets and became, in effect, their informal ambassador. A letter from Senator Borah became an entry visa to the Soviet Union. Of course, we all wrote stories that day saying Roosevelt was thinking of recognizing the Soviet Union. Shortly after becoming president he did.

He had picked me out to carry the message to Mrs. Roosevelt simply because when he looked around, mine happened to be the first face he recognized. His staff was minuscule compared to the numbers in the vast White House bureaucracy of today's Imperial Presidency. At Warm Springs that winter he had Marvin McIntyre with him to manage the press and Steve Early for about everything else. Bill Hasset, a marvelously literate and literary person, was somewhere in the background handling important correspondence and writing speeches. Missy LeHand was there somewhere, but rarely seen. The staff was small and we of the press were few in numbers. They were friendly with us and we with them. There was literally none of the sense of confrontation that developed in later years between press and White House, particularly in the Nixon years. Even the reporters from Republican papers that were automatically critical of Roosevelt were on friendly personal terms with Roosevelt, with his family, and with his staff. John Boettiger of the *Chicago Tribune*, owned by Roosevelt's arch enemy, Colonel McCormick, later married Roosevelt's daughter Anna. At Warm Springs that winter Anna went horseback riding almost every day. Several of us, myself included, often rode with her. The Roosevelt family always enjoyed easy relations with the press.

The Road to War

The story of the New Deal has been told so often, and so well, that there is little I can usefully add to it. I, my wife, Anne, and our growing family of (ultimately) three sons lived in Washington throughout the full Roosevelt–New Deal–World War II–Truman era, and indeed on through the first half of the Eisenhower administration. Most of the time we lived in Georgetown, having moved there long before it was "discovered." The Georgetown we knew, on through World War II, was a relatively quiet and pleasantly mixed place made up mostly of old families, white and black, dating from before the Civil War and often living side by side, with new families moving in partly for the architecture and partly because it was cheaper. My wife's family moved there in the mid-twenties, when her father, Adm. Spencer Shepard Wood, retired from the navy. They had lived until then on Twenty-second Street, just off Sheridan Circle in the then new embassy section. They bought a Georgetown house at 2808 N Street, which had once been the home of the first secretary of the U.S. Navy, but which had become a tenement. My wife's mother wanted to move there partly because she loved the house for its architecture, pure early federal and intact with original woodwork and firebacks (probably because its owners during the Victorian era had been too poor to "modernize" it). She wanted it also because it was cheap (either eight thousand dollars or twelve thousand dollars according to conflicting family recollection). Anne's father warned her mother that "if you move to Georgetown none of your friends will come to visit you over there." Anne and I moved there twenty years later, but even then one of our friends, Helene Morse (also in journalism), emerged one day from her newly bought, small brick house to be greeted by a neighbor child chanting, "We know you're rich, you don't wear pretty clothes." There were still a lot of blue collar working-class people in Georgetown in those days, their wives wearing "pretty clothes." The gentrification of Georgetown didn't really get decisive until World War II. Even then, wartime recruits to government often went there because it still was cheaper than modern housing along the Connecticut, Massachusetts, and Wisconsin Avenue corridors.

The domestic changes or reforms of the first Roosevelt years are blurred now in my memory. Washington was full of new hopes and enthusiasms and actions. But I gradually moved from covering congressional hearings and debates on New Deal legislation on the Hill down to the State, War, and Navy Department buildings clustered around the White House where people were watching the rampant new nationalisms of Japan, Italy, and Germany. Roosevelt took advantage of the new willingness of Congress to spend money to begin a navy buildup. Through my father-in-law I met several top navy people, including Adm. William H. Standley, chief of naval operations. My growing knowledge of and interest in both international affairs in general and naval matters in particular led to an assignment to cover the naval conference opening in London in December 1935. Thirteen years earlier, in 1922, in Washington the nine leading powers of those times had agreed upon a naval ratio of 5-5-3-1.67-1.67—meaning parity for the United States and Britain, three-fifths of that parity for Japan, and less than two-fifths each for France and Germany. In 1922 the Japanese were willing to accept that mark of inferiority. They no longer were in 1935. Their delegates went to London demanding full equality with the United States and Britain. When London and Washington refused, the Japanese walked out of the conference and into the race for sea power in the Pacific.

When did World War II begin? Probably in 1919 at the Versailles conference. The treaty shaped there imposed on Germany such penalties and restrictions as could only inflame public opinion and make the German people ready for the expansionist nationalism of the Hitler era. I find it fascinating that within two years of defeat in World War I and of the imposition of the penalties of the Versailles treaty on the Germans, their steel production moved ahead of British steel production. Neither defeat nor the penalties of the Versailles treaty halted Germany's rise as the strongest industrial power in Europe. The worldwide economic depression that hit Germany in 1930, followed by inflation, added further grievances in the collective German mind. The Germans blamed the unemployment that came with the depression, and the inflation that followed it, on the Versailles treaty, hence on the victors of World War I. By the time Hitler came to power in January 1933 Germany had both enormous grievances and steadily growing industrial power. Hitler did not create angry expansionist German nationalism. It was there waiting for someone to rouse and exploit.

In London at that naval conference of late 1935 I had my first glimpse of the parallel fact that Japanese nationalist expansionism was also on the rise. The Japanese were straightforward about it. They were on the march to empire. The walkout in 1935 should have been no surprise. They had taken Taiwan in 1895, southern Sakhalin in 1905, Korea in 1910, Shantung and the former German islands in the Pacific in 1918, Manchuria in 1931. By 1935 the idea of continuing to accept naval inferiority was to them ludicrous.

I should have realized then (I did not) that I was watching one of those moments in history that go under the technical diplomatic label of *bouleversement des alliances*—that is, "reversal of alliances." Japan had long been an admirer, a protégé, and in World War I an actual ally of Great Britain. The British had consciously nourished and strengthened Japan as a "long stop" on the far side of Russia. Containment of tsarist Russia was a prime British foreign policy objective throughout most of the Victorian era and down into this one. (The United States revived it in the cold war.) It was a residue of that containment of Russia policy that frustrated American secretary of state Stimson at the time of the Japanese invasion of Manchuria in 1931 and the subsequent and bloody Japanese entry into Chapei, a largely Chinese section of the great port city of Shanghai. Stimson tried hard in 1931 to persuade the British to go along with him in at least declaring that the two would refuse to recognize the consequences of those acts of Japanese military advance into China. Stimson got nothing out of the effort. There were transatlantic telephone conversations, exchanges of memos, hours of ambassadorial conversations. But to the British of 1931 a strong Japan as a barrier to Soviet expansion in the Far East was still more important than the territorial integrity of a China that was, anyway, in a phase of political chaos and fragmentation.

By 1935 it was too late for anything short of war to restrain Japanese expansion. The Japanese had gained five years of freedom to gather strategic military positions in China, train their army in actual combat in the process, and get their naval building program under way. Perhaps World War II could never have been avoided, but 1931 was probably the last clear chance to head it off. Until Japan invaded Manchuria, the world operated on the assumption that the League of Nations would prevent wars of military aggression. Japan, Italy, and Germany were all members of the league. All were bound by the covenant of the league against precisely what the Japanese did when they invaded Manchuria. The United States was not a member of the league, but it was committed to the territorial integrity of China by the Nine-Power Treaty of 1922. Japan, in 1931, struck the first blow against the limits on national behavior imposed by the whole network of existing treaties, including the covenant of the league. The failure of London and Washington in 1931 to come to the defense of the fabric of those treaties left them toothless and meaningless. If Japan could take all of Manchuria, push on into Jehol (the next province in China proper), and take over a whole section of the supposedly international city of Shanghai without hindrance, then there were no longer effective barriers to military adventurism and expansionism. If the "satisfied powers," the United States, Britain, and France (all with real interests in the Far East) would do nothing to save China from Japanese conquest, it would logically follow that the road was open for others.

Benito Mussolini of Italy had big dreams. He set up, in a prominent place on the broad avenue he drove through the center of ancient Rome, a map in marble for both Italians and tourists to see contrasting the Italy of that day with the ancient Roman Empire. He left no doubt of his desire, and intention, to build a new Roman Empire. On October 3, 1935, he sent his troops into Ethiopia. They conquered it for him within a year. It was easy, and the League of Nations, the British, the French, and the Americans did nothing.

Adolf Hitler became chancellor of Germany on January 30, 1933, while the newly elected but not yet inaugurated American president was still at Warm Springs. Hitler made his first overt move on the road to conquest in March 1935 when he announced that he would build his army to thirty-six divisions, a specific violation of the Versailles treaty. A year later, in his second major violation of that treaty, he sent his troops into the Rhineland. On July 17, 1936, Gen. Francisco Franco launched the Spanish civil war.

What I was watching in London in December 1935 was one more overt evidence of the collapse of the international system set up after 1918. I was equally unaware that I had also glimpsed the reason why a generation later American leadership took the United States first into Korea and then into Vietnam.

The world's diplomats never forgot the Manchukuo Incident of 1931 and its sequel. Firm collective action then might, at least in theory, have prevented the subsequent chain of events that led on to World War II.

The top leaders in Washington who committed the United States to war in Korea in 1950 (Truman, Acheson, Forrestal) and in Vietnam in 1962 (Lyndon Johnson, Dean Rusk) had been drilled in the theory that the time and place to stop aggression is when it first occurs. Manchukuo was the deed that cleared the way for all that came after. All I personally remember is that one day in London in 1935 the chairs for the Japanese delegation at the conference table were empty. They had gone away. My clipping files show no evidence that I, or other reporters present, realized the weight of what was happening.

From the Meiji restoration in 1868 Japan's associations had been with the Western powers, primarily with Britain and the United States. Japan was in fact one of the Allied powers in World War I. In 1935 the walkout from the London Naval Conference exposed the fact that Japan had broken off its old association with those Western powers and was casting in its lot with the newly expansionist powers, Germany and Italy. Japan had reversed its alliances.

A Diplomatic Detour

In April 1939 Robert Thomson Pell, a career U.S. State Department officer, invited me to join him in London on a mission that, had it been successful, would have noticeably changed the face of today's world.

The mission assigned to Pell, and on which he had been working for over a year, was to find a place outside Europe that would be suitable for the large-scale resettlement of people from Europe and then to negotiate with the German government for the orderly movement of Jews from Germany to the new place of settlement. By the time I reached London on a leave of absence from my newspaper, the *Christian Science Monitor*, Pell knew exactly what he wanted to do and how he proposed to do it. But by the time he sent for me his problem had grown bigger than when he was first given the assignment.

Before recounting what Pell, with modest help from me, actually did during the final months before World War II put a sudden end to our efforts, let me first review the general situation about the Jewish community in Central and Eastern Europe.

At the time Hitler came to power in Germany in 1933 there were about 600,000 German-born persons classified as Jews by the German government. In addition, there were in Germany about 150,000 more Jews born in countries to the south and east of Germany classified by the Germans as *Ostjuden* (Eastern Jews), of whom roughly 50,000 were Polish born.

Although Hitler's anti-Semitism was well known from his political book *Mein Kampf* and from his many public speeches, in which he had inveighed against Jews and declared his intention to drive them out of Germany, he did not, until the promulgation of the Nuremberg laws on September 15, 1935, take radical overt steps to push them out. In those laws he deprived Jews of their German citizenship and forbade both intermarriage and intercourse between Jews and Germans. Some Jews who were sensitive to the pressure from the Nazi regime chose to leave then when it was comparatively easy to do so, but there was no mass flight of Jews from Germany. This was a main reason for the *Kristallnacht*, the pogrom unleashed on the Jews on the night of November 9, 1938. Later, when I was working with Pell on the Intergovernmental Committee for Political Refugees, a deputation of Jews from Berlin came to London and quoted German officials as telling them to warn us that there would be more shock tactics like the *Kristallnacht* unless outside governments got on promptly with plans for receiving and settling more Jews in the outside world. Hitler was far more eager to have them leave than they were to go. (See appendixes C and D.)

On this point Princeton historian Arno J. Mayer, writing a carefully researched account of the road to the Holocaust (*Why Did the Heavens Not Darken?* Pantheon Books, 1988), notes:

> Notwithstanding the unrelenting pressure, there was no significant increase in emigration from Germany. The condition of the Jews still appeared to be short of catastrophic. The old established Jewish middle-class in particular remained confident that with time and mounting foreign pressure bureaucratic and economic rationality would temper the Nazi regime and cure it of its anti-Semitic mania. Their belief was partly sustained by their reluctance to pay the ever steeper emigration tax and their apprehension about their economic and social prospects in exile. (p. 165)

Professor Mayer goes on to note that from 1933 to 1938 "fewer than 150,000, or 30 percent of Germany's Jews had either emigrated or gone into exile." He also notes that during those same first five years of the Nazi regime only 27,000 German Jews had crossed the Atlantic to settle in the United States "though under the quota for native Germans nearly that many could have sailed every year." They did not use up their U.S. quota opportunities when available. Among those who did leave Germany, most preferred Paris to New York.

The event that did stimulate more Jews to leave and the outside world to do something to help them leave was, perhaps surprisingly, the German occupation of Austria on March 23, 1938. That was immediately followed by the arrival in Austria of special German police units that sought out and arrested leading Austrian Jews and many German Jews who had already migrated as far as Austria. The Nuremberg laws did not stimulate a mass Jewish exodus from Germany, but the spectacle of German police units moving into Austria and arresting many of the 190,000 Austrian Jews there struck a new degree of fear in some Jews and a heightened awareness among others of what might lie ahead. Hitler had already made clear his intention to seek the annexation of other territories inhabited by Germans.

The chronology is instructive. Hitler's troops marched into Austria on March 23, 1938. Less than two months later, on May 15, President Roosevelt proposed an international conference to organize an inter-governmental committee to deal with the refugee problem and named Myron J. Taylor, former head of U.S. Steel, to be head of the U.S. delegation. The conference was convened at Evian, France, on the south shore of Lake Geneva, on July 6 with delegations from thirty-two countries present. It elected Mr. Taylor its president, authorized the setting up of a permanent organization with staff in London, ordered a survey of the numbers and current treatment of Jews in Central and Eastern Europe, and provided for an organizing meeting of the committee in London on August 3. At that meeting George Rublee, a prominent American lawyer, was named director of the Intergovernmental Committee, Sir Herbert Emerson from the British Foreign Office was named vice director, and Pell was to be assistant director. Pell would run the staff in London. (Later, on February 13, 1939, Rublee resigned, Emerson became director, Pell moved up to be vice director, and I, in April, became assistant director.)

Postwar students of the road to the Holocaust have usually dismissed the Evian conference and the Intergovernmental Committee that it established as a failure. Professor Mayer writes: "Judging by the abortive Evian conference and its sequel, the outside world was not about to help Hitler get rid of 'his Jews'."

There was more to the Evian conference and its work than that. It was not summoned to obtain a sudden expansion of immigration quotas. No government at the time was politically capable of doing that. Evian did precisely what President Roosevelt expected of it. (See appendix A.) It set up an international organization with a mandate to do the two things that as a practical matter could be done under the circumstances of that time. Its mandate was to find a place or places for large-scale resettlement of Jews and to negotiate with the German government for the orderly movement of Jews from German-controlled territories to such places of settlement. It did both.

Pell, who was the key operating officer on the staff of the committee, set up a small office in London consisting of himself, an office manager, an accountant, and a secretary. He opened conversations with the German government. The urgency of his work was quickly underlined by two further events. On September 30, 1938, the two Western prime ministers, Neville Chamberlain for Britain and Edouard Daladier for France, went to Munich to meet Hitler and, in effect, surrendered Czechoslovakia to him. And a month and nine days later, on November 9, Hitler turned his brown-shirted storm troopers loose on the Jewish communities of Germany and Austria.

The first of these two events added the 350,000 Jews of Czechoslovakia to the 190,000 in Austria and approximately 300,000 still in Germany for a new total of 840,000 at Hitler's mercy. The second event, *Kristallnacht*, was a deliberate shock tactic aimed at the outside world to prod it into opening an escape route for those Jews. It was done as visibly as possible. While the storm troopers smashed shop windows, burned, looted, beat, and killed along the main shopping corridors of all the major German cities, they did it most methodically and openly along the Kurfursten-dam in Berlin itself in the full view of the diplomatic and the foreign press corps.

The Kurfurstendam was and still is an elegant, broad boulevard run-ning straight through the fashionable west side, which had developed during the expansion of Berlin in the Bismarck era. In 1938 it was lined with the most elegant shops, many of them owned by Jews. The riot-ing went on all through the night of November 9. By the evening of November 10 the whole world knew and, as intended, was shocked.

But by that time staff work had already been done at the State De-partment in Washington, with Pell at the center of it. The plan existed in outline. The first task was to push it through the White House and obtain the president's approval, then open talks with both the German government and the Jewish communities, of which the most important were those in London and New York.

The first operational move was a trip to Berlin. Pell and Rublee went over from London on January 11 for an opening talk with Hjalmar Schacht, who was then head of the Reichsbank and had until recently also been economics minister. At that meeting the two sides sketched out a two-part program calling for a trust fund to be set up in Germany to receive Jewish assets, a portion of which would be usable for emigration costs and another portion for the care of Jews in Germany before emigra-tion. Then there was to be a corporation set up in London, to be funded by Western Jewish communities, that would prepare places of settlement for the migrants.

When Rublee and Pell got back to London after those preliminary talks with Schacht, they received a long cable dated January 14, 1939, from Washington that spelled out in detail Washington's appreciation of the problem and proposals for dealing with it (the text of this telegram is reproduced in appendix B).

The appreciation was realistic. "The fact must be faced that there exists in Central and Eastern Europe a racial and religious group of some seven million persons for whom the economic and social future is exceedingly dark." "Indications are rapidly increasing" that this situation will reach "an acute stage" in the "near future."

The president, according to the cable, "did not believe that the migration of seven million persons from their present homes and their resettlement in other parts of the world is either possible or essential to a solution of the problem." But he did think that "the organized emigration from Eastern Europe over a period of years of young persons at the age at which they enter actively into economic competition, and at which they may be expected to marry, is not beyond the bounds of possibility."

The president then estimated that the migration of 160,000 such persons a year over a period of years "should reduce the problem to negligible proportions." He did not think that such numbers could be accommodated "by infiltration," but would rather require "creation of a new Jewish homeland capable of absorbing substantially unlimited Jewish immigration." He doubted that Palestine "could absorb and maintain the necessary influx of population." He noted that "a Jewish Colonization Bill concerning Angola was passed unanimously by the Portuguese Chamber of Deputies in 1912."

That was the American plan, as approved by the president.

Angola, then a Portuguese colony located in southwest Africa, is far enough south of the equator to be suitable for Europeans. It is larger in size than Texas plus California. There are tropical rain forests in the north and temperate plateaus in the interior. It has oil, diamonds, copper, iron, and ample crop lands for a population far above its present level of about sixteen million. At that time Angola had about 11 persons per square mile. (Israel today has a population density of 548.) A second attraction was that the Portuguese were as willing to receive several million Europeans in 1939 as they had been in 1912 when the Portuguese Chamber of Deputies unanimously authorized Jewish settlements in Angola.

Had the American plan that Rublee and Pell worked out in early 1939 been put into effect Angola would today be a thriving modern community inhabited by almost as many whites as blacks, and perhaps still a source of wealth for Portugal. In 1939 space, resources, and welcome all combined to make Angola seem in the eyes of American and British diplomats to be the most attractive place that could be found anywhere in the world for the resettlement of European Jews.

That was the blueprint. Pell's task was to sell it to the Germans, on tolerable terms, and then to the Jewish communities that were expected to provide the capital necessary to prepare towns and even cities in Angola sufficient to receive 160,000 settlers every year for the next fifteen or twenty years.

He had inevitable difficulties with the Germans. They wanted to load the plan with forced German exports. The departing emigrants would become salesmen for German goods. Rublee and Pell talked them out of that. By February 14 they had extracted from the Germans an agreement to set up a trust that would receive 25 percent of confiscated Jewish wealth and commit it to the costs of migration and also to social services for the children and older people remaining in Germany.

By late April, when I arrived in London, Pell was spending most of his time trying to set up the corporation that would manage the details of the migration and supervise the construction of the receiving places in Angola. The Germans were getting impatient. On May 18 Pell reported the arrival in London of a deputation of German Jews from Berlin who had been sent over by the German Gestapo with orders to warn Pell that there would be more shock tactics unless the corporation was actually set up and began operating.

Pell was having difficulty getting the London and New York Jewish communities to work together. Pell fixed more than one date for organizing the corporation only to find that one or another essential participant had a sudden reason to be elsewhere. We once located Lewis Strauss, representing the New York group, on a ship headed for Cherbourg when he had promised us to be in London. The London group headed by Lord Rothschild was reluctant to work with New York financier Bernard Baruch. There was a lot of foot-dragging during June and July. But by July 20 Pell was able to report to Washington that he had obtained the agreement of the Jewish communities to form the corporation and the agreement of Paul Van Zeeland, a widely respected former prime minister of Belgium, to serve as its president.

The work of the committee was substantially finished. President Roosevelt invited the top officials of the committee to come to Washington for a meeting with him "in early September." The ceremony there would be the official, formal launching of the project.

On September 1 the Germans invaded Poland. I was in Paris that day on a minor chore for the committee. I got back to London two days later. Pell had already left for Washington. My superior was Sir Herbert Emerson at the Foreign Office. I asked for instructions. He told me to dismiss the staff and take the files to a safe place "somewhere in the country." I called a taxi, piled the filing cases in, and drove them to the home of friends who lived on a farm near Maidenhead, "to be picked up after the war." I then reported to the American Embassy.

If World War II had not been started by Hitler on September 1, Paul Van Zeeland would have been in Lisbon talking to President Salazar of Portugal during that first week of September to settle on such details as the location in Angola of the first settlements and the future relationship of the Jewish community to the government of Portugal.

If World War II had not happened, Angola, not Palestine, would have become the officially designated homeland for those Jews willing to migrate out of Central and Eastern Europe.

If World War II had not happened, and if the Rublee-Pell plan had worked successfully, there would be no state of Israel in Palestine today and no problem of trying to reconcile the Israelis with the Palestinians. The Evian conference would not have been in vain.

I remember with particular respect two persons who worked with our committee in setting up the corporation that was to manage the construction of new communities in Angola for receiving the immigrants from Europe. One was Harold Linder, who at the time was vice chairman of the American Joint Distribution Committee, the principal organization for the management of charitable funds for the American Jewish community. He was tireless and effective in getting the American Jewish community involved in the establishment of the corporation. I remember the day we were trying to locate Lewis Strauss for an organizational meeting of the corporation. It was by telephone to Linder in New York that I was able to locate Strauss, and it was Linder who insisted that Strauss get to London for the meeting. The other person we found most helpful was Simon Marks of the Marks and Spencer stores in London. He was always the first to come forward with funds and organizational work.

A highlight of the work of the committee in London was one day when Pell told me to go down to the offices of the Rothschild Bank in the city (our own office was in the West End near Parliament) and see what I might be able to discover about why Lord Rothschild seemed to be reluctant to go ahead with the corporation. I chatted with a bright young lawyer who had been assigned as liaison with our committee. He told me that the bank was particularly concerned about having Bernard Baruch associated in any way with the corporation. Through Linder we were able to obtain assurance that Mr. Baruch would not be able to use the corporation to raid Rothschild holdings of mineral rights in Angola. That assurance seemed to clear the way for final agreement by the London group to the corporation.

Relations between Simon Marks, who was the most active younger member of the London group of Jewish leaders, and Lord Rothschild, the hereditary senior member of that community, seemed to be strained. Once the corporation was finally set up Lord Rothschild gave a dinner for everyone involved in the work. I was awed by the splendor of the Rothschild house and its marvelous collection of paintings and other art objects. I was also awed by the superb quality of the food that came from the Rothschild kitchen. Not so Simon Marks, who was seated across the table from Lord Rothschild himself. Simon took out a cigarette when he had finished his main course and was about to light it. Lord Rothschild spotted the move and firmly, and brusquely, told him no smoking while others were still eating. Simon protested, but submitted to the superior authority of the Rothschild name.

Pell assigned me to observe and report on the arrival of the German liner *St. Louis* at Antwerp on its return from a voyage around the Atlantic basin during which it had been unable to unload its passengers, all of whom were Jewish émigrés from Germany. Our committee had arranged for the exit visas, and we thought we had secured landing visas for them in Dominica. For reasons never explained by the Dominican Republic the landing was canceled. We were unable on short notice to arrange for any other country on the western side of the Atlantic to take them at that time. The ship headed back to Europe. Pell arranged during the interval to have its passengers disembarked at the port of Antwerp. A group from the Jewish Joint Distribution Committee was sent to meet the ship and arrange for the distribution of the passengers to various European countries, each of which had by then agreed to take a portion of the list. I watched as the ship was brought alongside the wharf. Passengers were seated in deck chairs being served their morning bouillon (a routine

ritual of life aboard transatlantic liners of that era) by white-coated stewards. Morris Troper of the JDC presided over the table at which delegates
from the various receiving countries took the passenger list and assigned
to disembarking passengers their new destinations. I seem to recall that
France took the largest number. I have never seen a report on the ultimate fate of those people. Those who were still in France, Holland, and
Belgium a year later were presumably caught up in Hitler's dragnet after
the fall of France.

And So to War

I was in the American Embassy on Grosvenor Square in London at midday on Sunday, September 3, 1939, listening with everyone else there to the radio when Neville Chamberlain announced Britain was in a state of war with Germany. As he finished speaking, the air raid sirens screeched. We all trooped dutifully to the cellar next door. There was no air raid that day. I was never clear whether the sirens sounded because a returning friendly airliner was mistaken for a German bomber or whether it was done deliberately to impress upon everyone that war had actually begun. If the purpose was the latter it had its effect, and that included a temporary job for me at the embassy.

My assignment in London had been by the State Department, which had placed me with the Intergovernmental Committee. When Sir Herbert Emerson, director of the committee, released me from my duties there, its work being suspended automatically for the duration of the war, I reverted technically to the State Department. Hence, I reported at the embassy and was given an immediate temporary assignment there. The embassy building, a pleasant Georgian-revival structure of red brick trimmed with limestone (now the Canadian Embassy, the American Embassy having since the war moved into a new, larger, and more assertive structure across the square), had at that time a small waiting room just inside the front door. I was planted there and told to "take care" of all tourists who came for succor to the embassy. The assignment turned into an intriguing lesson in panic control.

Not all American tourists panic when their European tours are suddenly interrupted by the outbreak of a war, but some do just that. It became a game for me to calm their fears, persuade them that they would probably get home before Hitler could get them, and explain just how that was to be done. Adm. Alan Kirk, the naval attaché at the embassy, had everything beautifully arranged well in advance. The two fine, fast transatlantic ships of the United States Lines were immediately diverted from routine schedules to take care of the sudden tourist migration. Instead of coming in at the usual passenger terminal at Southampton, which was needed now for naval uses, they were to come to Weston-super-Mare, a holiday resort on the Bristol Channel, which had plenty of hotels no longer needed for summer holiday visitors and no wartime function. All I had to do was persuade the tourists to go, the sooner the better (nothing being more useless than an alien tourist in a country trying to gear itself for war), to Paddington Station and take the next train from Paddington to Weston-super-Mare. An American Express Company agent would be on the platform there on arrival of all trains from London with lists of hotel rooms and arrangements for informing them well in advance of the next embarkation for New York.

The plan worked well. By the end of a week the crest of the tourist wave was cleared out of London and its individual elements bedded down in one or another of those many resort hotels at Weston-super-Mare, providing, incidentally, a welcome extension of the normal holiday season for the hoteliers of that place. Admiral Kirk then released me from all government obligations. I cabled to Charles Gratke, the *Monitor*'s foreign editor in Boston, reporting back for assignment, and he told me to go to Rome. That took a bit of arranging, which gave me time to see Anne off for Weston-super-Mare and home via the United States Lines and to practice journalism in London. I called on our ambassador, Joseph P. Kennedy, and learned that he was as pro-German and anti-English as an Irishman could then be and sometimes still is today. He argued that Britain was bound to lose the war and that the sooner it happened the better for all concerned. He opposed any U.S. help to the British on the ground that it would only prolong the war and thus the damage to all involved. Of course he said it to me "off the record," which I respected. I have since wondered whether I was being too journalistically responsible in honoring his injunction. Had I actually written for publication what he had said to me in private he would, of course, have denied saying it. Those private views were well known both in Britain and in American government circles. Would any good purpose have been served by printing them publicly? Probably not. I did not print that story, but when the British Cunard liner *Athenia* was sunk by a German submarine on September 3 with 112 Americans aboard, of whom 28 lost their lives, I wrote a British reaction story recording the inevitable hope among the British that the sinking would stimulate the American people and government to forget about neutrality and make American weapons available to the British and to the French. By that time my permit to travel through France had come through, my wife Anne telephoned from Weston-super-Mare, so I bought a rail and cross-channel steamer ticket and on September 13 set off for Rome.

The journey was unusual. The cross-channel steamer from Dover to Boulogne was less than half full. The train from Boulogne to Paris was eight hours late. I had plenty of time to read the notices posted in all public places instructing military reservists to report to their assembly area. Eventually I shuttled by taxi across an unnaturally quiet Paris to the station for Rome. There I boarded a sleeping car marked exclusively for Italy, passengers not being allowed to leave the train as it passed through Switzerland en route.

I do not remember how it happened that I chose as my hotel in Rome the Hotel de la Ville at the top of the Spanish Steps and scarcely more than a fifteen-minute walk to the American Embassy, but it was a happy choice. The Hotel de la Ville was old, probably built sometime around 1880. It was not shabby, but it looked settled and long used. Its marble floors were smoothed unevenly from many feet and daily scrubbing. The entrance hall was just big enough for a reception desk and the concierge. It was the kind of comfortable, nonflashy hotel that attracts what the English call "country gentry," not rich tourists. The latter would normally go to the new and glamorous Hotel Hassler next door, which later became German army headquarters. The de la Ville's amenities included an adventurous young bachelor first secretary from the American Embassy (his name is lost to my memory) who happened to have achieved an easy social relationship with Italian foreign minister Count Ciano (also Mussolini's son-in-law). The two would meet of an afternoon at the beach or of an evening at a nightclub. Also resident was John Whitaker, Rome correspondent of the *Chicago Daily News*, which at that time had probably the most consistently able staff of foreign correspondents of any American news service. John was one of the best, was well established in Rome, also was personally acquainted with Count Ciano, and was most generous in helping a newly arrived colleague. Thanks to those two and to others at the American Embassy, including the ambassador, William Phillips, I was able quickly to grasp the general Italian situation and write acceptably about it.

The situation in Rome at that time was that the Italian duce, Benito Mussolini, had been talked, or frightened, out of his commitment to

Hitler to go to war at once. The commitment was solid. Only three months earlier on May 22, there had been proclaimed from the Reich Chancellery in Berlin a "Pact of Steel" by which Germany and Italy bound themselves to each other. The text said that if either one of them "became involved in warlike complications with another power or powers, the other High Contracting Party would immediately come to its assistance as an ally and support it with all its military forces on land, at sea and in the air."

There was nothing ambiguous about the commitment or the situation. Since September 1 Germany had been involved in "warlike complications" in Poland. Italy was required by the Pact of Steel to support Germany with its "military forces," and both Britain and France had declared that they were at war with Germany. If the May 22 pact meant anything, it meant that Italy should at that point have been mobilized and have placed its troops on its frontier with France in order to divert French forces from France's German front. But when I reached Rome on September 14, there had been no sign of any martial move, or even martial posture, by Benito Mussolini. Italy had made no declaration of solidarity with Germany or any hostile move toward France on land or Britain at sea. Italy was staying out of the war.

Eight months later it would be a different story. By that time Hitler's early successes had stiffened Mussolini's spine and whetted his appetite for a share of the spoils of war. In May 1940, when German troops would be surging through France, Mussolini would remember his obligations under the Pact of Steel and deliver "the stab in the back" at France.

But in mid-September of that first month of the second great world war word had seeped out from Mussolini's offices that he had backed away from his war commitment. Hitler had opened the war too soon for Italian taste. Mussolini had been aiming at joining Hitler at war in 1942. He was not ready in 1939, and, besides, he had no liking for the way Hitler had chosen to open the war. Hitler's sudden pact with Stalin was a startling surprise (we know now from captured documents). But it gave Mussolini an out. His Pact of Steel had called for prior consultation. Hitler had not consulted him or informed him in advance of the deal with Stalin. And besides, the Hitler-Mussolini partnership had been founded on the ideology of fascism, which in those days meant anticommunism. It was ideologically impossible for Hitler to enter into any sort of partnership with communism, and yet he had; more than that, Hitler had compounded it by inviting Stalin to share Poland with him. This was another partition of Poland by which, beginning on September 17, Soviet troops moved into eastern Poland (and also into the three Baltic states: Estonia, Latvia, and Lithuania).

Mussolini was left looking like (and feeling like) the jilted lover. More than that, Hitler had invited communism westward into Poland, and Poland was next door to Rumania, which was once part of the ancient Roman Empire and of prime concern to any Italian government. Mussolini did not know how far the new Hitler-Stalin partnership might go. Was it temporary and applicable only to Poland, or might Hitler be thinking of dividing up the Balkans with his new friend in Moscow? The newspapers in Rome were full of discussions of the range of Italian interests. If the Soviet Communists moved into Rumania, would that be dangerous to Italy? I was writing about all this from Rome on September 18. By September 28 I was writing about Italian concern over "the looming shadow of Soviet Russia." It is interesting that this concern showed up equally in both the newspapers controlled by the state and those which reflected Vatican views. Church and state were at one in Rome in late September in their anxiety over Hitler's deal with Stalin and in their profound hope that Italy would manage to keep out of the war. Both types of newspapers also carried many articles relishing the prospect of a booming economy from selling goods to both sides in the war that Italy was to avoid.

It was at that time and in that mood that Mussolini welcomed Hitler's self-styled "peace offer" to Britain and France. The war in Poland was, in effect, over by mid-September. So far there had been no fighting along the western front. The sinking of the *Athenia* had been a mistake, unintended by the German high command, in fact contrary to orders. On October 6 Hitler spelled out in the Reichstag his proposed peace terms for Britain and France. He would call off the war against the West, he said, provided the British and French would accept the partition of Poland as final. They had accepted the disappearance of both Austria and Czechoslovakia. Why not also accept the dissolution of Poland? The French were tempted. The British were not. On October 12 Chamberlain, in a speech in Parliament, dismissed Hitler's purported peace offer as being "vague and uncertain" and called for "convincing proof" that Hitler really wanted peace. The Germans took the speech as being a rejection of the peace offer. So too did my editor in Boston. Two things were reasonably certain by that time. There would be a real war in the north of Europe. And Italy would keep out at least during the first phase. Gratke sent a cable. It was brief and to the point: "now go to Berlin."

I left Rome with a backward glance of affection. My last report from there contrasted the mood in Rome with the deep anxieties around me when I had been in London. I wrote: "But that was England and the north and here in Rome there is sunshine and then gentle rain and the church bells ring without undertones and there are young men still in the streets. . . ."

When I finished packing my bags, I took a last look out of my fourth-floor window at the now familiar courtyard of the Hotel de la Ville. Opposite, three floors down, was a broad balcony. John Whitaker was stretched out on a bench in the sun being massaged. He had a bad back. His neighbor in the adjoining room, Olive Monroe, was reading to him. She was a sort of den mother to the American correspondents, an expatriate American widow of sufficient means to be able to live in Rome for its art and beauty and associations. I remember pleasant meals with Olive, John, and others in the American community. When I think of John the word *gallant* comes to mind. He was slender, thoughtful, generous, quick to find the news, and able at presenting it. He had given me a letter to his *Chicago Daily News* colleague in Berlin, Wally Deuel, who would be as helpful to me in Berlin as John had been in Rome. I am proud of my profession. The roster of American correspondents who covered World War II is long and honorable. There was none better than John Whitaker. The scene lingers in my mind—John being treated by a masseur on a peaceful, sun-drenched day in Rome while Olive read to him. I never saw John again. He died of bone cancer before the war was over.

Another scene lingers. As my taxi drove from the hotel, I had a quick glimpse of the vast sea of flowers spilling down the Spanish Steps. Nowhere else in the world is there a flower market like that, certainly not in Berlin. I felt a twinge of nostalgia as I left Rome in flowers and sunshine and headed for war in the north.

Berlin: Before Election Day, 1940

I had no problem getting from Rome to Berlin in mid–October 1939. Current films about travel in those early days of World War II always manage to produce a sinister context for the scene. It was not like that. I went to the German Embassy, asked for a visa, got it within three days, told the hotel concierge to buy me a ticket to Berlin, and took the train to Berlin. There was nothing out of the ordinary about the trip itself. I went by night sleeper. I handed my ticket and passport to the sleeping car attendant. I woke up next morning in Germany. Incidentally, in current movies made about the events of 1939, people seem to fly. Some people did travel by air in those days, but not many and not often. It was stunt stuff. No one did it for comfort. It was low-level and very bumpy flying. I flew from London to Paris over the channel once in those early days of flying. I was so weak from vomiting during the flight that I had to be carried off the plane. Normal travelers went by train. It never occurred to me to think of going from London to Rome or Rome to Berlin by anything but train. My own train trip from Rome to Berlin produced only one abnormality. There were no baggage porters at the platform when I got off my train at the Friedrichstrasse Bahnhof in Berlin.

I did the easiest thing. I walked to the nearest hotel, which happened to be the Continental, around the corner from the station, took a room, and sent a hotel porter back for the luggage. I stayed in that hotel long enough to acquire "a German family," meaning a source of information from an ordinary local family living an ordinary local life.

As an American correspondent at a time when German policy was keyed to keeping the United States out of the war as long as possible, I settled into a privileged life. I was given the ration card of a "heavy worker." I could eat at a restaurant maintained by the Foreign Office where rationing did not apply. And I could import extra food from Denmark. I received a weekly package of a dozen eggs, a pound of bacon, a pound of butter, a pound of cheese, and a jar of honey. This was more than I needed for my own purposes. Thus I had the means of cultivating my "German family." I took them butter, eggs, or cheese in return for admission to the routine life and attitudes of a family of four living in a working-class section, Wedding. The widowed mother was a passionate Nazi who kept a wreath over a photograph of Hitler on the piano. The son was a pragmatic Nazi. He wore a Nazi party button because he worked at the post office and had to be a party member to keep his job. He was also of military age and hoped to keep out of the army. His party membership would help. (After the war I learned that he was eventually drafted, sent to Russia, and never returned.) Then there were two daughters, one a switchboard operator at the hotel, the other a clerk in a music store. The latter specialized in selling sheet music for the opera and symphony orchestras. The two daughters had no use either for Hitler or for nazism. I was present when one of the daughters deliberately knocked Hitler's picture off the piano. The brother laughed. The frightened and angry mother picked it up and scolded the daughter. From "the family" I gleaned a regular crop of street stories that were helpful in getting the public attitude toward nazism in perspective. They always had a new story for me, such as the following.

A company of brown-shirted storm troopers was marching down the street. A drunk on the sidewalk shouted, "Down with Hitler, to Hell with Hitler." The leader halted his troop, walked over to the drunk, and whispered to him, "Please, don't do that. It's dangerous. I think I have a Nazi in my rear rank."

The Continental Hotel was comfortable, but I was the only American correspondent there and the rooms were small. I decided to try apartment living. I moved to a furnished apartment in the Olivar Platz, about half an hour by bus from the center of town. By December it was getting cold. I was mentioned in a colleague's news report after he found me warming my fingers in hot water on the stove in order to be able to type. I soon gave that up and moved into the center of Berlin life at the Adlon Hotel, which was unscarred by war and still one of the best hotels in all Europe. Several other American correspondents were already there along with several officers from the American Embassy.

The Adlon was an elegant hotel in the art moderne style (probably about 1910) and located strategically at the corner of the Pariser Platz and the Wilhelmstrasse. If you turned left coming out of the front door of the hotel the American Embassy was next door in the Pariser Platz, with the Brandenburg Gate just beyond. The French Embassy (closed) was across the platz. If you turned right from the hotel front door, the British Embassy (also closed of course) was around the corner in the Wilhelmstrasse on the right, and a stone's throw beyond that was Bismarck's old Chancellery, which had become the Foreign Office. Hitler's new Chancellery was just a little farther along the Wilhelmstrasse. The Propaganda Ministry was a block away, to the left, from the Foreign Office. All were within short walking distance from the hotel.

The Adlon was at the crossroads where journalists, diplomats, spies, and government officials all congregated. Many a colleague found that he could get most of the news he needed at the Adlon grill. It was the center of activity, just as the grill at the Grillon in Paris became a similar center after the war. A visiting journalist gets to know such a center in every European capital. In Berlin in 1939 and 1940 it was the grill at the Adlon. I took a room in the back wing, overlooking Goebbels's garden. I watched his children playing in the garden. Bill (William L.) Shirer of CBS had a room on the same floor, but in front with double French doors to a balcony looking out on the Pariser Platz and facing northwest—the direction from which most air raids came. When an air raid happened, the American group would tend to gather in Bill's room to watch the action. The same group would gather in my room at news time. I had a radio receiver that could pick up the BBC from London. Radio listening in my room became a feature of our lives, both morning and evening.

During that first phase of the war American correspondents had an easy time living, getting news, and transmitting it. We were allowed to travel more or less at will anywhere under German control. We could talk to anyone. Ordinary civilians spoke to us freely in public or private. We of course identified ourselves as Americans. That was a precaution and a protection for both. I wore a small American flag pin on my lapel, while sporting a French beret basque as headgear and, as nearly as I could manage, a British Guardsman's bristling mustache.

There was no problem about the *Heil Hitler* greeting. A bus conductor, for example, was required to give the Nazi salute and say "Heil Hitler" to anyone boarding the bus. The permissible and acceptable response by a foreigner was the classic German peasant greeting *Gruss Gott* (God's greetings).

There was no precensorship of news for newspapers. We transmitted by telephone to the office in Bern, Switzerland, of Press Wireless, a communications service set up and owned by a group of leading American newspapers. The Press Wireless office recorded our copy on discs, transcribed them, and then filed them at the Swiss telegraph office. I could use any telephone, public or private, make a collect call, and read my news story.

There was of course postcensorship. The German Embassy in Washington read whatever was printed from us and reported back to the Foreign Office in Berlin. I was careful in what I wrote. We were forbidden to write about prospective German military movements and locations. In late 1940 one American colleague, Ralph Barns of the *New York Herald Tribune*, was expelled for reporting (accurately) that the German army was getting ready to invade Russia. But so long as one was reasonably discreet about such matters one could write freely—up to an invisible point. When I once discussed civilian morale and reported some lack of popular confidence in Hitler's wisdom, I was summoned to the Foreign Office and given a warning. Much more of that kind of writing and I would be invited to leave. But that was the worst punishment mentioned. Since, in that phase of the war, the Germans were winning the battles and wanted to promote the theory of their military invincibility, the more we wrote about the successes of German armed forces the more pleased they were. There was little going on in Germany at that time that the government wanted concealed, not even the concentration camps for Jews and other persons deemed dangerous to the regime.

The Germans were not then self-conscious or secretive about the concentration camps. The label *concentration camp* had not then acquired the sinister connotation it has today. Internment of enemy aliens in time of war was familiar in Europe. British and French immediately interned their enemy aliens on the outbreak of war in 1939. Those enemy aliens interned in Britain by the British on the outbreak of war in 1939 included German-born Jews. Americans put even their native-born Japanese into internment camps after Pearl Harbor. Jews in Germany were aliens under German law and Jews anywhere were enemies of Nazi Germany by declaration of Dr. Chaim Weizmann, president of the Jewish Agency. In a letter written to British prime minister Neville Chamberlain and published in *The Times* (London) on September 6, 1939, Dr. Weizmann declared that all Jews everywhere would fight against Nazi Germany. The letter was reprinted in Germany and cited by Hitler. There was nothing sufficiently unusual about the internment camps in Germany to attract the special attention of American correspondents in Berlin in 1939 and

1940. Only one, Otto Tolischus of the *New York Times*, asked for permission to visit a camp. His report, printed in the Sunday magazine section of the *Times*, found nothing startling going on in the camp. Sporadic killings of Jews occurred in Poland early in the German occupation. There was much more killing, frequently by anti-Semitic locals, as the German army moved into Russia in 1941. But the deliberate, organized mass extermination of Jews by Germans began only after a conference of top Nazis at Wannsee, a Berlin suburb, on January 20, 1942.

Broadcasting from Berlin was different from newspaper reporting. All scripts for news broadcasts had to be submitted before delivery to a panel of censors, one each from the Foreign Office, the Propaganda Ministry, and the Military High Command. My broadcasting career grew out of the fact that I was the only newspaper reporter in Berlin at the time who was allowed by his newspaper to do broadcasts on the side. Bill Shirer was the CBS correspondent. CBS wanted twice daily news reports from Berlin and also wanted Bill to make frequent trips out of Berlin, often to the military front when fighting was going on. He could not both travel and meet as many circuits as were wanted. He asked me to substitute for him when he was out of town or unable to meet a circuit. That was my introduction to news broadcasting.

For broadcasts to the United States we used the German radio's short-wave transmitter, which was located in a temporary building in the garden of a large, turn-of-the-century beaux arts–style villa, near the Adolf Hitler Platz at the far end of the Axis, the main east-west boulevard that continued the line of the Unter den Linden westward through the Tiergarten and beyond. The censors had a room in the villa. Once copy had been cleared there was still a short walk outdoors from the villa to the studios in the garden. This could become interesting during an air raid. There was always the possibility of a bomb (which did not happen near me during my stay in Berlin) or a bit of loose shrapnel. The censors delayed me only once. I had written in my script a reference to "Goering's medals." They contended that the word *medal* was derogatory. They asserted that medals were for children, that soldiers wore *decorations*. I replied that the highest decoration which existed in my country is the Congressional Medal of Honor. They accepted my point and I did the broadcast as written. Someone from the censor's office monitored the broadcasts to see that the script was followed. He could switch off the circuit if I were to say something not in the approved script.

Waiting at the radio station for circuit time could be eventful. One evening when the air raid alarm sounded and the lights went out I chose to remain upstairs in the room we used for writing last-minute scripts. It had French windows to the floor. I opened them to watch the air raid. I could see searchlights probing the sky, shell bursts, and finally the plane, presumably British. I became aware of another person standing beside me. A male voice remarked, casually: "You've got to admire the courage of the chap up there, flying all the way from England and not a very good chance of getting home again." I agreed with his comment. We chatted about such matters. The all-clear sounded. The lights went up and I turned to see who had been my conversational companion. A long scar across his cheek, plus his English accent, left no doubt. It was an Irishman named William Joyce who did regular pro-German broadcasts for the German propaganda service to England, where he developed a substantial audience of people who found his extravagant version of events a diversion from standard BBC fare. He was known in England as Lord Haw-Haw. He claimed to have been born in New York, but after the war the British hanged him in the Tower as a traitor.

A third Irishman, or man of Irish descent, appeared in Berlin somewhere about that same time. Tall, handsome, and expensively tailored, he became known in the American community as the man of many hats. He kept a suite of rooms at the Adlon. A table in his entrance hall was covered with his collection of hats, mostly either black or gray homburgs. His name was John Hartigan and he said he had come to Berlin for former president Herbert Hoover to report to Mr. Hoover on conditions in and prospects about Germany. When picking up my mail at the concierge's desk one day I was handed an envelope and told, "Mr. Hartigan said to give this to you, that it might interest you." I took it to my room and read a long report addressed to Mr. Hoover, which began with "Dear Chief." The text came close to being a repetition of what Ambassador Kennedy had said to me privately in London. It took as its premise that Germany was bound to win the war, that the longer the war lasted the greater the damage to Western civilization, and that the United States should avoid anything that might delay the German victory. He recommended that Mr. Hoover repeat the program he ran during World War I for feeding Belgian children. He said that taking the load of feeding Belgians off the shoulders of the German economy would help get the war over sooner. Just as I finished reading, the phone rang and Mr. Hartigan informed me that he had by mistake left the wrong envelope for me. He retrieved the report to his "chief."

Wayne Chatfield Taylor, a representative of the American Red Cross (later its president), arrived one day from Freiburg. He said Freiburg had been bombed. He was on a train in the switching yards when the attack took place. He noticed that the planes doing the bombing had flown at Freiburg from the East. He was puzzled. The Propaganda Ministry announced that Freiburg had been bombed by Allied planes. It became the excuse for reprisal bombing of England. After the war we confirmed from German records that the planes doing the bombing were German planes coming from the East.

Everyone seemed to come to the Adlon. One day it was the former crown prince. My memory file contains a glimpse of Louis Adlon, owner and manager of the hotel, dressed in his formal uniform of striped trousers and cutaway coat, clicking his heels, bowing deferentially, and addressing his guest as *Hochheit* (Highness). The crown prince had dropped in for lunch. The Hohenzollern monarchy had been abolished by the Weimar Republic, but at the Adlon Hotel members of the former imperial family were treated with meticulous deference. I noticed that the most popular cigarette at the tobacco counter at the Adlon and elsewhere around the western part of Berlin was named Schloss Oels, which was the crown prince's personal estate.

During the German campaign in France a rift developed within the American correspondents' group. Tours to the front were led by a dashing young German army officer attached to the Propaganda Ministry, Karl Boehmer by name. One group of correspondents liked him personally and cultivated his friendship. They were rewarded. There were always two or more cars for the American correspondents. Boehmer would take Guido Enderis of the *New York Times*, Pierre Huss of INS, and Louis Lochner of the AP in his own car. Toward the end of the day he would head back to the cable-head at high speed, having ordered the following cars with UP, *Herald Tribune*, *Chicago Daily News*, CBS, and other correspondents to follow at the official army speed limit, which was about twenty-five miles per hour. This gave the favored three a time advantage over the competition. Those who went in the favored car justified the friendship with Boehmer as being practical journalism. Those who suffered felt that their colleagues had used improper tactics to gain a time advantage. The American group was unable to find common ground in approaching the German authorities. Those who refused favors felt that the others were being unduly pro-German.

We date World War II from the invasion of Poland on September 1,

1939. On that day Hitler's armies stormed into Poland. There were then twenty days of sudden violence and destruction in Poland and many a person, mostly Polish, lost life or limb. But it was over after twenty days, and then there were six months of no more major fighting anywhere. I, having arrived in Berlin after the fighting in Poland had ended, found myself reporting not the biggest and most destructive war in history, but rather a lot of questions and uncertainties as to whether there would be anything more than the war in Poland.

There were many odd things to explain. Mussolini had failed to join the war as Hitler had expected him to do and as he was contractually committed to do. The French had failed to launch an offensive against Germany in the West as their commitment to Poland had required them to do. It was as though the Italians and the French and the British all still hoped that by doing nothing the war might gradually cease to be a great and general war. And indeed that well might have happened had it not been for Hitler himself. Suppose he had elected to be satisfied with the conquests he already had in his pocket in late September 1939—Austria, Czechoslovakia, and Poland? There had been no bombing of cities yet, no bombing of anything except Poland. The war on land was nothing except occasional, perfunctory small-arms fire along the French-German frontier. At sea the British passenger liner *Athenia* had been sunk and a daring German U-boat skipper, Guenther Prien, had penetrated the British naval anchorage at Scapa Flow in Scotland and sunk the British battleship *Royal Oak*. The two German pocket battleships, *Deutschland* and *Graf Spee,* sortied into the Atlantic and sank a dozen British merchant ships. The British aircraft carrier *Courageous* was torpedoed on the high seas southwest of Ireland. But these were acts of German initiative. During the first six months of World War II there was not a single important act of military initiative by Britain or France, and no serious plans by either for launching any such act of military initiative. Had Hitler done nothing more after the defeat of Poland he would have been the undisputed master of Central Europe with the written consent of the Soviet Union and the tacit consent (by inaction) of everyone else.

Hitler's strategic position would have been safe. The British were blockading his ports on the North Sea, thus cutting him off from direct trade with the outside world. But he had indirect access through Sweden, which acted as a middleman for trading purposes, and his new relationship with the Soviet Union gave him access to the raw materials of that vast country. He could not be starved of either food or necessary raw materials so long as Stalin was willing to cooperate with him. There was no reason then to doubt Stalin's willingness to do just that.

But Hitler was not ready to settle for being master of Central Europe by Soviet consent. Throughout that first winter of the war he was busy building the tanks and planes and training the men for further conquest, the meanwhile letting his civilian population get a taste of the spoils of war. Berlin markets swelled with hams from Poland and sausages from Czechoslovakia. I took a midwinter trip to Vienna and Prague. There was no sign of open resistance to the German occupation. People seemed subdued, but busy. Food, clothing, and all usual consumer goods were in ample supply. Factories were busy with German war orders. Hitler's war machine was efficient. It harnessed conquered peoples to the German economy with no apparent effort. Almost overnight the newly conquered were working for the conquerer. Hitler's war machine was economically profitable, so profitable that its obvious success smothered the doubts and anxieties on the home front in Germany itself. There was plenty of such doubt and anxiety in the beginning, particularly among some of Hitler's top generals. But it is difficult to argue against success. Few tried to do so after the blitzkrieg in Poland.

Jacob Beam, one of the able young diplomats in a remarkably well-staffed American Embassy at the time, had an unpleasant experience that winter. He went back to Washington on a brief visit and found himself a social pariah for telling people in political circles something of the true state of affairs in Germany. They wanted to hear that there were severe food shortages, mass public dissatisfaction, shortage of essential war materials. The last thing Washington upper circles wanted to be told was the truth, that Hitler controlled the world's most efficient war machine, made up of superbly trained and highly motivated soldiers and the most modern weaponry in ample supply. Diplomat Beam came back to Berlin shaking his head and telling us correspondents that we had not done a good job of telling people at home how powerful Hitler's Germany had become. Wishful thinking is difficult to overcome. Jake Beam found himself being accused of being pro-Nazi when he tried to tell people in Washington that the German tanks were not immobilized from lack of oil and grease.

Such illusions, and with them the possibility that the war would never really begin, were wiped out one April morning (April 9, 1940) when Danes and Norwegians woke up to find German troops on their airfields and in their seaports. In Denmark it was an almost bloodless conquest (thirteen Danes killed). The government at once capitulated and ordered an end to resistance. It was all over before midday. In Norway it would take longer. The king and government escaped German capture. Many Norwegian military units resisted. The British could, and did, come to their aid. Fighting lasted almost to the end of April and cost the Germans 1,317 killed, ten destroyers and three cruisers sunk, and three capital ships damaged and out of action for months.

I was asked to go to Copenhagen after the Danish capitulation and do a broadcast from there for NBC. I flew up from Berlin in a German army transport plane and went first to the American Embassy, then to the local newspaper offices. By the end of the day I was ready to write that "I never dreamed that I should ever see such heartache in a people." The Danes were crushed, physically and mentally. True, their position had been hopeless. Resistance would have been useless. But they had repeatedly been promised by the Germans that their neutrality would be respected. The king was personally assured on the day before the invasion that his country was safe. Then he woke up the next morning to find German soldiers surrounding his palace. Hitler was not to be satisfied with Austria, Czechoslovakia, and Poland.

Nor was he to be satisfied by adding Denmark and Norway to his holdings. Early in the morning of May 10, the Belgian and Dutch ambassadors in Berlin were summoned to the Foreign Office and informed that German armies were entering their countries "to protect them from the French and British." The invasion had in fact already begun. It would continue over the next six weeks until northern France had been overrun, the French government had retreated from Paris to Bordeaux and sued for an armistice with the Germans, and the British had taken the last of their troops off the beaches at Dunkirk. The battle for northwestern Europe was over. The battle of Britain was about to begin.

Hitler's Last Chance

The Battle of Britain was about to begin, but the beginning of it was less certain at that time than it seems in retrospect. Well before the fall of France the German Navy had done advance planning for an invasion of Britain. On the very day (June 21, 1940) that the French were signing the articles of capitulation in the forest of Compiegne, I, on a press tour of the battlefields, saw and got three photographic shots of a huge river barge being hauled on rollers up and over the Danube-Rhine watershed by a tractor with a German naval officer in full uniform standing on the bow and shaking a fist at us. And Dr. Goebbels had long since used the bombing of Freiburg as a propaganda justification for the bombing of British cities, but there had been no general German bombing of British cities up to that time.

Was there to be a battle of Britain?

The scene in the Reichstag on the evening of July 19 was one that no one present could ever forget. It was Hitler triumphant, at the peak of his career, savoring to the full his victories, dispensing rewards to his generals, and—offering peace to Britain.

Hermann Goering sat in the Speaker's chair in his capacity as president of the Reichstag. Hitler, as chancellor, sat at the head of the government bench, wearing civilian, not military, uniform. Everyone in Berlin of any importance was there—including the Diplomatic Corps and the foreign press. Hitler went to the rostrum just below the Speaker's desk. Before starting to speak he turned offhandedly and placed a small box on the corner of the Speaker's desk, then turned to the audience and began with a review of his military conquests from Poland to the six-week campaign through the Low Countries and France. Then he announced the honors to his generals. He conferred the rank of field marshall on nine army generals and three air force generals. (The kaiser in World War I conferred field marshall rank on only five of his generals.) While Hitler was speaking of the others, Goering's hand crept over to the little box on the desk and surreptitiously stole a quick glance inside. Hitler came last to Goering, announcing that Goering was now reich marshall, a title never granted before. Then there was playacting. He started to resume his speech, then, as though struck by an afterthought, he stopped, turned, picked up the little box, opened it to show a diamond-studded object inside, and handed it to Goering telling him, and everyone, that it was the Grand Cross of the Order of the Iron Cross. Next, with all settled back in their seats again after the cheering, Hitler turned to the future and to the subject of Britain, his remaining undefeated enemy. He spoke at length about the political situation in Britain. He asserted that it was only the politicians who were determined to carry on the war. He excoriated Churchill specifically and he concluded with the following climactic declaration:

"In this hour I feel it to be my duty before my own conscience to appeal once more to reason and common sense in Great Britain as much as elsewhere. I consider myself in a position to make this appeal since I am not the vanquished begging favors, but the victor speaking in the name of reason.

I see no reason why this war must go on."

I was standing at that moment beside Alexander Kirk, the American chargé d'affaires in Berlin at the time. The slender, impeccably dressed deputy ambassador cultivated a languid air. As the enormous applause for Hitler's speech died down a very excited German diplomat, the head of the American desk at the Foreign Office, came rushing up to Mr. Kirk and said, "Oh, Mr. Ambassador, isn't it wonderful, now we can have peace." Alexander Kirk was at that instant in a diplomatically delicate situation. He did not dare either agree or disagree with the German. He just looked at him, patted his mouth to cover a still visible yawn, and said, "I am hungry. Where might I find food?"

Without any possible doubt Hitler thought he was offering an acceptable peace to the British. His own past remarks about the future world and repeated informal statements from Foreign Office and Propaganda Ministry officials had sketched out his general terms. Hitler would want back the former German colonies taken by others after World War I—principally in Africa. Otherwise, he proposed to let Britain keep its empire, including India. Unstated was the essential condition. Britain would have to accept the fact of Hitler's control of all of Western Europe. For the first time since the reign of Charlemagne, more than a thousand years before, Britain would look across the Channel at a Europe with a single ruler, Adolf Hitler.

Three days before the Reichstag speech of July 19 Hitler gave orders to prepare for an invasion of Britain to be carried out "if necessary." But it is doubtful that he ever seriously intended to send his soldiers across the English Channel. He had always wanted to avoid a real war with the British. In his fantasy world there would be an almost German-British condominium, he taking the whole of continental Europe while the British ran the rest of the world through their empire. He was astonished that the British did not take seriously his peace invitation of July 19. His own mind had already turned to the problem of Russia. At the end of July he was exploring the possibility of invading Russia before winter set in and by the end of August he was moving troops from the West to the East.

The chronology of events is particularly relevant at this point. The peace offer to Britain was made in the Reichstag speech on July 19. On August 1 he ordered Goering to seek the defeat of the Royal Air Force, but he surrounded that order with severe restrictions on methods to be used. There was to be no "terror attack" on civilians, specifically no bombing of London. He went to his mountaintop retreat—the Berghof (Eagle's Nest) at Berchtesgaden—on August 8 with his top generals and all the film footage which could be found of the recent Russian campaign in Finland. They spent days studying those films for knowledge of current Russian weapons and tactics. During the next two weeks there were other meetings with top generals, at all of which he emphasized the danger from Russia and the possible necessity of early military action against Russia. On August 26 he ordered ten divisions moved east, and on August 27 staff officers went east to prepare a suitable headquarters for him for the campaign against Russia.

What a different world we would be in today had Hitler refrained from taking any hostile action against Britain. He did take hostile action. His navy was on the offensive in the North Sea and the Atlantic. His bombers were attacking British seaports. Suppose that instead of taking actions that were intended to push the British toward peace by air and sea blockade he had done nothing hostile at all but had turned from Britain and concentrated on attacking Russia. Would the British have taken major offensive action against Germany? Perhaps, but unlikely. The more likely scenario is that the British would have sat on the sidelines watching the downfall of the Soviet Union. And in that case, would the United States ever have come into the European war? It is highly doubtful that Britain and America would have joined in an attack on Germany in order to save Communist Russia. It took the actual bombing of the U.S. fleet at Pearl Harbor to bring the United States into war with Japan. And it took a German declaration of war to bring the United States into the European war. The United States never did declare war against Nazi Germany. The United States declared itself to be in a state of war with Germany because of the German declaration of war against the United States—and *only* after the Germans declared war against the United States.

Why then did Hitler finally unleash Goering's Luftwaffe against London? His strategy through most of August was to try to force the British to peace by a blockade enforced by direct bombing on the seaports and by submarine attacks on merchant shipping but with minimum damage to civilians and civilian life.

Herein lay Hitler's first serious mistake in World War II. He assumed that the blockade plus the threat of an invasion could induce the British to seek peace. What it did in fact was to subject the British government to a rising popular demand for British offensive action against Germany. That is the way it worked. At night on August 26 British bombers appeared for the first time over Berlin, but did no serious damage. On August 29 they came again; this time twenty German civilians were killed. And they came again on the night of August 30. That, in turn, brought public pressure on Hitler for retaliation.

British bombers over Berlin two nights in a row were too much for Hitler. On September 4 he finally authorized the Luftwaffe to attack London massively and by night. On September 5, in the big Sportpalast, he delivered a rousing speech that in effect was his declaration of unrestrained warfare against Britain. Those nights of British bombers over Berlin had drawn his attention back from Russia. The British had to be punished for their folly in attacking his capital instead of making the peace he had offered them. At that speech I was in the foreign press section—in line with the speaker, but back against the wall. I could not see the entrance door from where I sat. I became aware of a strange rhythmic sound at the far end of the hall beyond my range of vision. The picture of a mass of dogs barking crossed my mind, but it was rhythmic. Dogs don't bark in rhythm. Then I could see Hitler walking down the center aisle. The noise was of massed thousands of voices chanting *Heil Hitler, Heil Hitler,* endlessly, in a wave which moved down through the hall as he walked forward. I had to pinch myself, literally, to keep from slipping into the rhythm and joining in the noise. It was difficult to avoid being drawn into the emotionalism of the moment. He mounted the rostrum and started speaking, mocking Churchill, mocking British ideas, mocking British folly, and swearing vengeance for the damage the British had been doing, first in the industrial Ruhr, then in Berlin itself. Make no mistake. Hitler was a powerful orator and a persuasive speaker. He could rouse an audience to a screaming pitch of enthusiasm and conviction.

The next day, September 6, his bombers were sent to London and pounded the docks and oil refineries at the east end of the city. That was a foretaste. Two days later they flew again to London in the biggest mass flight of aircraft ever up to that time—625 bombers escorted by 648 fighters. The east end of London was in flames. Traffic in and out of the city was almost impossible. London was badly hurt. England was wounded, but not fatally. Hitler had committed himself to the air battle of Britain, but not to an invasion. It was still theoretically possible. The seaports along the Channel coast were full of invasion barges. Most of Hitler's best army divisions were still along the coast ready to try to cross the Channel. But the order was never given.

On the morning of September 18 my secretary came to my office in Berlin trembling and pale. She said, "Have you heard the news, there has been an invasion attempt. It has been beaten back. The losses are terrible." I immediately went out, took the S Bahn, an elevated rapid transit line that circles Berlin with stops at all the major main line stations and from which one could see the switching yards behind those main stations. In several of them were long lines of hospital cars with the red cross on their roofs. Obviously, something big had happened.

It was not an actual invasion. It was a practice exercise. British bombers had caught barges loaded with infantry during the exercise. But it was enough to show the German high command that the RAF had not yet been driven from the skies. The German navy had required the assurance of three days of German command of the skies over the Channel for an invasion. The invasion exercise was on September 16. We learned after the war that on the next day, September 17, Hitler officially postponed the invasion "until further notice."

The bombing of London was the fatal mistake from which Hitler never recovered. He had struck Britain a less than mortal blow at a time when his real target was the Soviet Union. Those first great bombing attacks on London destroyed any last chance of a peace with the British. He had bombed himself into the one thing his generals most wanted to avoid, a two-front war.

By goading the British he assured just that. He wasted the best of Goering's Luftwaffe pilots in the Battle of Britain. German air losses in that dreadful battle could have made the difference between success and failure on the Russian front had they been saved for that purpose.

In Berlin during those months of the Battle of Britain we caught occasional glimpses of what was going on. At the American Embassy an able young colonel named John Lovell recruited us of the American press, along with members of the embassy staff, to watch for the numbers on the collars and shoulders of German soldiers on the streets of Berlin. When a new number showed up we would report it to John. By this means he kept a record of German units coming back through Berlin from the West. He knew what units had been on the western front during the battle of France and the Low Countries. If they showed up in Berlin it probably meant a short leave there on their way to the East.

Colonel Lovell's intelligence work was extensive and highly successful. I learned how successful one day in December 1940, well after the fall of France. At the time I had moved out of the Adlon and joined several American military attachés who were living near the zoo in a house which had, before the war, been the Cercle Français, or French Club. It was under American Embassy protection. It had a caretaker and wife who had been trained in French cuisine. At breakfast that morning Colonel Lovell remarked that dinner that night would be interesting. He would be happy to have me join. I did. At dinner time there arrived military attachés from countries to the east and southeast of Germany. After an excellent French dinner, which included fresh endive for salad (curiously I remember that and nothing else about the meal), Lovell invited us to the library. Once we assembled he spread a map of Eastern Europe on the table and announced that he would give his colleagues his estimate of the German order of battle and its capability, and would then invite the others to do the same. He marked off on the map his estimate of the various German armies with the presumed number of divisions in each and then said that in his opinion the German deployment was equally ready for a move either south or east, but he thought more probably they would go east. Then in turn he called on the Hungarian, Rumanian, Yugoslav, Bulgarian, and Greek attachés to give their estimates. Each in turn went to the map. One or another would offer a minor change in the estimate of numbers of divisions. All seemed to think that the deployment meant an intention to strike directly eastward at the Soviet Union.

Lovell called last on the Soviet attaché. He stood up, went to the map, and said he agreed so closely with the estimates of the others about location and numbers of German units that it was unnecessary for him to offer any changes. He noted that the others seemed to think it more likely that the deployment meant the Germans would go east. He thought it more likely that they would go south, but, he added, doing a little dance turn, if they do go east, "das will kein Spaziergang sein" (it will not be a Sunday promenade).

It was obvious that that particular Soviet army officer was fully informed about Hitler's troop dispositions and their implications. We all saw on the map the bulk of Germany's combat army including its best front-line divisions and almost all of its armor. Hitler had obviously left only a light holding force behind him along the English Channel. There could not be the slightest doubt from those dispositions that Hitler was ready by December 1940 to send his forces into the Soviet Union. Stalin could not by then have been ignorant of what Hitler was intending. If he was surprised when the blow actually fell (on June 22, 1941), he could blame no one but his own wishful thinking.

Meanwhile, life and work in Berlin for an American war correspondent had changed radically. Franklin Delano Roosevelt was running for reelection, but his reelection was not certain. An extremely popular candidate, Wendell Willkie, was running against him on the Republican ticket. The Germans had a special reason for thinking that a Willkie victory over Roosevelt would make a difference in the U.S. relationship to the war in Europe.

During 1940 I was a frequent Sunday afternoon visitor at the home of U.S. Comdr. Paul Pihl and his wife Charlotte. He was the U.S. naval attaché for air. She was the sister of Wendell Willkie. She held a regular salon. Her "Sunday afternoons" were popular with the Foreign Office set and with top officers of the Luftwaffe. I met at her house most of the men who commanded the air battle over France in 1940. Many times I heard her say that if her brother were to win the 1940 election he would keep the United States out of the war. I have no way of knowing to what extent her statements on this subject influenced German high policy, but I do know that up until election day 1940 American correspondents in Berlin were given general freedom of movement, freedom of access to German officials and to people on the street, and freedom to report.

That general permissiveness for American correspondents ended abruptly when Roosevelt won and Willkie lost. From that moment the German government treated us as future enemies. Freedom of movement was restricted. It became much harder to discover and report beyond the official German communiques.

At that time Alexander Kirk made a quick trip back to Washington for consultation and to renew his credentials as American chargé d'affaires in Berlin. On his return to Berlin he sent for me and urged me to go home and try to tell the American people why their country would be at war someday with Nazi Germany. He said that people at home had no real idea of what the war was all about. He said I ought to write a book about it, and in a hurry, because surely sooner or later we would find ourselves in the war against Germany.

I agreed with him about the inevitability of future U.S. involvement. I was surprised at how unaware public opinion was at home. I was beginning to feel the urge to write a book. And I had begun to feel that the amount of background material I could gather by staying on much longer in Berlin was limited. I felt that perhaps the time had come to get home and write down all the things I had not felt free to say when writing from Berlin itself.

Kirk also called in Wally Deuel and said much the same to him. Bill Shirer had already gone back and we knew his book, *Berlin Diary*, would soon be out. If Kirk had had his way, he would have had all the American correspondents in Berlin back home writing their books. As it was, Bill Shirer's book was published on June 20, 1941, nearly six months before Pearl Harbor and thus in ample time to be widely read well before the United States was in the war. The book I wrote as soon as I got home was ready for the printer on the day Hitler invaded Russia, June 22. I had included a chapter of speculation about Hitler's probable attack on Russia. We just had time to pull out that chapter. Since the event had happened, it was hardly necessary to speculate about it. My book, *Pattern of Conquest*, thus had almost as much time as Shirer's to prepare American public opinion for what we both felt was bound to come. Wally Deuel's book was the most scholarly and sophisticated of the three. Also, he was a perfectionist. He did not get his book ready for the printers until after the Japanese bombed Pearl Harbor on December 7 and the Germans declared war on the United States on December 9. By that time Kirk's educational mission had been accomplished as well as it could be done in advance of the event by those of us who had been living in Berlin through the beginning of Adolf Hitler's drive for world power.

When I had recommended to my editor Charles Gratke in Boston that I come home and he agreed, on the last day of January 1941 I took all my accumulated reserves of food, chocolate, tea, coffee, clothes, soap, toothpaste, and surplus clothes to the office of Friedrich Preller, who represented the Christian Science Publishing Society in Germany, and told him to distribute as needed among the Christian Science community. Then a few German friends accompanied me to the railway station and saw me tucked into the night sleeper for Geneva.

I felt both relief and regret as the train pulled out. The Berlin experience had had its dramatic and also some happy moments. There were friendships that lasted through the war, and experiences that could never be duplicated. There was an evening when I was invited to dinner by the Werner Azendorfs. He was a German journalist with an American wife, who stayed on with him in spite of the war "for better or for worse." They lived in Potsdam. I went to dinner that night by a small, bumpy, squeaky trolley car. I remember the trip and the posters inside the car warning Germans to beware of spies. It was shortly after Christmas. They had had a goose for Christmas dinner. The flesh of the goose was gone, but they served proudly as the main course what was left—goose fat. It had been rendered and flavored with onions and apples. We spread it on chunks of heavy peasant bread and felt that we were having a feast. I enjoyed that dinner and that evening. I am happy to know that they both survived the war.

On going out at night in the *Verdunklung* (blackout) one wore on the coat lapel for recognition a luminous button of individual design known as a *Glühwurmchen*.

In the lobby of the Adlon every new face became the subject of lively speculation. Is he, or she, a spy, and if so for whom?

Life in Berlin had flavor. After the bombing began, there was an extra edge of danger. One night I was in bed when bombs fell somewhere near. I felt no sense of conscious mental fear, but I noticed that my knees were knocking together.

There is nothing like food rationing to improve the flavor of a meal.

All the human senses are stimulated by danger and privation. Remove danger and privation and life thereafter seems bland.

Berlin Postscripts

The trip to Geneva was uneventful. German trains always did run on time, and they continued to do so well into the war and long after I left Hitler's Germany behind. Wartime Germany was a remarkably smooth-running, efficient, and effective institution. The brilliant success of the early military operations had quelled dissent and had been achieved with less than full mobilization. There was no visible shortage of manpower or of any normal civilian amenity. Berlin was amply supplied with excellent restaurants. Their menus gave no evidence of shortages of supplies. Nor did the shops. The wine cellars of the Adlon had been replenished with the finest of French vintages. The shops were overflowing with the latest of ladies' finery from Paris. Hitler would have had it made if only he had not spent so many of his best pilots over London, if only he had lulled the English by doing nothing hostile to them instead of goading them into real war. Looking back over those days I am amazed that Hitler committed the fatal folly of turning the English into angry, active enemies instead of leaving them to be disapproving spectators of his war with the Russians.

The Berlin I left on the last evening of January 1941 was undamaged and unhurt. Everything was functioning there, in all of Germany, and in all of the countries that Hitler had already annexed to his new empire. I had made a quick midwinter trip to Vichy in the unoccupied part of France. The venerable Marshal Petain was presiding over a country morally defeated but physically functioning. France is France. It functions in war or peace. General de Gaulle in London had proclaimed the continuation of the war, but the vast majority of the people of France simply went about their normal lives, which included making tanks and guns. The only difference was that they were being made for the Germans. France was hitched easily and quickly to the German war machine.

My train out of Berlin left the station on time, crossed the frontier into Switzerland on time, and brought me to Geneva on time. There several of us who had come out of Berlin together had a layover of several days waiting for the American Express Company to put together a special train to take Americans through France to Spain and Portugal. The group included Sigrid Shultz, who had been the *Chicago Tribune*'s bureau chief in Berlin and whose mother had been an opera singer with much of her career in Berlin. Sigrid had grown up speaking German as easily as English and knowing through her mother's connections members of the Hohenzollern family and of the former Imperial Court circle. Through them she gained information not easily found from Nazi sources. Sigrid was my original source for knowledge of the practice of *euthanasia,* sometimes translated as "mercy killing," which began in Germany during the summer of 1940. We found confirmation of the first reports in the form of death notices in local newspapers that were remarkable for the frankness of the wording. During September and October they often contained such words as *unbelievable, sudden, unexpected.* They often disclosed the fact that cremation had taken place before next of kin were informed. By piecing together the information in these notices we were able to learn that Gestapo and SS units had carried out a program of emptying institutions of three categories of persons: the aged, insane, and incurable. We didn't learn how many were killed. Our estimates ranged from perhaps twenty thousand to one hundred thousand. But we did know that by the time Bill Shirer and Wally Deuel left in early December 1940 and Sigrid Shultz and I left in late January 1941 such institutions, including those maintained by the Jewish community, had been cleared out as part of a general policy of preparing Germany's hospitals for the business of war. The death notices usually named one of three specific places where cremation had occurred. They were Grafeneck, a castle near Muensingen in the Black Forest south of Stuttgart; Hartheim near Linz in Austria; and the Sonnenstein Public Medical and Nursing Institute, near Pirna on the Elbe, south of Dresden. The inmates of hospitals, nursing homes, and sanatoria all over Germany had presumably been moved to one of those three places for cremation. The assumption most of us made from known evidence was that they had been moved in buses or vans fitted with gas jets and that the inmates probably died during the trip from the original institution to one of the places where the bodies were cremated. Beginning in November death notices were limited to giving only name, place, and date. The revealing and distressed adjectives were forbidden.

The practice of euthanasia in Nazi Germany in 1940 was brought to the attention of the Vatican with the question whether it is legal to kill persons who "because of mental or physical defects are no longer able to benefit the nation." The response was given in the December 16, 1940, issue of *Acta Apostolicae Sedis*, the official monthly publication of the Vatican: "In the negative since it is contrary to natural and divine positive law."

These were matters we talked over on the train ride to Geneva and during our layover there waiting for our next train. I also took advantage of the time to look up Noel and Herta Field, a remarkable couple who played a mixed role during the cold war. Noel was an American with a Swiss education and a Swiss wife. He was equally comfortable in English, French, German, and Swiss German. He was also highly idealistic with a passionate urge to do something splendid for humanity. I met him first at the London Naval Conference of 1935, where he was one of the State Department's experts on the American delegation. He resigned from the State Department at the outbreak of war in Europe and went to Switzerland for the Unitarian Service Committee. His official and ostensible job was helping war victims, but he had other connections. On an earlier trip into Switzerland he had told me that he was primarily concerned with rescuing Spaniards who had fought against Franco in the Spanish civil war. At the end of the war in Spain Noel and Herta had settled in France, but now, with Petain and Laval allowing the German Gestapo to roam at will over southern (and still supposedly unoccupied) France, they were in danger again and moved to Geneva. Noel was busy trying to get the known anti-Fascist leaders into Switzerland and then leading them on into the anti-German underground in Eastern Europe. He told me that he was even making clandestine trips into Nazi Germany in his undercover work. During an earlier trip out of Berlin I had been in Berne and checked Noel's story with Allan Dulles, who was running the OSS (Office of Strategic Services) American intelligence operation there. Allan said that he sometimes used Noel to carry materials into Germany but that Noel was probably working for others as well as the United States. Clearly, Allan did not entirely trust Noel.

I rather liked Noel and Herta. They were passionate, dedicated, earnest—although the goal of their dedication seemed fuzzy and remote. I enjoyed talking with them. She was as intense as he, and as imprecise as he about her purposes and aspirations. We learned, years later, that they were members of the Communist party, but unusual. When Noel left the State Department and joined the party, he was asked questions about his work in the State Department. He refused to answer such questions on the ground that he wasn't working for them, the Communists, at that time. He would work for the Communists from the time he joined, but would not betray his own country. His remarkable standards got him into further trouble with the Communists. During the early stages of the cold war, when Stalin was fixing his grip on the satellite countries of Eastern Europe and purging the early Communist regimes in the process, Noel went to the airport in Warsaw for a flight to Prague. At that time all passengers leaving Warsaw by air went through a departure room that had no windows but several doors. (I was in it on several occasions.) A traveler who entered that room could not be seen by anyone who had come to see him off at the airport. Nor would he be seen by anyone waiting for him on the far side of that room. Noel entered that room and was next discovered, years later, in a prison in Prague. His wife Herta tried to follow him and also disappeared from that same room at the Warsaw airport. Noel's brother Herman went to Europe to try to find Noel. He too disappeared.

During the Khrushchev thaw the Fields were released from prison in Prague. Herman came home, but Noel and Herta chose, for reasons I cannot fathom, to remain in Prague. They were visited once by Flora Lewis of the *New York Times*, who found them to be as unrealistic and muddled as ever. They had been through the KGB wringer, but still they did not wish to return to the United States. My guess is that they both had an idealistic view of the ideal Communist state and felt themselves alienated by what they considered to be the materialism of Western society. To the best of my knowledge they never left Prague. I would like to know what happened to them in the end.

I have brushed against three Communists in my career. In thinking about them I am struck by how different they were. Noel and Herta (I lump them together in memory) were truly dedicated persons. They were quietly intense, their whole lives centered upon their sense of their cause. I am sure they were utterly sincere. At an American college they would have been labeled "do-gooders." In the Europe of World War II they worked against nazism and fascism with the devotion and intensity of medieval saints working against sin and the devil. Had they lived in the time of the Reformation they would certainly have been passionate followers of John Calvin, and a century later they would probably have been working for the Inquisition.

Guy Burgess, one of the four British intelligence officers who worked clandestinely for the Soviets (the others were Donald Maclean, Kim Philby, and Anthony Blount), was totally different. My wife and I met him at a British Embassy party in Washington. All he talked about, or seemed to care about, was his Lincoln Continental. He took us for a quick ride (during the party) to show off its power and "cornering." He had the instincts and manners of an eighteenth-century English rake, a person who loved defying conventions and shocking conventional people. He would do anything outrageous and foolish. He was sent to London from Washington after being repeatedly arrested for speeding on the main highway from Washington to Richmond. He was an embarrassment to the embassy. And of course he was later a traitor. But I doubt that he ever believed in anything.

And then there was Lady X, whose first husband had been an American banker and her second an English peer of the realm. She was warm-hearted and generous and loved to show off her Communist party card. She was neither rake nor saint, but just a good-natured female who loved everyone and joined the Communist party as others of her kind would join the Red Cross or a society for preventing cruelty to children or animals. She had enormous energy, and it found its outlet at one time in work for the Communist party. That was before World War II and before being a Communist was treasonable. She served England loyally during the war. The last time I heard of her she was mothering waifs and strays.

There was no common denominator among those three cases.

But enough of that. I was in Geneva. The day came for our train. By that time a substantial number of Americans and persons with travel papers for the United States had gathered in Geneva. We boarded a train that made no stops through France. We had an uneventful run, making our first stop in Barcelona, then on to Madrid, and finally to Lisbon.

At Lisbon our "group," which had grown to about a dozen, went to hotels in Estoril, down river and on the coast from Lisbon, where we would wait for our American Export Line ship. We had a few days. I reported in at the American Embassy where "Bertie" Pell, Sen. Claiborne Pell's father, was ambassador. I told him that I would be happy to talk to anyone from the British Embassy who might want to hear my tales of life in Berlin. One telephone call and I was sent over by car to the British Embassy, where the ambassador spent the afternoon digging out of me anything and everything I could tell him about conditions back in Germany, which I was happy to do.

During my Berlin days I had had earlier meetings with British officials when I had gone out to Berne for a breather. I always checked in there with the military people and with Allan Dulles at the American Embassy. I was asked there whether I would be willing to meet with some of their British friends. I agreed, of course, but laid down a condition. If I was to talk with them, I wanted it to be in the open, where the Germans would undoubtedly see me doing it. I thought it safer for my position as a journalist in Berlin. As a result, whenever I was in Berne I would have dinner with British air commodore Ferdinand West V.C. (1918) at a restaurant frequented by the diplomatic corps. He proposed that I write postcards to a fictitious person in Berne whenever there was a British air attack on Berlin. There was to be a code that would indicate the number of significant bomb hits and location. It was an intriguing idea, but I decided against it on the ground that the value he could get from such postcards was less than he could get from me when I would come out and be free to talk with him. He agreed, reluctantly. He did so want to have someone writing a postcard after every British bomb hit in Berlin. I like to think that the debriefing the British ambassador in Lisbon got out of me was worth more to His Majesty's government than the postcards would have been.

Executing Kirk's Plan

Immediately on getting back to the United States from Europe I wrote a series of twelve articles on wartime Germany for the *Monitor*. The managing editor, Paul Deland, was enthusiastic about the result and sent a note recommending the series to an old personal friend of his, Theodore Roosevelt, Jr., who at that time was an editor at Doubleday in New York. I was invited to the Doubleday office for a chat and emerged with a commission to expand my *Monitor* series into a book to be ready for publication as soon as possible.

I finished the *Monitor* series in March. My wife and I, with our first child, Bill, then just two years old, rented a little brick colonial house on Prince Street in Alexandria, across the river from Washington, and I started reshaping into book form the material gathered during fourteen months in Germany. It was the easiest writing I ever did. The book virtually wrote itself. The material was vividly fresh in my mind and already organized by the *Monitor* series into subject areas. Also, I had left Berlin with a title in mind.

One day in Berlin, shortly after the French surrender, I had walked into George Kennan's office at the American Embassy to find him filling in boxes on a large chart laid out on his table. Across the top he had set up columns for each country Hitler had already conquered—from Austria to France. Down the side he had written such words as *money, religion, schools, police, and civil rights*. When I asked what he was doing, he replied, "Trying to see whether there is a pattern in their treatment of their victims." He was making a chart of the pattern of German conquest. I had my title, *Pattern of Conquest*.

I remember the month in Alexandria as both hard work and a happy family interlude. I was writing at home. The center of Alexandria was full of bits of history. Between stints of writing we three went walking along the waterfront. It was probably the only time that young Bill ever had both his parents exclusively to himself because the oncoming war would soon occupy most of my time, and when the war was over our second son, Jonathan, had joined the family. Bill saw very little of his father during his early childhood.

The book was finished and off to the printers by the middle of May. I went back to regular news writing, which at that time was almost entirely about the war and the steadily increasing American role in the war. Alexander Kirk had felt that the American public needed to know more than it did; by the time my book was finished not only was the public getting a steady and growing flow of information about the war, but the government was already well embarked on a massive expansion of American military power and its use.

On April 11, 1941, the U.S. Navy extended the U.S. "security zone" from 60 degrees west to 26 degrees west, thus pushing the U.S. sea frontier virtually to Iceland. On that same day, the U.S. destroyer *Niblack* dropped a pattern of depth charges on a presumed German submarine. This meant in its effect that the U.S. Navy was protecting the flow of supplies and ammunition for Britain halfway across the Atlantic and was ready to shoot at any German submarine taking hostile action in the American-protected zone. (No two-way shooting occurred at that time because Hitler had specifically and repeatedly forbade the German navy from any hostile act against American shipping, whether commercial or naval.) On June 3 I and ten other American newspaper reporters who had recently returned to this country from the various foreign war zones left LaGuardia Field for a ten-day tour of the nation's defense plants. What we saw on that trip made it abundantly clear that American industry was ready to produce shells, guns, tanks, warships, and war planes in quantities far beyond what Britain had ordered or was expecting. The United States was gearing itself for getting into the war. The buildup had been started after the fall of France in June 1940. What we eleven saw on that trip of American factories and shipyards in June a year later was impressive. I wrote as follows:

> The factories are built. The assembly lines are beginning to move. The builders of the new plants are being elbowed out of the way by the men who operate them. . . . We haven't crossed most of the German production curves yet. But we have built in one short year an arms capacity . . . fully as great as what Germany began the war with and probably in many elements well beyond German capacity today. . . .

America is under way and the thrill of its awakening power keeps time with the rising throb of the furnaces and forges, lathes and drills, riveters and welders of a Nation finding itself in the face of danger.

The major U.S. role in the war in Europe started with President Roosevelt's reelection in November 1940 by a margin of 449 electoral votes against 82 for Wendell Willkie. When Congress reconvened in January after the election recess, his first proposal was for the massive supply of U.S. war materials to Britain on a "loan" basis. This took the form of legislation known as the Lend-Lease Act, which came into operation on March 11, 1941. In April the United States took over from the British the military protection of Greenland. It became a base for U.S. sea and air protection of convoys going to Britain. In May the United States sent fifty oil tankers to Britain. On June 24 President Roosevelt used his executive authority to extend aid to Russia, which had been invaded two days earlier. On July 25 President Roosevelt decreed that the Philippine army was part of the U.S. Army and sent General Douglas MacArthur to the Philippines to take command. He also froze Japanese assets in the United States, which effectively imposed an embargo on shipment of oil and scrap metal to Japan. In early August he sailed aboard the U.S. cruiser *Augusta* to Argentia Harbor in Newfoundland, where he was joined on August 14 by Winston Churchill. They signed an eight-point document known as the Atlantic Charter, which amounted to a set of joint Anglo-American war aims. The United States was by then virtually in the war on Britain's side. By September 12 I was datelining my copy "With the Second Army in Louisiana."

American naval forces had been getting plenty of training and testing running convoys in the Atlantic, but there had as yet been no large-scale practice for the ground and air forces that were coming into being with conscription. By early September nearly half a million of America's new soldiers were concentrated in two rival armies along the Red River basin in western Louisiana, and I was among them, in uniform, as a simulated war correspondent. At the end of a week the Second Army, the bigger of the two with more tanks and designated as the attacking force, had been so badly outmaneuvered that the umpires called a halt for regrouping. Gen. Ben Lear, who commanded the Second Army, had been routed and twice had to abandon his headquarters one jump ahead of his enemies commanded by Gen. Walter Kreuger.

So decisive, and surprising to spectators of the maneuvers, was the superior operation of the Third Army that Bob Allen (Robert S. Allen, co-author with Drew Pearson of *Washington Merry-Go-Round*—first a book, then a popular column) decided we had better try to find the explanation. We acquired a jeep, put a white flag on it, crossed the battle line, and took off for General Kreuger's headquarters near Lake Charles. We wanted to meet the general whose army had done so well.

A pleasant young aide met us at Kreuger's headquarters but had to tell us that the general was off in the field somewhere. We had started to turn away when he said, "But his chief of staff is here; would you like to talk to him?" The aide was so polite that we could not very well say no although it was the general we wanted to see. We followed along. As we were about to enter the office he turned and said, "Oh, by the way, his name is Eisenhower, Colonel Eisenhower." The name meant nothing to either of us.

We went in and found ourselves in a lively chat with a bright, interesting, and interested officer. Bob mentioned that I had recently come back from Germany. Immediately the young colonel started asking me questions about the German army. He interviewed me as much as we interviewed him. Bob and I were both impressed. Bob wrote a column in praise of Colonel Eisenhower.

Years later, when Eisenhower was president of the United States, I asked him whether he happened to remember our first meeting. He did. He said he always thought that he probably owed his promotion to that column of Bob's. Perhaps. The column certainly did not hurt Colonel Eisenhower's record. The fact is that "Ike" was the planning officer on Kreuger's staff. He had previously (the sort of thing we all learned much later) planned MacArthur's retreat to Bataan. He was already well known in the army as a skillful planning officer. His plan for the maneuvers in Louisiana showed superior skill at managing a large body of troops in the field. In the public eye Kreuger was the winner in those maneuvers, but inside the army the top people all knew that it had been an Eisenhower plan that won the day. Kreuger benefited, as he should have. He went on to be MacArthur's ground forces commander in the Pacific. Ben Lear disappeared from public sight. I went back to Washington with a realization that the United States was preparing to go into a big war in a big way. The European theater was the only place you could possibly use an army as big as the one we saw in Louisiana in those maneuvers (which ended just two months before Pearl Harbor).

It did not occur to me at that time to question whether my country should be moving on a course that assumed we would soon be in the big war in Europe. I took it for granted that nazism was evil and a German victory contrary to the American national interest. Not everyone at the time felt the same way. There was a bitter national debate over the president's policy of supporting Britain. The *Chicago Tribune* and the Hearst newspapers joined in warning against the United States "being dragged into war to save England."

I never got actively into the debate. I simply took it for granted in my own mind and in my writing at the time that the British were fighting our war and that we would sooner or later play a more active role in defeating Germany and its allies. Not until I started writing this book did it occur to me to ask myself why I was so automatically and reflexively pro-British and anti-German in spite of the fact that I inherited a German name and my immigrant Harsch ancestor was a German peasant who came over from the Rhineland in 1743. The only thing I know about him is that he chose to leave Germany (taking with him, according to family legend, his only moveable possession, a cow) for the prospect of being able to own land someday in William Penn's colony in a new world. Did he have any sense of being "German"? He came from the Palatinate, near Zweibrücken. Perhaps he thought of himself as a Palatine rather than as a German. If he did have any sense of being a German it had disappeared from the family culture long before my time.

I grew up in an entirely English culture. The Bible I knew from childhood was the King James version (although I still have a copy of a Lutheran Bible in German from an earlier generation). One grandmother was a Hannum. Her mother was a Parker. The other grandmother was a Bowers, whose family liked to think that they were descended from King Charles II via Nell Gwyn. The stories and poems read to me as a child came totally from the great body of English literature. I grew up familiar with Tennyson, Wordsworth, Byron, the Brownings (both of them), Dickens, Thackery, and Hardy. Goethe and Schiller were names unknown to me until college days, and then slightly. I lived in an English culture. Subconsciously I thought of England as the motherland. I wanted from an early age to go to an English university, which I succeeded in doing (Cambridge, 1928, 1929). I was brought up in a religion (Christian Science) whose founder, Mary Baker Eddy, once wrote in *Poems*: "Brave Britain, blest America! Unite your battle-plan. . . ." In September 1941 it seemed natural and proper to me that we Americans were organizing ourselves for joining the battle shoulder to shoulder with our British "cousins." To me, at that time, those who called themselves America Firsters were somehow treasonable.

In reading over my wartime reporting from Germany and afterward in the United States, I do not find one word or phrase that expresses doubt about the rightness of Britain's cause and the rightness of American support for that cause. The nearest thing to pro-German sentiment that I personally encountered was the attitude of Joseph Kennedy (father of Pres. John F. Kennedy) and John Hartigan (described earlier), both of whom reflected what I assumed was normal Irish anglophobia. Col. Robert R. McCormick of the *Chicago Tribune* was also an anglophobe and campaigned to keep the United States out of the war, although he gloried in the exploits of his division, the famous First, during World War I and its first action in that war at Château-Thierry.

I can recall the arguments among classmates in the opening days of school after the outbreak of World War I in 1914. "Who are you for, the French or Germans?" I think I remember that the choices were about even although there was no count of hands. Toledo, Ohio, where I was born and grew up, probably had as many people of German origin as British. I remember open pro-German sentiment during World War I. My Boy Scout troop once marched off to a house that we had heard had in it photographs of the German kaiser and his wife. The owner came out and allowed a deputation to come in and see. True enough, there were the photographs on the wall. We milled about outside feeling we ought to do something, but went home. While overt pro-Germanism was unusual by 1939, opposition to Roosevelt's pro-British policies, taking the form of isolationism, was vociferous and the battle in Congress over lengthening conscription service from one year to two and a half years was hard fought and the outcome close. It cleared the House by a single vote. A substantial majority of Republicans voted against extending conscription service and against Lend-Lease.

By October 1941, when I went back to Washington from the Louisiana maneuvers, those arguments had been settled. Massive American aid was flowing across the Atlantic in ships escorted by the U.S. Navy as far as Iceland, where the British took over for the balance of the voyage. The United States had taken over the protection of Greenland in April and of Iceland on July 9. The North Atlantic as far as Iceland had become an American-protected zone, in which the Germans were forbidden by the U.S. Navy to sink ships carrying goods to Britain. The United States was in fact giving Britain naval support and giving the U.S. Navy war experience, but without shooting until September 4. On that day a submarine, the German U-642, fired two torpedos at the destroyer *Greer*. President Roosevelt issued an order to "shoot on sight" any German warship found in the waters under U.S. protection, which meant the western half of the Atlantic Ocean.

In other words, by October 1941, the U.S. Navy was actually in a shooting war with the German navy, U.S. industry was working up to full production of the weapons for a major war, and the U.S. Army had had its first large-scale maneuvers. The United States was substantially ready to enter the war on Britain's side.

Air Raid, Pearl Harbor

Once the Louisiana maneuvers were out of the way my editor, Charles Gratke, had another idea about using me. German armies were surging into the Soviet Union. No one knew whether Soviet soldiers could stop them. They were moving so fast during October that the war in the East could be over before snowfall. Gratke thought it was too late in the year to send me directly to Moscow. It might be all over for the Russians by the time I could get there. So he suggested that I take off in the opposite direction, spend the winter reporting on Japan and China, and then, in the spring, if Russia was still in the war, head for Moscow by the back door, through Persia (Iran). It seemed a sensible plan of action. I asked for a breather on the way and decided to take Anne, my wife, with me as far as Hawaii. We would leave our son Bill with my parents, who had a house in La Jolla where he could be safe and in good hands for his mother's short vacation. We went to California by train, the three of us. We put Bill in my mother's willing arms, and Anne and I went up to San Francisco to board the USS *Lurline* of the Matson Line for what we expected to be a pleasant holiday before I would go on, by air, to Japan.

We landed in Honolulu on December 3 and went to the Halekulani Hotel, where we found ourselves in a pleasant little cottage all to ourselves in a palm grove. The hotel consisted of a cluster of individual cottages grouped around a central building containing the reception and dining rooms. It was directly on Waikiki Beach next door to the Royal Hawaiian, where the richest tourists went. Beyond that was the Moana for the less rich tourists. The Halekulani was largely residential. Most of its rooms and cottages were occupied by naval officers and families. We were assigned a table in the dining room between the tables of Admiral Pye, who was Deputy CINCPAC (deputy commander in chief, Pacific), and Adm. Fairfax Leary, COMCRUPAC (commander, cruisers, Pacific). We felt at home. We knew the Fairfax Learys from

Jamestown, Rhode Island, where they had a summer house. Anne's family had long summered at Jamestown, where they owned two houses at that time and where Anne's father, Rear Adm. Spencer Shepard Wood, was senior admiral in the community, hence was host at the annual gathering of admirals in the area.

Honolulu was a simpler place then than it became after the war. Agriculture, mostly pineapples, was still the major industry of the islands. It was a tourist town, yes, but not on today's scale. There were four ships of the Matson Line that brought probably an average of four or five hundred tourists a week to Honolulu and took back to the mainland as many. But the three hotels on Waikiki Beach were sufficient for that flow of tourists. Now more tourists arrive and depart every day, by air, than used to come in a month by ship. Hawaii's original character has been overwhelmed by tourism. When Anne and I arrived there on December 3, 1941, the arrival itself was a festive occasion, a band playing Hawaiian music on the pier, a floral wreath around one's neck. We spent our first two days exploring the city and enjoying the beach. I checked in at a navy press office in town and asked for an appointment to see Adm. Husband E. Kimmel, who was Navy commander-in-chief, Pacific. I was given an appointment for eight o'clock on Saturday morning (December 6). We hired a small car and decided to do a tour of the island after my appointment at the naval base. We packed a picnic lunch, swimming clothes, and towels and left the hotel on Saturday morning in time for the appointment. I was there punctually. Waldo Drake, press officer for the Pacific command, met me in the reception center and took me to the admiral's office. He and his staff were waiting for me in a conference room. We sat in a circle with a large, low coffee table in the middle. Waldo remembered in his account of the meeting that the admiral sat most of the time with his white buckskin shoes perched comfortably on the table. I remember an easy, relaxed atmosphere with the admiral starting off by asking me about Germany. He and other members of his staff were obviously eager to glean any knowledge they could from a reporter who had been in Germany at the beginning of the war. It was my experience with Colonel Eisenhower over again. After about half an hour of being the subject of the questioning I turned to the admiral and asked if it was my turn to ask a question. He agreed, and I remarked that I was totally new to the Pacific area and the general situation there. So would he please tell me whether there was going to be a war in the Pacific. Without a pause, immediately, almost casually, he replied, no. His explanation (which I think I remember almost word for word) was the following:

Since you have been traveling you probably don't know that as of six days ago the German high command announced that the German armies in Russia had gone into winter quarters. That means that Moscow is not going to fall to the Germans this year. That means that the Russians will still be in the war in the spring. That means that the Japanese cannot attack us in the Pacific without running the risk of a two-front war. The Japanese are too intelligent to run the risk of a two-front war unnecessarily. They will want to wait until they are sure that the Russians have been defeated.

I was fascinated. Of course I asked a lot of follow-up questions. I have no way of knowing to what extent the admiral was saying what he thought prudent to say to a visiting reporter, rather than what he actually thought. I only know that he was relaxed, and so was his staff. They all seemed to think it worthwhile to hear whatever I could tell them about Germany. They showed no sign of being under strain or pressure. No one on the staff disagreed with what the admiral said about the prospects of war in the Pacific.

As soon as the meeting broke up I joined Anne in the car and we set off for a tour of the island. We turned left out of the naval base to do the round tour from left to right, the city of Honolulu having been left behind us between Waikiki Beach and the naval base at Pearl Harbor. We drove along beside large pineapple plantations on our right and beaches on our left. At the end of the island we passed a plantation and noticed a small airfield with a few fighter planes parked on it. We headed back on the far side of the island, passing Kailua Beach in the early afternoon. We stopped once for lunch and several times for swimming. Whenever we saw a particularly inviting beach we stopped and tried it out. We had a lovely day with no worries because, after all, the admiral had assured me only that morning that there would be no war in the Pacific. It was a good day. We had a pleasant dinner at the hotel watching the lights of shipping moving in and out of the harbor. The dining room was full of naval officers in their white uniforms and their wives in summer frocks, all behaving as calmly and unworriedly as the admiral and his staff were that morning. We went to bed at the end of a day we had both much enjoyed.

I woke up the next morning hearing some distant banging. I woke Anne and said, "You have often asked me what an air raid sounds like. Listen to this. It's a good imitation." She woke, listened, remarked sleepily, "Oh, is that what it's like?" We both went to sleep again. After a while she woke me and said it was time for our morning swim. We dressed for swimming, went to the beach, about a hundred yards from our cottage, and went swimming.

After an easy swim we turned to shore where a man was standing looking intently toward Pearl Harbor, which was about twelve miles down the shore on the far side of the city of Honolulu. We looked too and saw a great column of black smoke. I said, "What's going on?" He replied, "Oh, they must be having some sort of an exercise, but I guess it's over now."

That answer is at least a part of the explanation of the absence of strain or anxiety at the admiral's office the previous morning and at dinner the previous evening. Everyone in the islands was accustomed to war games. They had been going on forever, more frequently of late, of course, but war games were war games, and the boys were always playing them. Just another war game was the natural assumption. The man who had been watching, and the two of us, assumed just another war game. We went to our cottage, changed into daytime clothes, went to the dining room, and started eating breakfast. Mrs. Pye was at her table on one side of us and Mrs. Leary at her table on the other side. Everything seemed normal. The room was dotted with officers in white uniforms eating a leisurely breakfast. Then a woman came into the dining room in semi-hysterical condition. She said, "The battleships are burning." Someone stood up and tried to reassure her that it was just another exercise. "No," she almost screamed. "They are Japanese. I saw the red balls under the wings. They shot at our car. I was driving my husband to his ship. The battleships are burning."

One by one, around the room, officers stood up. Some seemed to shake themselves as if trying to adjust to a new reality. The room emptied quickly. I remembered that I was a reporter and that perhaps I ought to be doing something journalistic.

I bade Anne a quick good-bye at the door. She looked a bit anxious as I drove away. By that time she certainly knew that we were in something other than "just another war game." My first concern was to get myself some war correspondent credentials. I went first to the navy press office, where they gave me a card identifying me as an accredited war correspondent, then to army headquarters at Fort Shafter. I found the G-2 (intelligence) office and asked for similar army credentials. A colonel obliged. While he was doing the paperwork, voices came on a radio intercom. In best army voice and idiom someone was making startling statements, such as "paratroops landing on Diamond Head," and "troop ship approaching Kailua Beach." The colonel gave me my accreditation card, reached for his revolver belt, buckled it on, checked his gun, and went out the door. I last saw him headed for wherever he expected the action to be. He must have been taking seriously the information coming over that intercom. Why I didn't is beyond me, but I just went to my car and drove to a place on Red Hill from which I knew I could look down on Pearl Harbor and see what was actually going on. I saw enough to know that this was the real thing and that many of the ships in the harbor had been badly damaged. Previously I had noticed particularly the location of the battleship *Oklahoma* because Anne's father had both commissioned her and flown his flag as admiral for the first time from her main mast. My eye located her. She was turned over, her bottom up and keel showing.

I turned away, drove to the telegraph office, and started writing a cable to Boston. Since it was a Sunday morning and my paper did not print on Sunday, I had not felt in any great hurry to get word to Boston. Just as I finished writing, a man came out of the back room and told the clerk at the desk to accept no more cables. He said all transmission of normal cable traffic had been stopped. I left what I had written anyway and told them to send it as soon as they could. By that time it was too late to do what I should have done sooner and what an AP reporter's wife did do. Her husband was a regular correspondent there and had a house overlooking Pearl Harbor. He was out of town that morning on one of the other islands. But his wife was there, picked up the telephone, called her husband's San Francisco office, and told them from her own front door what she was seeing. By the time the censorship order was issued she had already given the AP a wonderful eyewitness account of the havoc those Japanese bombs were causing.

The final wave of Japanese attacking planes must have flown away about the time of our swim. By the time I left the hotel all was quiet, relatively. After looking at the horror of Pearl Harbor with ships still burning and visiting the cable office, I went to the navy press office, then back to Fort Shafter. By that time it was known that there were no Japanese ships near the islands. The attacking planes had disappeared back into the northern mists. I settled down to routine journalistic jobs. The first thing I did was to investigate reports of enemy sabotage. Reports were a dime a dozen. The only evidence I ever found of an actual act of sabotage was that army voice on the intercom. Some Japanese agent with a gritty American army accent and idiom had managed to plug into the interservice intercom that connected all military installations.

By the end of the day I could reassure Anne that the islands were not being invaded or in any serious danger of being invaded. The war had started, yes. Pearl Harbor had been attacked. The navy had been grievously wounded. The loss of American life (we learned later) had been 2,403. The loss of aircraft was 149 (mostly on the ground). Six battleships were sunk or aground. But patrolling aircraft were unable to find any Japanese ships or aircraft in or near the islands. The worst had happened. We were in no personal danger. My main task was to learn all I could about what had happened and have it ready to go as soon as the cable office was back in operation.

One of the officers in the navy press section invited Anne and me to join him and his wife in a pleasant cottage they had rented at the top of the pass on the road that crosses the island from Honolulu to Kailua on the far side. The air was cooler up there on the pass, the garden blazed with tropical flowers. We settled into a routine: mornings spent collecting experiences and information and writing, afternoons on the beach at Waikiki, and evenings in friendly discussion. Each day I left another cable at the cable office. And then one day as we were chatting on the beach the horizon began to fill up. Soon there were many ships. They gradually materialized into the four big passenger ships of the Matson Line—*Lurline, Monterey, Mariposa,* and *Matsonia*—escorted by at least a dozen destroyers and cruisers plus various supply ships. An entire army division had arrived to reinforce the garrison of the islands.

With the reinforcements came about thirty official war correspondents. My monopoly on the story was broken. Up to that day I was the only reporter on the island who had already had experience as a war correspondent. I was overwhelmed by the inrushing regiment replete in official war correspondent uniforms, some of them elegantly tailored. They all rushed from the ships to the Royal Hawaiian Hotel, madly interviewing taxi drivers and hotel bellboys on their way to their typewriters. The cable office reopened in time to receive reports too often filled with lurid accounts of poisoned wells and cut power lines, little of which had foundation in fact. There had been Japanese agents in Honolulu who had reported daily to Tokyo on the ships into and out of Pearl Harbor and the exact location in the harbor of the main units. But there was no sabotage except for that one voice on the intercom. The Nisei, persons of Japanese background who were born in the islands, later proved by gallantry on many a battlefield in Europe their loyalty as Americans.

But what to do next? I had wrapped up the Pearl Harbor story before the inundation of other reporters from the mainland. My editor said, "Now go to Singapore." That seemed sensible. The four Matson liners had soon unloaded their cargo. I put Anne aboard the *Lurline* for her return voyage. Her job was to look after our son. I saw her off and then asked Waldo Drake to get me to Singapore. He laughed and said he would see what he could do. One day he sent for me and asked whether I would like a ride. I said, "To where?" He said, "I can't tell you, but if you want a ride report to the *Enterprise* at 0800 hours tomorrow morning." I said, "Waldo, you know where I want to go. You wouldn't send me on a wild goose chase, would you?" He just smiled and said, "If you want a ride be at the gangplank of the *Enterprise* by 0800 hours tomorrow morning and, by the way, do *not* say anything to your editor."

Waldo had given me a problem. My orders from my editor were to get to Singapore. Would it be better to wait for some ship I knew to be going to the Far East or take a chance on what might turn out to be a cruise to nowhere? In the end I decided to take a chance that Waldo had in mind some plan to help me on my way. Besides, there was no point in staying in Honolulu. The action had been there for one brief and violent day. But that was over. The news was far to the east of Honolulu and Pearl Harbor. By that time I had had word from Anne that she was safely back in La Jolla with Bill and my parents. The family lived in a two-story, Spanish-style house, high on the hill above the town, surrounded by lawn and rose gardens and looking out over the Pacific Ocean. I was fortunate. I could go off to war feeling comfortable about my wife and child. Anne would have plenty to do taking care of Bill, who by that time was two years old. She would be well occupied. Our second son, Jonathan, was born nine months after our trip to Honolulu.

"Cutting a Dido"

Waldo had mentioned offering a ride on the same cruise to a colleague who had come out with that wave of reporters from the mainland, one Herbert Renfrew Knickerbocker of the *Chicago Sun-Times*, known as "Red" for obvious reasons of coloration and temperament. He was to me a legendary character, having won journalistic fame in World War I. I found him wrestling with the same problem I had. He too had been told by his editor to get to Singapore. We examined the pros and cons of whether to board the U.S. carrier *Enterprise* at 0800 hours the next morning. Red was fairly sure that Waldo would not deliberately send us on a voyage that would automatically bring us back to Honolulu. We packed and, next morning, were at the foot of the gangplank to the *Enterprise* at the appointed hour. From the pier, looking up, the first sight of a modern aircraft carrier is an impressive object. Almost with awe we mounted to the deck, identified ourselves, and were assigned to an escorting officer, who first issued us cabins in "officer country" (as war correspondents we had the assimilated rank of army major or navy lieutenant commander). After stowing our gear we were shown our battle station, which was the "fighting top," a modern variation of the old crow's nest well up on the main mast. There we made the acquaintance of a marine officer who, in case of battle, would command the light weaponry of the ship from that high vantage point. He mentioned casually that in battle it would probably be the first thing shot away. But for us it was an excellent place for watching the lively deck action of a carrier at sea in wartime.

By that time the ship had cast off its lines and was underway heading for the open sea. We were escorted to the front of the flight deck, where Adm. William Halsey (later known as "Bull" Halsey) was standing looking out to sea. He was in an emotional mood. This was the first sortie of any of our naval forces out of Pearl Harbor against the new enemy since the disaster of December 7. The upturned *Oklahoma* lay astern of us. The *Arizona,* a burned-out wreck, was over to starboard. Two other battleships, badly marred and sitting in the mud, were alongside Ford Island. There were tears of anger in his eyes when he told us that he was going out there "to get those yellow-bellied bastards" and even the score for what they had so recently done to us. By that time we had passed the entrance to the harbor, and our escort of a cruiser and several destroyers had formed around us. We were a Task Force, standing out to sea in search of any enemy we could find but primarily headed for the Marshall Islands to avenge as far as possible the "Day of Infamy."

We settled comfortably into the routine of shipboard life, lively conversations in the Ward Room, the early-morning routine of launching the dawn patrol, the marvel of launching and taking in planes at sea with a deck that does roll and pitch a little no matter how big the ship or how calm the sea.

A week after we had left Pearl Harbor behind us the admiral sent for us again, this time to his cabin. When we were seated, he informed us that he had had a signal from Admiral Nimitz telling him that we both wanted to go to Singapore and authorizing him to assist us in that purpose, provided that it did not interfere with his own operations. He said that there would soon be a destroyer coming alongside to refuel and that it would be going into Samoa. If we liked he could put us over to the destroyer in a breeches buoy; we could get at least as far as Samoa and might pick up something from there to take us toward Singapore. He himself was off to strike at the Japanese in the Marshall Islands. He would like to have us with him, but it was our choice. We thanked him, said we would let him know our decision shortly, and went off to wrestle all over again with the choice of covering the first American offensive strike of the Pacific War or taking a chance on getting to Singapore from Samoa.

Red was always for going on, not going back. He convinced me that it would be a great mistake to go back to San Francisco and start all over again. We packed, went to the main deck, and watched the lines being rigged both to refuel the destroyer and to pass supplies over. The two ships were steaming at about thirty knots, a space of about one hundred feet between. We could only marvel at the seamanship of the vessels and those handling them. The two ships must have moved in parallel for nearly an hour. The distance never varied by enough to cause danger or lose the cargo passing between, which included the two of us.

We thanked the admiral for his courtesy, and mentally thanked Waldo for having in fact had our assignment to Singapore in mind when he sent us to the *Enterprise*. We found ourselves on the deck of the USS *Lampson,* a modern destroyer equipped as a flotilla leader, under command of Comdr. P. V. Mercer, a spirited officer who enjoyed everything about his beautiful ship and the life he could lead within it.

He welcomed us aboard, then explained his mission and its relation to us. He was assigned for the moment, he said, to cover the arrival of reinforcements for Samoa. He would soon be putting us ashore at Pago Pago, the capital of American Samoa. We might find some ship heading in the direction of Singapore. Meanwhile we soon had a glimpse on the horizon of what had become a familiar sight—again the *Lurline* and her three sister ships of the Matson Line, this time no longer in tourist white but in wartime camouflage. They had come out from the coast with a division of U.S. Marines. Before that first day was out, we had gone ashore at Pago Pago, found quarters in a Navy bachelor officers' quarters, and watched the four Matson liners come into harbor and begin to unload tanks, guns, supplies, and U.S. Marines. It took several days to unload everything from those ships. Red and I had in the meantime learned from the local navy people that no ship of any kind had been in Pago Pago since the attack on Pearl Harbor and, so far as they knew, nothing was expected or expectable. That was disconcerting. It became more disconcerting when the first of the Matson liners, having finished unloading, turned around and headed out to sea and back to San Francisco to carry more American soldiers to some other future battlefield. One by one each of the four finished unloading and headed back home. Again a dilemma. Which was worse, to risk staying on Samoa indefinitely or go back all the way to the Pacific coast and start over again? Red argued that since we were halfway across the Pacific it would be humiliating to turn up back in San Francisco and have to start over again. I agreed, reluctantly, to stay.

So we watched with mixed feelings as the last of the Matson liners disappeared over the horizon and then settled back to make the acquaintance of the local U.S. Navy establishment. Samoa at that time was governed by the U.S. Navy. There was a permanent but small regular staff of navy people primarily concerned with local government and with operating navy communications. There was also a local native militia wearing a special uniform consisting of a wraparound skirt or kilt of navy blue material. I studied the native houses, which consisted of a built-up platform of stone and crushed shells on which was a marvelously fitted frame roof on poles. The roof was thatched with palm leaves. Panels of woven palm leaves hung, movable, in the spaces between the upright poles. Bedding consisted of many layers of woven palm matting. The structure was well off the ground, allowing for easy ventilation, and seemed ideally suited to the gentle climate. I marveled at the joining and fitting of frame and poles, all done without metal of any kind. The joints were bound with plaited vines. At the time Red and I arrived, all the natives, so far as we could observe, lived in such houses. We had several days of savoring an idyllic native life—mixed with anxiety about getting to Singapore—and then a welcome sight. The USS *Lampson* was back in the harbor, and its captain was soon walking up the path to the navy compound. He greeted us and asked whether we would like a ride. But where? He said he could not tell us where, but he would be delighted to have our company if we chose to be at the pier at good old 0800 hours in the morning. Once again the dilemma. He knew where we wanted to go. Would he invite us if he were only going back to Pearl or San Francisco? We hesitated only slightly over that one. We knew it might be our last chance for a long time to leave Samoa behind us. We were at the pier at 0800 hours in the morning. As we climbed aboard, the lines were cast off and we headed once more for the open sea.

We were quickly assigned to comfortable cabins. Since the ship was a flotilla leader it had a special cabin for an admiral, but none being aboard, one of us had it (I can't remember which). The captain's large, regular cabin went to the other of us since the captain used a little cabin next to the bridge whenever the ship was in a war zone, which indeed it then was. As soon as we had stowed our sparse luggage we reported to the bridge. The ship was passing the headlands. The skipper gave the helmsman a course setting, ordered full cruising speed, settled back in his swivel chair, turned to us, and said, "Now, would you like to know where we are going?"

Adm. Fairfax Leary had been appointed to command all Allied naval forces in the Southwest Pacific with headquarters at Wellington, New Zealand. He was leaving Pearl Harbor at that very hour by flying boat. The *Lampson* had been assigned to his command. It was at that moment the only ship yet assigned to that command. Hence, Admiral Leary would have nothing from which to fly his flag until we got to Wellington. Hence, said Skipper Mercer, he intended to try to beat the flying boat to Wellington.

For the next week the USS *Lampson* raced for New Zealand, making probably the fastest run ever over that course. Twice we were called to battle stations when another ship was seen on the horizon. The gun on the foredeck was loaded and the battle flag run up (biggest flag I had ever seen until then). But in both cases the other ship turned out to be a freighter of Allied nationality with suitable identification signals. Then one fine day as we approached Wellington the skipper summoned the ship's crew to the quarterdeck. He explained that we would be the first American ship to enter that harbor since the United States had entered the war. It behooved us to come in in style. He told them of the British cruiser *Dido,* which had become famous for the brisk, smart way it was handled until "cutting a Dido" had come to mean in any navy the smart handling of a ship. He said he intended to "cut a Dido" on our way into the harbor. He did.

We were soon in a channel. I happened to pass the chart room a few minutes later and noticed that the executive officer was sweating over his chart. I asked him if he was having a problem. He replied that "the Skipper is taking us in by dead reckoning. He is two buoys ahead of me. I can't keep up with him." The captain was taking us through a long and by no means straight channel at cruising speed, without waiting for the usual navigational checks. Ahead we saw docks and piers and ships. The largest was obviously a cruiser. The skipper kept up speed almost to the last moment, reversed engines, and slid up alongside the cruiser perfectly. He had "cut a Dido" and everyone cheered, on both ships.

Confusing the Enemy

Red and I made our farewells to Skipper Mercer, to his fellow officers, and to his fine crew. We climbed over the cruiser HMAS *Australia,* walked through the shipyard, hailed a taxi, and asked to be taken to the main hotel. As we were getting our luggage out of the taxi, a young man jumped out of another car and rushed up to us saying, "Are you Messrs. Knickerbocker and Harsch?" With surprise at being greeted by name we admitted that we were, and he then said, "Would you like to meet the prime minister?"

We said, yes, of course, we would be honored and delighted, but could we check in at the hotel first? He allowed us about five minutes to sign the register and then bundled us off as fast as he could to the prime minister, Peter Nash, who, immediately and without the usual preliminaries, said: "How long do you expect to stay here?" We replied that we wanted to get on as quickly as possible and could he use his best influence to get us on the first possible flight to Australia.

At that he relaxed visibly and said he was relieved. He looked relieved. He said he regarded journalists as birds of ill omen and was afraid we were there because we thought the action might soon be in New Zealand. He would be delighted to help us on our way to Australia. He told his secretary to see to it that there would be seats for us on the first plane out, a flying boat (Short–Sunderland) scheduled out two days later to Sydney. We then asked about filing our stories and what we could report. He told us that would be up to Admiral Leary, who, he said, had just arrived a few hours before we did and was in the same hotel. (Skipper Mercer had not been able to beat a flying boat, but he came remarkably close to doing so.) So as soon as we politely could we got back to the hotel (named the Wellington, of course), checked in at once with the admiral, and asked him what we would be allowed to report of our trip. He gave us general instructions and told us to file our copy through his intelligence officer, who would act as military censor. At that point Red and I parted for our respective rooms to write. And we wrote. The copy poured out. We met next in the censorship room, handed in our copy, and then, and only then, showed each other what we had written.

That produced a surprise because we had interpreted the admiral's instructions quite differently. I thought I was free to say where we were and how we got there. Red thought we could freely write about what we had seen in Samoa. Red wrote a beautiful color story of watching the marines with all their tanks and guns coming ashore on a tropical island, without saying where. I wrote, under a Wellington, New Zealand, dateline, February 9: "The Battle of the Supply Line from America's factories to the far Pacific battle front has been won. Japan has suffered its first serious reverse. An American Admiral commands the terminus of the supply route. The way stations have been secured. Blue jackets are here." The story further said that Admiral Leary was in command of all Allied forces in the area and had arrived. It said I had reached Wellington on a U.S. destroyer. It said that during the trip from Pearl Harbor I had been on other U.S. Navy vessels, including a carrier. It said I had seen reinforcements landing at way stations along the supply line.

The above interpretation of our arrival in New Zealand (seized upon of course by the headline writers) came in my copy after an opening paragraph that expressed the enthusiasm all of us who reached New Zealand aboard the USS *Lampson* felt at the time. It read: "A trim destroyer cut the outer corner of this harbor, 23 knots boiling under her fantail, pushed hard on a destroyer's equivalent of brakes at the last moment and slipped without maneuver into a berth while New Zealanders first rubbed their eyes and then waved their hats at the Stars and Stripes."

Red's story and mine were entirely different. But both were passed by the censor. Both were handed on by our respective newspapers to the Associated Press for general distribution to other newspapers. Most editors twinned the two together. The combination made for remarkable reading. The Japanese must have been puzzled when they received their copies, as they would. AP stories of that kind would go at once to neutral countries, where the Japanese press service could pick them up. My own newspaper carried my story with an italic precede that read:

"For weeks the editors of *The Christian Science Monitor* had no word of Joseph C. Harsch. After his eyewitness reporting of the Japanese attack on Pearl Harbor, Mr. Harsch was instructed to proceed to the battle area of the Far Pacific.

"Silence, broken only by one carefully censored note, followed. It was from Pago Pago, in the American outpost of Samoa. It could only say that the ship he arrived on 'had guns on it.' Again silence."

The prime minister of New Zealand kept his promise. Two days later we boarded a large and most impressive flying boat in the harbor of Wellington. We were back to first-class civilian travel, British style: stewards in white jackets, napkin over left hand, holding silver tray, right hand dispensing goodies. We had an uneventful, comfortable, nonstop flight to Sydney, landing in the middle of Sydney Harbor, where our boat was boarded by a group of local reporters who asked first, "What do you think of our bridge?" and second, "What do you think of Australian women?" Reporters who cover ship arrivals and ask questions like that used to be a Hollywood cliché. It literally happened to the two of us that day in Sydney Harbor.

The more important fact was that Red and I had actually reached the far Pacific from Pearl Harbor without having had to go back to San Francisco for a fresh start. But we were not in time to get to Singapore. We landed in Wellington on February 9 and reached Sydney on February 12. Singapore had not yet fallen, but there was no longer any way to get there. The Japanese, having on December 10 sunk the only two Allied capital ships in the area, the British battleships *Prince of Wales* and *Repulse,* were blockading the harbor. The airport was closed by Japanese bombs. Everything that could get out of Singapore had already gone. The Japanese were closing in for the kill. It fell on February 15. The nearest we could get to Singapore would be Java, then a Dutch possession. We went to the office of the Dutch consul general and asked if he could help get us on the next plane for Batavia (now renamed Jakarta), the capital of the Dutch East Indies. He was most obliging, called the Dutch airline KLM, and informed us that there would be seats for us on a flight in the morning. We were most appreciative, assuming that getting seats the very next day must have taken much influence. Next morning, February 16, having written a report for Boston on the Australian reaction to the fall of Singapore, Red and I reported in at the KLM desk at the airport and were soon boarded on a DC-3. We were surprised to find no one else in the passenger cabin. When the engines were revved up and the plane began to roll, Red and I were still the only passengers. Not many people were rushing to get to Batavia that day.

We had a two-day flight from Sydney to Batavia. We stopped overnight at Alice Springs in the middle of Australia, where for the only time in my life I actually saw people walking around with "their heads in a cloud." The cloud was made up of swarms of flies. The aborigines were accustomed to it. The whites wore broad-brimmed hats and netting. The hotel was frontier style—a single-story affair under a corrugated iron roof. Alice Springs had not then become a tourist resort. On the seventeenth we stopped to refuel at Broome on the northwest coast of Australia, a place equally Spartan in its traveler amenities (corrugated iron roofs again) put on the edge of a long curving beach of purest white sand caressed by a lagoon of limpid translucent turquoise. It was a pearl fishing port, but the boats were all bunched together on the shore, sequestered from Pearl Harbor Day on because the pearl divers were all Japanese. I looked down with awe at the sheer beauty of beach and lagoon as we circled and then headed north for Java. As we passed over the Timor Sea the captain sent word back that we were then over the most heavily shark-infested waters in the world. Soon he invited us to the cockpit and pointed out a column of smoke rising on the far horizon to the right. That, he said, was coming from Bali, where the Japanese were at that moment making a landing. He also informed us that the Japanese were on Sumatra. Red and I looked at each other. We had our first glimmer of appreciation of what we were doing. Here we were headed for Java. Bali lies to its right, Sumatra to its left. My instructions from Boston had been "to proceed to the battle area of the Far Pacific." I was nearer my assigned goal than I had yet fully appreciated.

"Strategic Redeployment"

We landed at Batavia on February 17 without further incident, checked in at the Hotel des Andes, and immediately went to the bar, where we knew we would find any colleagues or friendly diplomats who might be around. There were no British, Dutch, or American colleagues, which seemed slightly surprising to us (we still had much to learn about the war in the Pacific). But there soon came in a group of cheerful but dusty and bedraggled young British officers. "Have a drink," we said. "Don't mind if we do," they replied. "Where are you from," we said. "Sumatra," they said. "We were the last of the rear guard. We blew the last oil well this morning and just came across the straits. The Japs have the whole island now."

First thing in the morning Red and I went to the government press office and asked, among other things, about arrangements for journalists getting out if things should get too serious. "Oh, don't you know?" the officer said. "There aren't any. We thought you knew before you came." He responded to the look of puzzlement on our faces by explaining that the Dutch government had long ago grouped all correspondents in three categories. Those on the first category list would go at the first sign of danger. These had gone a month ago. The second category was those who wanted to stay almost to the end but wanted to be sure of getting out. They had gone a week before. The third category was of those who would stay no matter what, meaning even through a Japanese occupation. He assumed when he heard we were coming that we were going to be joining those who would spend the rest of the war in Java, no matter what.

Red and I thanked him for his information, went to the airport, and boarded a flight to Bandung, the summer capital, which was also Allied military headquarters. We found the American section and the senior American officer there, Gen. George H. Brett. While we were chatting, he pointed to an officer in British uniform coming out of the next building and getting into a car. "That," he said, "is General Wavell" (Allied supreme commander at that time). "He is leaving right now for India." As for the Americans? He explained that he had a B-17 bomber left over from the havoc at Clark Field in the Philippines on Pearl Harbor Day, when most of the American planes were caught on the ground. He would be using it the next day to transfer his air force command to Australia. He regretted that his passenger list was full. While we were chatting, an air raid alarm sounded. General Brett led us into a slit trench. Far overhead we watched our first air battle in the Southwest Pacific. We counted about twenty planes in the air; then there were fewer and several parachutes blossomed and some wreckage came hurtling down. The wreckage, unfortunately, had Dutch markings on it. The implication was starkly obvious. The Japanese already enjoyed decisive air superiority over Java. Red and I thanked the general for his candid information. Now we knew that there was not going to be any serious defense of the Dutch East Indies. It behooved us to give thought to how we might spend the war in some place other than a Japanese prisoner–of–war camp. Bandung is a short shuttle flight from Batavia. We were back at the Hotel des Andes in time for dinner. This time we found the bar bustling with American and British colleagues in uniform. They had come ashore from the British P&O liner *Empress of India,* which had just arrived in the harbor of Batavia loaded with the Australian Sixth Division back from the war in North Africa. The original intention was to use that division to help defend Singapore. But with the fall of Singapore it was diverted to Java. By the time it actually reached the harbor of Batavia the military situation was too bleak to provide a reasonable case for putting it ashore in Java. The Australians had already lost their entire Seventh Division at Singapore. Our colleagues who had come out with the Sixth informed us that the order to deploy that division in Java had been canceled and the ship would be sailing on to Australia the next day with everyone who had come out from Egypt aboard. My account written at the time of what happened next reads as follows:

> So we left Java like refugees from any doomed city after the regular transportation had finished. As the decision was made word came that a ship of uncertain capacity might sail that night. After a dash to the port by taxi, we found a 1400-ton Malayan coaster lying at the coaling docks with a Chinese crew on strike. We were offered deck space if

the ship sailed. British soldiers volunteered to stoke the ship to get up steam. At the last moment, however, the Chinese crew agreed to work after all and we put out of the harbor at dusk, wondering whether we would make the Sundra Straits before the Japanese attack.

Many of our co-passengers were refugees from Singapore who had already been through one escape in the midst of bombs and were therefore understandably anxious.

We sat on deck that first night watching the dim lights of our escort and other convoyed ships around us. Nothing happened. Next morning we passed out of the straits, leaving green Java behind and most of the passengers went around shaking hands quietly, some tearfully. Then we settled down to a long voyage on a slow ship which had not been on the high seas since the time 29 years ago that she sailed from Dundee.

Incidentally, Red had come down with me to the port intending to go along, but at the coal docks had second thoughts. He decided to take his chances on finding something else later. He stayed on in Java another two or three days and picked up a freighter going out of Tjilatjip on the south coast. His ship was bombed on its way to Australia but made it without major damage to Port Darwin, whence Red made his way back by train to Melbourne.

I can now add some details of my own retreat from Java that were forbidden by military censorship at the time. The ship was named *Klang*. Her other passengers consisted largely of the white employees of the former Singapore Broadcasting Corporation and a dozen British soldiers from the paymaster service who had brought out the records of the British forces who had been serving in Singapore. The *Klang* had previously been running a regular passenger and light freight service up the coast from Singapore to Kuala Lumpur. She was a coal burner, and she had a native Chinese crew. The reluctance of the crew to go to Australia was understandable. They knew that Australia had an Asian exclusion policy. Australia held no charms for them. They came aboard, literally, at bayonet point. When we steamed out from Batavia harbor, we found ourselves in the company of the *Empress of India* and several other smaller, assorted ships, mostly commercial vessels. We had an impressive escort, the U.S. cruiser *Marblehead* plus several American and Dutch destroyers. After they took us safely through the straits between Java and Sumatra, the escorts turned and headed back through the straits. (The next day they joined the combined American, British, and Dutch naval forces in the battle of the Java Sea. The cruiser *Perth* was sunk, as were most of the Dutch vessels. The *Marblehead* was severely damaged but limped to the nearest safe port in India.) Our convoy scattered in separate directions. We watched the stately *Empress of India,* far faster than we were, disappear in the general direction of Australia. Soon we were alone, steaming along at a sedate seven knots, on an empty ocean with perhaps our greatest asset the fact that our ship was so old and so small that it was hardly worth a Japanese torpedo.

For ten days and nights we sailed on, seeing nothing but empty sky and empty sea. I made the acquaintance of British army "compo tea," a mixture of powdered tea and sugar, and British army baked beans. I was grateful for any food on that voyage but have not since felt the need for either. That voyage ended at night in the outer harbor of Fremantle, the seaport for Perth in Western Australia. As the anchor went down, the English captain and Scottish engineer (the only white members of the crew) reached for their respective bottles of whiskey and were soon dead to the world. Shortly thereafter an Australian naval launch came along-side and an officer shouted through a trumpet an order to "clear for action" as an enemy ship was reported approaching. The British army sergeant took command. He ordered us to bring out the mattresses and arrange them along the railings on the outer side of the vessel. He ordered women and children below and deployed his men along the railings. They had rifles and a single machine gun. With these arrangements complete we waited for whatever might happen. Nothing did. The launch came back and announced an "all clear." The twelve soldiers stowed their rifles and we all went to sleep. Next morning early a U.S. submarine tender came into port followed by several U.S. submarines (survivors from the battle of Java Sea). The *Klang* and the U.S. ships moved into the inner harbor, and most of the crews were soon ashore. For the sailors from the submarines and their tender it was the first shore leave after the outbreak of war. By evening I did not see a single American sailor unescorted by a female Australian.

The quick camaraderie made for amicable relations between the United States and Australia for that first day, but on the second day the scene changed radically. The *Empress of India* also arrived in the harbor at Fre-mantle, having taken longer to get there in spite of her greater speed. (Her delay was presumably due to a longer route chosen to safeguard her precious cargo. With the possibility ahead of a Japanese invasion of

Australia the government there could not afford to lose a second division from its meager army.) The soldiers of that Australian Sixth Division had been through the battle of Tobruk in North Africa. They were proud of their title Desert Rats. They were home, and they too came ashore, but to find their own Australian girls on the arms of the American sailors. There ensued one of the unrecorded battles of World War II, but fortunately one fought only with derogatory remarks and fisticuffs. The police did their best to keep the competition relatively peaceful, but Perth had a lively time until American sailors and Australian soldiers moved on to their next assignments on other fields of battle. My own strategic redeployment from the early disasters of the Pacific war was by then complete.

General MacArthur's Frustrations

For understandable reasons Gen. Douglas MacArthur and I had different reactions when we found ourselves (at some distance apart, I in Java, he in Manila) facing the rushing tide of the Japanese advance.

For me it was perfectly simple. I still remember with a shiver the sense of claustrophobia I felt during my last night on Java. The Japanese were closing in on me from three sides. My escape routes were being cut off. When Red and I went down to the coal dock at Tanjang Priok looking for our escape ship, only her mast and bridge showed above the dockside. She was small, dingy, and rusty; and her crew was mutinous. But she was headed for Australia. I went aboard and never looked back. That was the night of February 21, 1942.

By that time Douglas MacArthur was already a national hero with a personal and family reputation to uphold. His father had won the Congressional Medal of Honor for planting the battle flag of the Twenty-fourth Wisconsin Infantry on the crest of Missionary Ridge at Chattanooga in the Civil War. He himself won distinction commanding the much-decorated Rainbow Division in World War I. And now he had frustrated and delayed the Japanese advance in the Philippines by two months. The Japanese had expected him to fight a battle for the city of Manila. Instead, he executed War Plan Orange, an old plan recently revised by Col. Dwight D. Eisenhower when he was planning officer on the MacArthur staff. MacArthur's handling of the maneuver part of that plan has been universally regarded by military critics as brilliant. His problem was to bring two separate armies at opposite ends of the island of Luzon back, phase by phase, alternately, to the Bataan peninsula while both were in daily danger of encirclement. He began the withdrawal operation on Christmas Day. It was completed on January 6 with negligible losses. He ended up with eighty thousand men in previously prepared positions. On February 28 those forces were holding the lines successfully, and they continued to do so for another two months. Not until April 9 did the white flags go up on Bataan and May 6 on the fortress of Corregidor.

Back at home, and everywhere else, the successful retreat to Bataan was, inevitably, contrasted to the less successful retreat of the British army in Malaya. Singapore fell on February 15. Japanese general Masaharu Homma had been given two months for the conquest of the Philippines. By the time Corregidor fell on May 6 he was three months behind his schedule.

But what the public at home and elsewhere did not know was that General MacArthur had only executed part of Plan Orange, and then only when it was too late to execute the entire plan. Under the plan, as redrafted by Eisenhower, MacArthur should have stored on Bataan enough food and supplies of all kinds for his army to be able to hold out for two years. According to William Manchester in *American Caesar*, his biography of MacArthur, "One depot alone, at Cabanatuan on the central Luzon plain, held fifty million bushels of rice—enough to feed U.S. and Filipino troops for over four years." The food was available within easy transport distance of Bataan. But MacArthur had always scorned the Orange Plan and he refused to give the orders to put it into operation until there was no longer time to replenish the storerooms on the peninsula. He had successfully brought eighty thousand troops into a peninsula that is some forty miles wide and nearly sixty miles long. It was a powerful defensive position. With enough food and ammunition it might well have been held until the navy could come to its rescue. A year should have been enough. But by the time the redeployment of his troops to Bataan had been completed he had not only his eighty thousand soldiers, but also an additional twenty-six thousand civilian refugees to feed and there was very little food. He had to put them all on half rations at once. Bataan was doomed, but not by enemy action. The army on Bataan (fifteen thousand were American, the rest Filipinos) was starved out.

Douglas MacArthur may have had two things on his conscience when, on February 23, he received a cable from Washington ordering him to proceed to Melbourne to take command of all U.S. troops in Australia. The desperate condition of his troops on Bataan was certainly his fault for having failed to stock the peninsula with food before bringing the people there. An earlier matter that has never been satisfactorily explained may also have been troubling him. Gen. Lewis H. Brerton, who commanded U.S. air forces in the Philippines area, was wakened and informed of the attack on Pearl Harbor on December 7 (December 8 in Manila) probably about an hour after the beginning of that attack. He first saw to informing all his air force units that a state of war existed. He had already, on the day before, put them on combat alert. He then went to General MacArthur's headquarters, where he was received by Gen. Richard K. Sutherland, MacArthur's chief of staff. In his diaries, published in 1946 under the title *The Brereton Diaries*, he describes what happened next:

> After General Sutherland had given me all available information I requested permission to carry out offensive action immediately after daylight. I told Sutherland I wanted to mount all available B-17s at Clark Field for missions previously assigned and to prepare the B-17s at Del Monte for movement, refueling and bomb loading at Clark Field for operations against the enemy on Formosa. General Sutherland agreed with my plans and said to go ahead with preparations; in the meantime he would obtain General MacArthur's authority for the daylight attacks.
>
> When I left General MacArthur's Hqs. I was under orders to prepare our heavy bombers for action but not to undertake any offensive action until ordered.

That order "not to undertake offensive action" was given Brereton at a little after five o'clock in the morning (Manila time). Three hours later Japanese planes were attacking various targets on northern Luzon. The diaries continue:

"I personally called General Sutherland and informed him that hostile aircraft were operating over Luzon and that if Clark Field was attacked successfully we would be unable to operate offensively with the bombers. I again requested authority to carry out offensive action." Permission was not granted then. It was granted at "about 11 AM." Brereton immediately ordered his Clark Field bombers, which had been circling around for safety, to land and load. They were on the ground loading when "at approximately 12:13 PM an estimated 54 Japanese bombers, flying in two waves, attacked Clark Field from high altitude." More waves of dive bombers and strafing planes followed. The attack continued for approximately an hour. "Preliminary reports gave 17 B-17s destroyed or damaged and 16 out of 21 P-40s of the 20th Pursuit Squadron destroyed."

To summarize, according to *The Brereton Diaries* General Brereton, at about five o'clock in the morning (Manila time) of the day of Pearl Harbor, requested permission to launch a bombing offensive against Japanese warships and troop transports coming from Formosa. Had permission been granted at that time, the bombers lost on the ground at Clark Field six hours later would, instead, have been in the air somewhere near Formosa attacking the enemy that had already struck the first blows of the war at Pearl Harbor. The six-hour delay in granting permission to take offensive action cost the United States twelve B-17s (the actual net loss) or roughly a third of the total of U.S. heavy bombers in the Philippines.

Why that costly six-hour delay?

General MacArthur's own *Reminiscences* contains the following comment on the affair:

> Sometime in the morning of December 8th, before the Clark Field attack, General Brerton suggested to General Sutherland a foray against Formosa. I know nothing of any interview with Sutherland, and Brerton never at any time recommended or suggested an attack on Formosa to me. My first knowledge of it was in a newspaper dispatch months later. Such a suggestion to the Chief of Staff must have been of the most nebulous and superficial character, as there is no record of it at headquarters. The proposal, if intended seriously, should certainly have been made to me in person. He has never spoken of the matter to me either before or after the Clark Field attack.

William Manchester devotes seven pages in his book on General MacArthur to the mystery of how and why those twelve valuable bombers and their fighter escorts were destroyed at Clark Field nine hours after the original Japanese attack on Pearl Harbor and six hours after General Brerton had asked permission to send the bombers on their expected and expectable mission. One possibility is that MacArthur was responding to the wistful hope of Manuel Quezon, president of the Philippines, that Japan might refrain from attacking his country if no offensive action was launched from his country. Another possibility is that like Napoleon at Waterloo his mind was simply overloaded and that for a span of several hours he was incapable of clear thinking and firm decision.

The losses at Clark Field on Pearl Harbor Day ended whatever chance might otherwise have existed to fend off the incoming invasion of the Philippine Islands. The B-17s, known as Flying Fortresses because of their defensive weaponry, were the latest and best heavy bombers of that era. Had all of Brerton's thirty-five bombers been used offensively at the outset of the war in the Pacific it is possible that they might have sunk enough Japanese troop transports to spoil the invasion. Infantry is helpless until it gets ashore.

(Back in Washington Admiral King studied MacArthur's performance both on that day at Manila and later during the retreat to Bataan. From that time on King refused, absolutely, to trust any substantial part of the U.S. Navy to MacArthur's command.)

In the tunnel, on Corregidor, on February 23, General MacArthur read the telegram from Washington saying that his commander-in-chief, the president of the United States, ordered him to leave the Philippines and go to Australia to take up a new command there. Small wonder that it took him nearly two weeks to make up his mind. To go would mean leaving behind for ultimate surrender to the Japanese his army of fifteen thousand Americans and sixty-five thousand Filipinos. In their eyes he would be abandoning them, deserting them. He knew that they already referred to him as "Dugout Doug" because he had only once crossed the three miles of water that separated Corregidor from the Bataan peninsula to visit his troops there. He was safe in the tunnel while they fought in the jungle. And they were on short rations and would eventually be starving. The time was long past when that army could either be reinforced or withdrawn. An occasional submarine would get through. The American high commissioner in the Philippines, Francis B. Sayre, and his wife went out by a submarine. So did President Quezon of the Philippines. A few others for various reasons of personal importance would get out that way. Several reporters went out on a small ship that managed to evade the blockade. But the vast majority of the soldiery would have to stay, be captured, and suffer dreadful conditions on the death march to prison camps. Many would die before the war ended. Small wonder that their general anguished over the decision to leave them. He talked with his staff about resigning his commission and joining his men on Bataan as a common soldier. He had apparently resolved that he would kill himself rather than surrender. Did he also realize that his two big mistakes—not stocking Bataan with food and not letting Brerton's bombers take the offensive immediately on the first day of war—were largely responsible for his immediate dilemma? He anguished from February 23 to March 6. But then the habit of obedience to orders got the better of any impulse to romantic heroism. He decided to obey orders and go.

My own "redeployment" from Java to Australia was a luxury by comparison with the MacArthur journey. Yes, I had to sleep on deck. Yes, I had to subsist almost entirely on British army baked beans and "compo" tea. Yes, I had to make do with a saltwater shower. But we saw not a single Japanese aircraft or submarine on our "retrograde maneuver." It was just smooth cruising on a glassy sea under a warm but not intolerable sun. It was a holiday cruise.

For the MacArthurs it was hellish in every way. At about seven o'clock on the evening of Wednesday, March 11, the general led his wife Jean, his three-year-old son Arthur, and Arthur's Cantonese amah, to what was left of the south dock at Corregidor and boarded PT-41.

PT-41 was built for speed, not for comfort. It was seventy-seven feet long. It had powerful engines. At speed, it could plane over the waves. But in a rough sea such boats made for miserable riding. Everything that night combined to make it miserable. A heavy sea was running, and waves broke over the foredeck and drenched everyone in the cockpit. The best account I have read of what happened to the MacArthurs on that trip is from Manchester's *American Caesar*:

MacArthur, his son and Ah Cheu were in agony. Ironically, it was Jean, about whom the General had been most concerned, who was the least distressed on the 41 boat. Arthur and his nanny lay below on the two officers' bunks, Arthur running a fever. On the floor beside them MacArthur sprawled on a mattress, his face waxen and his eyes dark-circled. He kept retching, though his stomach had been emptied in the first spasm of nausea. The anguish of his defeat, and the mortification at being sent away from his men, were now joined by the unspeakable physical suffering. For a 62-year-old man it could have been fatal. His limbs were so rigid that he was unable to move them. Jean, kneeling beside him chafed his hands hour after hour.

By Thursday morning PT-41 was halfway from Corregidor to the big southern island of Mindanao and the Del Monte airfield, which was still in American hands. They hid out during Thursday morning in a jungle-fringed inlet but by early afternoon decided to take the risk of running by daylight. They twice saw Japanese warships, but managed to avoid being spotted in turn. By seven o'clock the next morning they were coming into the harbor that served the Del Monte pineapple plantation near the airfield. By midday all were physically restored and comfortable at the plantation guest house under the care of U.S. Brig. Gen. William F. Sharp.

The flight from Del Monte to Australia was almost as miserable as the trip to Del Monte. The Japanese had landed in southern Mindanao and on various islands between Mindanao and Australia. Their planes were patrolling the area. The first B-17 sent to rescue the MacArthur family was in such poor and obviously unreliable condition that MacArthur refused to board it. He demanded, through Washington, two B-17s in reliable condition. The American command in Australia had no such planes, but managed to borrow two from Admiral Leary's command. The air was turbulent. The pilots had to fly low and dodge known Japanese airfields and bases. They made the trip safely and landed at Batchelor Field, about forty miles south of Darwin on the northern tip of Australia, but Mrs. MacArthur emerged from the ordeal declaring that she would never set foot in an airplane again. Two commercial airliners, DC-3s, were sent to carry them south in more comfort, but Mrs. MacArthur's distaste for flying was such that the general demanded a motorcar for the thousand-mile trip from there to the railhead at Alice Springs. Only when the doctor told the general that his child might not survive the trip by land did he finally relent and order the whole party into the two DC-3s. They took off just minutes before Japanese bombers attacked the field. The flight to Alice Springs seems to have been relatively comfortable and uneventful, but on arrival there, in spite of heat and those swarms of flies I had met on my way to Java, the general insisted on waiting overnight in a tin-roofed and iron-bedstead hotel for a narrow-gauge, very slow and primitive train to take them the next thousand miles south.

That was the day, March 18, when the Australian government, the Australian people, and I all learned that we had a new commanding general, that he, MacArthur, was actually in Australia, and that there were American troops in Australia.

The U.S. government had not said a word to anyone about MacArthur's escape from the Philippines as long as he was traveling by sea, air, and land to Alice Springs. It was announced only when he was there and safely out of range of Japanese aircraft operating from the island chain north of Australia. Not even the prime minister of Australia, John Curtin, was allowed to know about the escape until MacArthur had actually landed safely at Alice Springs.

From Alice Springs to Adelaide in the southeastern and populated part of Australia by slow train was a three-day affair. The lapse of time required for the trip made for a buildup of maximum excitement in Adelaide and an emotional explosion of relief and expectation. The first was justified in that the United States had accepted responsibility for the defense of Australia. The second was on more slender foundation. The crowds roared a hero's welcome for him when his train clanged its way into the station in Adelaide, but by that time the general himself had begun to realize that his dream of leading a relief expedition back to Bataan was just a dream. He had a broad command. He commanded all Allied forces in the Southwest Pacific. That included what was left of Admiral Leary's fleet after the battle of the Java Sea, the Australian and New Zealand navies (also what was left, which was not much), the Australian Seventh Division just back from North Africa, Australian militia units, and bits and pieces of American units that had made their way down from the Philippines and continued to dribble in from time to time. However, there were by that time thirty-seven American war correspondents in Australia, making for a splendid reunion of old friends in Melbourne by the time Red got down from Darwin. The group who had come with the Australian Seventh Division from North Africa and a second batch from Honolulu who had arrived with two field artillery units and some air force ground support crews provided General MacArthur with an impressive American press corps. Seldom in history have so many correspondents covered such a small army. The Japanese must have assumed from the torrent of copy flowing back to the United States that MacArthur's army was almost as big as he had expected it to be when he left Corregidor. It did grow by two American divisions (the U.S. Forty-first on April 6 and the Thirty-second on April 15) during the first six weeks of his command. He also had the Australian Seventh Division and a reconstituted Sixth. But that was far from enough manpower for him to think seriously of fulfilling the promise he made to the troops on Bataan that he would be coming back to rescue them. An army of four divisions was not enough to defend Australia should the Japanese be able to land a substantial army on the huge and largely empty continent.

The big news story of those first weeks after MacArthur's arrival does not show up in the copy we thirty-seven American correspondents sent back (censorship was rigid). It was an argument between General MacArthur and the Australian political leaders over how to defend their country. After the general had been there long enough to understand both the physical problem and his actual resources, he became convinced that the only possible way to save Australia was to head off Japanese landings. He proposed to take the offensive in the island chain to the north of Australia, particularly on the big island of New Guinea where the Australians had a foothold at Port Moresby. But the Australian leaders in the government were much more interested in saving the southeastern section of the country that included the three biggest cities—Adelaide, Melbourne, and Sydney—and most of the manufacturing. They talked of the Brisbane Line, a defense line to be drawn from just north of Brisbane and curving down to the south coast to the west of Adelaide. General MacArthur's first big battle was to persuade Prime Minister Curtin that the Brisbane Line could never be held by the four divisions then in Australia against the numbers of troops which the Japanese could put ashore along an undefended coastline. He won the policy battle, but only after the U.S. Navy had fought and won the battle of the Coral Sea. That is where Australia was saved.

The Japanese task force that was turned back in that battle was convoying a landing force intended to capture Port Moresby on the southern side of New Guinea. Once the Japanese had taken and consolidated a position there they would be able to provide land-based air cover for a further landing on the north tip of Australia itself at or near Darwin. I learned of the importance of that battle of the Coral Sea by a roundabout route.

Getting the first American troops ashore in Australia had involved difficulties with the Australian trade unions, which were accustomed to frequent work breaks, called "smokos." An American general was overseeing the unloading of his artillery. An Australian crane operator shut down the power on his crane at the precise moment ordained for his "smoko," leaving a piece of field artillery dangling in the air. The general grabbed a bayonet from one of his soldiers, strode over to the crane operator, and told him, firmly, to get back on that crane and get that gun on the ground. The bayonet in the general's right hand emphasized the command. The crane operator got back on the crane, but the shop steward complained. I recounted this at dinner that night to Frank Packer, editor of the *Sydney Telegraph*, a Tory paper that was delighted to have ammunition to throw at the Labour party government. He said he could not print the story on his own, but that he could reprint it from my newspaper if I would write it, which I did. He reprinted it as an example of how slack the Labour government was about the war effort. This had a remarkable consequence. I was invited for the weekend to the residence of the very British governor general (a relative of the royal family in England). On May 9 I was riding with him over the broad grazing lands around Canberra when an aide galloped up to the governor general and handed him an envelope. He opened it, read it carefully, turned to me, and said, "This is very good news. The Japanese have been turned back in the Coral Sea." The purpose of the weekend invitation to Government House had obviously been to persuade me that the Labour government was actually doing its best in the war effort. My story about the American general, the bayonet, and the Australian crane operator had hit home. The prime minister's office obviously had enlisted the governor general's help in persuading one American reporter to think more kindly of the Australian government. It gave me a measure of how anxious the Australians were at that time about their future and how dependent they felt upon the military power of the United States. The chances are that but for the victory of U.S. arms in that battle of the Coral Sea (which lies just northeast of Australia) the Japanese would have soon been ashore and heading for Melbourne and Sydney. That in turn would have made the ultimate defeat of Japan a more difficult and much longer operation. Australian morale was at a low point just before that battle.

Had I had any knowledge of investment opportunities I could have made a fortune in Sydney that spring. The very rich of Sydney lived largely on Bellevue Hill. I was given dinner there several times by another editor who lived on Bellevue Hill. Most of the other houses in his neighborhood were empty. He explained that their owners had all gone to the "outback," which meant sheep ranches far to the west. A Japanese submarine had slipped through the defenses of Sydney Harbor one night and lobbed a few small shells at Bellevue Hill. No serious damage was done, but a panic was on. I could have bought any house on that hill at that time for a song.

The battle of the Coral Sea had saved Australia, but that was of little comfort to General MacArthur. The American ships that fought and won in that battle were under the commands of admirals Frank J. Fletcher and William H. Halsey, who in turn were under the command of Adm. Chester Nimitz at Pearl Harbor. Admiral Nimitz in turn was under the sole and exclusive command of the U.S. chief of naval operations in Washington, Adm. Ernest J. King. The naval war in the Central Pacific was a U.S. Navy operation. General MacArthur commanded in the Southwest Pacific, but the perimeters of his command were revised from time to time to make sure that none of the ships that operated out of the Hawaiian Islands under Admiral Nimitz ever came under MacArthur's authority. He was given a small navy of his own, but it was always small. He never had more than a fraction of what he wanted and kept demanding, both directly to Washington and indirectly in Australia. As soon as he had persuaded the Australians to accept the local strategy of defending

Australia in the island chain to the north and had begun moving troops for what was to become the dreadful struggle for the Kokoda trail over the mountain backbone of eastern New Guinea, he turned his attention to the goal of reversing the strategy that had been adopted at the first big meeting of the principals of the Anglo-American alliance in Washington at Christmastime 1941. Prime Minister Churchill had come over from England with his top military staff. For a week at the White House they hammered out the basic strategy that called for concentrating the major Allied effort on the defeat of Hitler's Germany in Europe while fighting a defensive strategy in the Far East with minimum resources. Europe was to have top priority. General MacArthur's personal feud with the Japanese was put on the back burner of the Allied effort. To try to overturn that strategy he first cultivated Prime Minister Curtin and leading members of the Australian Parliament. He persuaded the Australian government to press Churchill in London to revise the strategy and send more forces of all types—land, sea, and air—to Australia. Then the general held a series of background briefings for Australian correspondents, which re-sulted in long and passionate articles in the Australian press calling for a revised strategy in order to take advantage of the great opportunities that allegedly were being wasted, in the MacArthur view, by not allocating more men and weapons to his command.

Douglas MacArthur was a persuasive man. When his purpose was to charm and persuade, he was exceptionally able. I, like many others, was "sold." I had concluded that under the Europe First strategy laid down at the Washington conference there would probably be a long stalemate in the Far East while Europe's fate was being decided. I had therefore recommended to my editor that I return home to cover "the other war." But before I left I was invited ("commanded" would be more accurate) to the MacArthur presence. When he heard that I was going back home, he sent for me and set the time for the day before I was leaving. His words to me were to be the last thing I would hear and would remember as I headed back for Washington.

He received me in an office that must have been at least sixty feet long, for it was long enough for a tall man, which he was, to pace steadily from one end to the other while delivering a sculptured sermon on the opportunities being wasted in his theater of operations by the mistaken Europe First strategy.

I sat enthralled on a sofa taking notes. He paced to and fro, slowly and pensively, talking steadily, not fast but also not leaving an opening for a question, occasionally taking a puff on a cigarette held in a carved ivory holder. Here is a sample of what I wrote after that brainwashing, which it was. It is verbatim MacArthur.

The number of planes without which it would be impossible to recapture Lea, Salamoa, Rabaul, and even the Philippines and the Dutch East Indies probably is less right now if they were available today than the attritional air losses if this front was maintained on the defensive for the next six months.

If General MacArthur possessed 2,000 extra combat planes today while the Japanese fleet is heavily involved in the Northern Pacific area he could almost certainly retake everything between here and Manila, but if the planes were doled out to him gradually on the concept of defensive strategy the same number of planes would be lost through attrition in a shorter time than probably the American public has any idea and at the end we would be no better off than now.

Since we are bound to lose war materials anyway it is far better to lose some in an offensive action than merely sitting back and watching events and leaving the offensive in Japanese hands.

That was the message I was to take back to Washington. Not only did he persuade me of his views, he also made me feel that somehow the future of the free world depended on my carrying that message to the very top in Washington. I was instructed to go at once to the White House when I got home and explain it all there.

Thus primed and prepared, I boarded a returning troop transport leaving from Brisbane and headed home by sea via the Panama Canal.

I should have realized at once that the idea of my being a conveyor of essential information to the White House in Washington was essentially silly. After all, I was going there not by air, or even by fast destroyer, but in a very slow troop transport going home virtually empty by way of the Panama Canal. I can only say that MacArthur's persuasiveness was so immense that the idea that I was carrying an important message stayed with me for the entire time of my slow passage home. It took me a month from Brisbane, Australia, to the Panama Canal. There I left the ship, hopped a military air transport flight to Newark, New Jersey, and caught a train to Washington. Immediately on reaching home I telephoned the office of Admiral William D. Leahy, chief military adviser to the president and chairman of the Joint Chiefs of Staff, and asked for the earliest possible appointment with him the next morning. It was granted. In the morning

I went first thing to his office in the Federal Reserve Board Building, which had been preempted for the war. I delivered my message from the general to the admiral. He listened patiently, then with a growing smile. At the end he said, "Harsch, we haven't forgotten General MacArthur. I think you will learn something before the day is out which will interest you, and reassure him." I thanked him, walked out of the building, and saw a newsboy crying "Extra." The bold headlines across the top of the front page announced, "Marines Land on Guadalcanal."

But the marines who landed on Guadalcanal were under the command of Adm. Robert L. Ghormley, who in turn was under Admiral Nimitz at Pearl Harbor, and he under Admiral King in Washington. Those marines and the army divisions which came in later to help in the battle for Guadalcanal were never under MacArthur's command. They helped him. The fighting on Guadalcanal took the pressure off his troops battling their way around New Guinea, but they were never under his command.

That was the story of the rest of the Pacific war. The navy, under Admiral Nimitz at Pearl Harbor, carried the main burden of the war in the Pacific. The succession of sea battles beginning with the Coral Sea broke the back of the Japanese imperial fleet. The marines went ashore for the desperately hard island landings—Tarawa, Saipan, and Iwo Jima. General MacArthur followed along on the southern fringe of the navy's advance. His island-hopping strategy exploited, brilliantly, the opportunities which the navy won. But it was Nimitz's great aircraft carriers and his fliers and his combat marines who opened the way for the moment when General MacArthur could wade ashore on the beach at Leyte and be able to say, "I have returned." And even then, it was Nimitz's old battleships salvaged from the disaster at Pearl Harbor that turned back one Japanese fleet in the Surigao Straits while the Jeep carriers turned back a second coming through the San Bernardino Straits; they saved General MacArthur and his troops on the beach at Leyte from suffering a second disaster in the Philippines.

FDR's Other Generals – and Admirals

Right through to the end of World War II Douglas MacArthur continued to be the most visible of America's wartime military commanders. His special place in the public eye stayed on with him through the war and continued long afterward. We will come back to him later as the virtual viceroy of Japan and then as the man who first nearly won and then nearly lost the Korean War. Meanwhile, in Washington I had a remarkable opportunity to learn something of other men who played less spectacular but more important roles in building and using the largest and most powerful military force in the history of the world.

At the top among those who met regularly together in the offices of the Joint Chiefs of Staff and with the president in making the major decisions of strategy and priorities the most respected among his colleagues was George Catlett Marshall, chief of staff of the United States Army. To everyone in this group, even to the president of the United States, General Marshall was *General Marshall*. He was addressed that way, never by first name or nickname. General Arnold, who ran the air force, was known as "Hap" among his peers. Admiral King, who ran the navy, was either Ernie or King. But to all of them General Marshall was just that. One explanation can be offered. A group of us met with Admiral King for dinner shortly after the appointment of General Eisenhower as European supreme commander was announced. Most of us had expected that honor, and that deep responsibility, to go to Marshall. It was generally understood that he wanted it and expected it. But the appointment went to Eisenhower. Why? Admiral King replied, "You can blame me." He told us that he had gone to the president and said he knew that Marshall was the best person for the European command and deserved it. But, he told us, he argued to the president that the presence of General Marshall on the Joint Chiefs of Staff in Washington was essential to the smooth running of that institution. I think I remember his exact words. From memory they went like this: "I told the President that we had to work with the British. I loathe the Limeys. Whenever General Marshall is in the room I behave. He makes me be reasonable with the British. As long as General Marshall is on the Joint Staff I will behave and manage to get along with the British. I can't be responsible for my own behavior without him. We need him here to keep me in line, and to make the whole combined Joint Staff operation work."

There may have been other equally compelling reasons for the Eisenhower appointment. "Ike" had written the final plan for the retreat to Bataan. He had been the guiding force in the highly successful performance of General Kreuger's army in the Louisiana maneuvers. His work in both planning and operations was widely known and respected. He had long been marked for advancement. Admiral King's presentation to the president may have merely fortified a decision already made for other reasons. The end result was that General Marshall remained in Washington throughout the war, largely out of sight of the general public but a major force in making the Combined Joint Chiefs of Staff work, and work well, and in shaping the major decisions of high policy.

It may be that the decision to give first priority to the war in Europe would have been taken without General Marshall's presence in Washington, but he was a consistent advocate of that decision and he policed it. He was also deeply committed to the proposition that there had to be a major Allied return to the continent of Europe, and as soon as possible. The British came forward with every possible alternative to a cross-channel invasion of the continent. They wanted to fight in the Mediterranean. They liked an invasion of Italy. A Churchill favorite would have been a landing along the Dalmation coast and a push up through the Lublijana Gap at what Churchill called "the soft underbelly of Europe." The British favored everything and anything except a straight plunge across the English Channel and a landing on a coast that had already been heavily fortified by the German army and would be defended with undoubted skill by unquestionably the best trained and most highly motivated army on earth. It was due largely to General Marshall's conviction that the decision was taken to cross the Channel. General Marshall was the dominant figure among the American chiefs of staff. He had the full confidence of the president. By keeping him in Washington the landing in Normandy took place beginning on June 6, 1944, and its success marked the beginning of the end of Hitler's German Reich.

I have a vivid personal memory of General Marshall's methods. A group of about twenty-five of us (American newspaper correspondents concerned largely with the course of the war) requested and were granted a group briefing session. We were to talk with him for background information, not a publishable interview. When we filed into his office, a row of chairs of our precise number had been set up in a semicircle facing his desk. He opened the proceedings by saying that he would first hear our questions. He pointed to the end man to his left. When the first had finished his question, his finger pointed to the next. He went across the line, saying nothing, just listening to each in turn state his question. When the questions were finished, he leaned back in his chair, paused for perhaps half a minute, and then started talking. He must have talked for certainly half an hour, perhaps for much longer. He talked steadily, without a pause. When he had finished, he had in fact responded helpfully to every question that had been asked. He then said, "Thank you, gentlemen, good day." We trooped out. We had had no chance to ask supplementary questions. They were not needed. He had told us all that he could, fairly and without evasion. We were satisfied. As we left, he turned to an aide, who brought him some papers. The last to leave saw him in deep discussion of whatever was his next business. It was a no-nonsense visit, no idle chatter, no waste of the general's time.

One can only theorize about how differently the war might have gone had George Marshall not remained in Washington on the Combined Joint Chiefs of Staff. He himself was not in the chair. That role fell to Admiral Leahy as the president's personal representative on the staff. Marshall never was more than chief of staff of the U.S. Army. But so strong was his personality and his skill at grasping concepts and articulating them and presenting them with recognized objectivity that he was the most powerful single figure on that staff. Without him at the center in Washington it is possible that the cross-channel invasion would have been abandoned, or so long delayed that the Germans might conceivably have defeated Russia and thus gained the ability to meet British and American armies with German strength all on the western front. In that case would Hitler ever have been defeated?

Another possibility is that without Marshall in Washington the navy would have obtained more men and material for the great thrust across the Pacific. That could have led to the swifter defeat of Japan, but it could also have meant delaying the cross-channel invasion. Again, the possibility was for a collapse of Russian resistance and a longer war in Europe. Admiral King was also a powerful advocate, but he usually deferred to General Marshall.

The Normandy invasion was an expensive operation. It took much courage even to conceive of carrying it out against the German army of 1944. True, that army had already taken several damaging defeats. It had lost the battle of Stalingrad and a quarter of a million German soldiers there between September 1942 and February 1943. And Germany's best general, Erwin Rommel, was defeated at Al Alemain from October 23 to November 4 in that same year 1943. Yet when the Normandy invasion finally took place in June 1944 the German army that defended the French coast exacted the lives of two and a half British or American soldiers for every German life lost. The British with their still vivid memories of the carnage on the battlefields of World War I in France and Belgium wanted anything but to face that still powerful German army on the beaches of the Channel coast. It took the persuasiveness and tenacity of George Marshall to overcome British resistance to the idea of crossing the Channel.

Least known to the outside world of the four members of the American military high command but perhaps essential to its remarkably smooth operation was Adm. William D. Leahy, whose title was chief of staff to the commander-in-chief, that is, to the president. He was also senior in rank to the others, having been chief of naval operations (King's title during the war) from 1937 to 1939. President Roosevelt had known him since World War I and immediately on Leahy's retirement from active duty in 1939 sent him to Puerto Rico as governor and then, in January 1941, as ambassador to Vichy France (that part of France not yet occupied by the Germans but under the leadership of France's World War I national hero, the aged Field Marshall Henri Petain).

Admiral Leahy's prime assignment was to coordinate, channel, and interpret the thinking and planning of the heads of the services—army, navy, and air corps—to the president. But unspecified was the further and equally important task of helping them iron out their own differences, which were sometimes substantial. King recognized his own bias against the British. So did the others. Admiral Leahy, in his memoirs (titled *I Was There*), says of King: "He was an exceptionally able sea commander. He also was explosive and at times it was just as well that the deliberations of the Joint Chiefs were a well-kept secret. The President had a high opinion of King's ability but also felt he was a very undiplomatic person, especially when the Admiral's low boiling point would be reached in some altercation with the British."

The problem was not limited to King's anglophobia. In Leahy's words, "King would have preferred to put more power into the Asiatic war earlier." The Pacific war was the navy's special war. The Japanese attack on Pearl Harbor had been aimed at the U.S. Navy. It had hurt the U.S. Navy. To many a naval officer and enlisted man World War II was war between the Japanese and American navies. The war in Europe to a true U.S. Navy man of 1941 was incidental and irrelevant. Fighting it was a chore imposed on them for unfathomable reasons. The war they wanted to fight was in the Pacific.

It is particularly interesting that it was Marshall who proposed putting Leahy into the White House and on the Joint Chiefs. King had agreed probably largely because Leahy was also navy, although on the retired list. In effect, the addition of Leahy balanced the institution of the Joint Chiefs at two army and two navy, because Gen. H. H. ("Hap") Arnold was also army, and as such subordinate to Marshall. (The air corps remained part of the army until the reorganization of the armed forces after the war when the U.S. Air Force was set up as a separate and independent branch of the armed services.)

The amazing and wonderful and fortunate thing for the United States is that this combination of personalities worked. Victory proved that it worked and worked well. We of the group of reporters who met with all four of them from time to time (usually at a private group dinner with Leahy, King, or Arnold; at the office with Marshall) came to know them well enough to form judgments. King and Marshall were the powerful and assertive personalities. Arnold was a quiet one. Leahy writes of Arnold that "we generally accepted his views on air strategy as correct and I cannot recall that he ever proposed a move that was not acceptable to the other Chiefs." Arnold was not assertive or abrasive or self-important.

Admiral Leahy was the one I knew best. The others I met only at the group sessions. But I had been personally introduced to Admiral Leahy by my father-in-law, Adm. Spencer Shepard Wood. I could, and often did, drop in at the White House to talk with him. His outstanding characteristics were forthrightness and impersonality. One cannot imagine Admiral Leahy insisting on protocol rights (as Marshall once did when he and King, in separate airplanes, were approaching the same landing field and Marshall insisted that King's plane circle until the Marshall plane had landed). Leahy, like Arnold, was free of self-importance. He seemed to have no sense of self at all. In group photographs he is usually in the second row or at the end. He never asserted himself. He was the reconciler of differences, the watchdog over the president's wishes in meetings with the Chiefs, the explainer in his daily meetings with the president of the Chiefs' problems and proposals.

Admiral Leahy's strength and his usefulness to the president probably lay in his marvelous forthrightness. He was totally devoid of affectation, pose, or evasion. His thinking and talking were as straight and uncompromising as the way he wore his cap—absolutely flat and in the middle. No jaunty angle for him. At a dinner toward the end of the war he was speculating about what captured territories we would want to keep. I stupidly said, "But, Admiral, we don't take territory after a war." He replied, "When did we ever not?"

One day I walked into his office. He looked up from his desk and said, "Harsch, how do you think the American people would react to half a million casualties on the beaches of Japan?" I gulped. He had let me know what was worrying the planners as they approached the end of the war. That was shortly before the Yalta conference. His question explains why the Joint Chiefs pressed Roosevelt so hard to get a promise from Stalin to enter the Japanese war. The admiral filled in some details. He said that if Russia were in the war and we could use Soviet air bases in Siberia for refueling, our bombing would be more effective and might make it unnecessary to storm the main islands of Japan.

He always considered the use of the nuclear bomb on Japan a mistake. He contended that Japan was so near starvation, from the sinking of most of its merchant fleet, that use of the bomb was unnecessary. I asked whether he had objected to its use. He replied that since he did not think it would work he never bothered to enter an objection. He said, "I told the king it wouldn't work." (*King* in this case meant King George VI of England.)

He also said, "I was brought up on the doctrine that we do not make war on women and children." He disapproved of all bombing of cities.

He explained why he did not think the nuclear bomb would work. He said he knew all about explosives but nothing about nuclear energy. This was a new technical world outside his knowledge and experience.

After Roosevelt died, Leahy explained the workings of the Joint Chiefs of Staff to the new president, Harry Truman. Truman listened intently and then remarked, "Why, Admiral, if the South had had a staff organization like that, the Confederates would have won the Civil War. Lee would not have had Johnson, Beauregard, Longstreet and the other generals running around on the loose." Leahy added that "the same statement could be made in regard to Lincoln's difficulties. Lincoln tried to create a chief of staff and a chain of command. Congress thwarted his effort."

Those quotations, taken from Leahy's memoirs, are interesting both as the author's commentary on the success of the Joint Staff operation in which he served and also for the incidental light it throws on Truman's enormous knowledge of American history. On a number of occasions later, during Truman campaign trips and in small gatherings in Washington, I came to know that Harry Truman knew what he was talking about when he referred to Lincoln's troubles with his generals and his inability to get a proper military staff. Also, Truman knew all about Lee's problems with his subordinate generals. I doubt that even Woodrow Wilson knew as much American political and military history as Harry Truman did.

Roosevelt was indeed fortunate that by the time he came to high office the armed forces of the United States had thrown up to the top an ample supply of men of command caliber. The grand strategy of the war was worked out between Roosevelt and Churchill. The team of Leahy, Marshall, King, and Arnold translated the decisions on strategy into operating plans, which in turn were turned over to the generals and admirals on the fighting fronts. Of these not all had faultless records. The most flamboyant were Halsey at sea and George Patton on land, both of whom scored brilliant successes and both of whom made at least one serious blunder—Halsey during the battle of the Leyte Gulf (when he let the Japanese draw him off on a wild goose chase) and Patton when he slapped a shell-shocked and mentally broken soldier. In the end the best of the battle leaders on shore were Eisenhower and Omar Bradley, both of whom would rise after the war to the top as chairmen of the Joint Chiefs of Staff. And, of course, Ike went to the White House. Both were the kind of soldier who makes very few mistakes.

The same could be said of Nimitz at Pearl Harbor, who was a genius at anticipating the enemy's intentions (helped by cryptographers who were breaking the Japanese codes) and at appraising Japanese capabilities accurately.

In thinking back over that middle period of the war I find myself using the word *placid* for the scene in Washington. To me those days seem placid, placid by contrast with what went before and after. There was tremendous tension and excitement and controversy in Washington during the days leading up to the war, the tension arising out of German behavior from 1933, when Hitler came to power, on down really to the day of Pearl Harbor, which suddenly ended the conflict over what the United States should or would do. Then there was the tension of the early war period when everything was going for the enemy in both Europe and the Pacific.

But by the time I got back to Washington from the South Pacific in early August 1942, the Japanese advance in the Pacific had been stopped at the battle of Midway, and American landings on Guadalcanal marked the beginning of the counteroffensive. In Europe the Russians were beginning to stand and hold their positions. Neither Moscow nor Leningrad had fallen. The German advance toward Baku and its vital oil fields was stalled. In Africa Rommel had on August 30 launched what was supposed to be his final offensive. It was designed to break British resistance in Egypt and put Cairo in German hands. But by that time the British had gained decisive superiority in the air and Rommel was running short of fuel for his tanks and planes. At the end of four days his advance had been blunted and his troops thrown back to their starting line. The tide had turned on every front.

What did that mean in Washington? It meant an absence of controversy. There was no longer any dispute about what was to be done. The United States was in the war. Its enormous military effort was beginning to make a difference on the battle lines. The country at home was united, perhaps more decisively than ever before in its history, united in its purpose and in the means. Remember, scarcely a third of the people in the colonies favored the American Revolution. A third would happily have remained loyal to the British crown. The War of 1812 was highly controversial at home and openly opposed in New England. The Civil War was bitterly controversial from first day to last. The country was more or less united about World War I, but the United States was in it for less than two years and then played only a supporting role. World War II was something unusual in U.S. history. The attack on Pearl Harbor had silenced political opposition. Washington was like the eye of the hurricane. It was sending its armies and its fleets out around the world, but at the center was harmony and the absence of tension and contention. We settled into a daily routine largely dominated by listening to the news from the battlefronts. In Washington itself there was virtually no news.

Unnatural Harmony

I had left Australia in June 1942 for the purpose of getting nearer the action. I got to Washington in August to find that city in a state of unnatural harmony. Partly this was because the fighting fronts were all far away. True, German U-boats were sinking merchant ships along the Atlantic seaboard, sometimes even within sight of land, but no American city was bombed or shelled. The main action of the war was an ocean away. The nearest was the bombing of London. There was no sense of near danger in Washington, no great excitement about the war, and no privation. English friends arriving in Washington from London were shocked to find a place so tranquil and "normal."

There was another reason for the relative tranquillity, one that a newsman would sense more than others. It was the absence of normal political contest. The way in which America came into the war, by Japanese bombs, had virtually neutralized the Republicans and forced them almost into political silence.

In writing now about these events of a half century ago, I find it particularly difficult to remember and realize how strong was the opposition to U.S. involvement in World War II up until the day Japanese bombs fell on the ships moored in Pearl Harbor. The marvelous unanimity of American public opinion during the war was not something that existed in potential before December 7, 1941. Opposition to U.S. involvement in the war during its opening phase, when it was seen generally as another European war between Germany and England, was enormous. Some measurements of public opinion showed 75 percent of Americans opposed to going to war against Germany. Americans, most of them, were not pro-Nazi or even consciously pro-German. But the aftermath from World War I had been disillusioning. Victory in that first great war had achieved none of its proclaimed purposes. It had not ended wars or made the world safe for democracy. The great American public remembered the promises and the disappointments afterward and wanted to stay out of this second round of war between Germany and England. Besides, there was a lot of anti-English feeling.

Fifty years of closest collaboration between the United States and Britain during and after World War II have all but wiped out anglophobia in this country, but it existed widely up to Pearl Harbor and it was not limited to the Irish. My good friend Quincy Howe, a member of one of Boston's most ancient and honored Yankee families, wrote a book called *England Expects Every American to Do His Duty*. That book was only one of many advocating a policy of total American isolation from the outside world and external quarrels. It was published in 1937, two years before Hitler's Germany invaded Poland and launched the second World War. It was part of the literature of a movement called the Emergency Committee to Defend America First, known usually as just America First. The agenda of the America Firsters called for stockpiling in the United States sufficient supplies of strategic raw materials to keep the American economy going through a five-year outside war; withdrawal of American forces from the Philippines, Guam, Hawaii, and other outlying bases except for the Panama Canal; and, in event of war, a ban on all trade with all belligerents.

They were serious, those America Firsters. They truly wanted the physical isolation of the United States from the outside world. Their founders included such important figures as Gen. Robert Wood, president of Sears Roebuck; Robert Hutchins, president of the University of Chicago; Gen. Hugh Johnson, who had run the NRA; and Eddie Rickenbacker, World War I hero. Add John L. Lewis, the top labor leader of his day and head of the CIO. Add Joseph P. Kennedy, who was a member even though he was also U.S. ambassador to the Court of St. James in the Roosevelt administration. Most popular speaker for America First was Charles Lindbergh. Add another war hero of those days, U.S. Marine Corps major general Smedley D. Butler. He won the Congressional Medal of Honor twice, once for capturing the city of Vera Cruz from Mexico in 1914 and again for capturing Fort Riviera in Haiti in 1917. He lectured widely for America First and advocated an amendment to the Constitution:

1. The removal of members of the armed forces from within the continental limits of the United States and the Panama Canal Zone for any cause whatsoever is hereby prohibited.

2. The vessels of the United States Navy, or of the other branches of the armed service, are hereby prohibited from steaming, for any reason whatsoever, except on an errand of mercy, more than five hundred miles from our coast.
3. Aircraft of the Army, Navy, and Marine Corps is hereby forbidden from flying, for any reason whatsoever, more than seven hundred and fifty miles beyond the coast of the United States.

Quincy Howe's book included a chapter titled "The British Network," which, by his definition, consisted largely of the English-speaking Union and the Council on Foreign Relations and which was laboring mightily, he said, to bring the United States into an alliance with Britain for the purpose of saving the British Empire.

Howe argued that the empire was doomed anyway and should go in order that "other nations will have their chance to find their place in the sun." He also argued that "a self-sufficient America promotes democracy" while "the moment the United States fights the war of aggression into which the British network is now forcing it . . . it will establish a dictatorship on its own soil."

Another early and enthusiastic supporter of the America First movement was Col. Robert Rutherford McCormick, editor, publisher, and principal owner of the *Chicago Tribune*, which had the largest circulation of any standard-size newspaper in the United States and was the dedicated voice of Midwest Republicanism. On the opening day of World War II, when Germany invaded Poland, a *Tribune* editorial declared, "This is not our war." Whether anti-British sentiment was a part of the colonel's isolationism is disputed. He denied that he was an anglophobe. His critics claimed that he bore a resentment against the English dating from experiences in an English boarding school at a tender age. (He went later to Groton in the United States, where he was a year ahead of Franklin Delano Roosevelt. They had only a passing and casual acquaintance there.) Whatever the anglophobia factor may have been, he was probably the strongest single voice for keeping the United States out of World War II, and as a staunch conservative Republican he was opposed to the New Deal. Before Pearl Harbor the colonel was primed and practiced in fighting Roosevelt and all his works. And he had associations of enormous additional potential influence. His cousin Joseph Patterson ran the *New York Daily News*, which was a commercial and popular success in New York and had gained the largest circulation for a tabloid-size newspaper in the country. Another cousin, and the sister of Joseph Patterson, was "Cissie" Patterson, who owned and ran the *Washington Times-Herald* from an editorial office only three blocks from the White House to the east and led a socially powerful life from a town palace on Dupont Circle four blocks from the White House to the west. The combination of the colonel in Chicago with his eastern cousins in New York and Washington could have made life miserable for President Roosevelt—if the three had combined against him.

But the bombs that fell on the battleships at Pearl Harbor on December 7, 1941, were Japanese, not German. They smothered anglophobia, neutralized isolationism, and gagged the colonel in his Tribune Tower in Chicago. The *Chicago Tribune* carried an editorial on its front page, at the top, two columns wide the next morning. It said: "All that matters today is that we are in the war and the nation must face that simple fact. All of us, from this day forth, have only one task. That is to strike with all our might to protect and preserve the freedom that we hold dear."

Colonel McCormick could not overtly oppose a war that had been started by Japanese bombs. And no Republican in Congress would have dared to take up open opposition to the war without the encouragement of at least the *Chicago Tribune*. So there was unnatural harmony in Washington. The press and Republicans in Congress joined the government in seeking the defeat of both Tojo's Japan and Hitler's Germany.

This explains why there was an easy and cooperative relationship between the working press and the top leadership. It made possible those dinners we had with Admiral Leahy, Admiral King, and General Arnold and the office meetings with General Marshall. It also made for easy and helpful relations with the press and information officers at the various departments of government, most of whom were journalists on wartime leave from their newspapers.

Supplementing the work of American government people and agencies were the Allied embassies with able staffs of press officers eager to be helpful. Particularly memorable were the British military experts. Col. Douglas Saunders of the King's Royal Rifles (head of the J. Walter Thompson Advertising Agency in London after the war) was stationed at the embassy and available for background military help at all times. A marvelously affable and personable "Eddie" Woods sortied daily from the embassy to the bar at the Mayflower Hotel to be available to journalists who frequented what was then the top hotel in Washington. And farther downtown probably the most popular single person at the bar of the

National Press Club was Charles Campbell, whose office was one floor below but seldom used. When asked why he spent so much time in the bar he once replied in a husky whisper, "My secret assignment from the king is to drink John O'Donnell to death." John O'Donnell worked for the *New York Daily News* and at the beginning of the war was as critical of Britain and of U.S. involvement in the war as an Irishman could be. But he and Charles Campbell became devoted friends. It tempered John's native Irish anglophobia and also made for easier Anglo–American relations.

By such means Americans writing about the war from Washington were themselves well informed and able to write knowledgeably about the course of the war. Censorship was scarcely necessary. It was handled by having an Office of War Information. No one was required to submit copy for precensorship. But a Washington writer was expected to check in with someone at the OWI if he had doubts about whether a certain subject was sensitive or might be of value to the enemy. It was a voluntary form of censorship. It worked remarkably well.

I have been leafing back over my clipping files to see what I was writing in that sort of an environment. Now that the war is fifty years behind us I find those particular writings to be on the dull side. After all, we learned long ago how the story ended. The interim assessments are unnecessary now. But I do find that what I wrote then was based on broad and accurate information. The American public was kept well informed during the long pull from Pearl Harbor to victory.

The first ruffling of the surface of this unnatural harmony in Washington was General MacArthur's challenge to the policy of fighting Germany first. The Republicans were starved for an issue, any issue, on which they could challenge Roosevelt without seeming unpatriotic. While the isolationist Republican right wing was still in its inner thoughts unhappy about being in a war against Germany, public opinion had by then been influenced against Germany by newsreels of swaggering jackbooted Nazis, by the shrillness of Hitler's rhetoric, by the barbarism of *Kristallnacht,* by news of concentration camps, and by rumors of still worse things being done to Jews. The Holocaust did not begin until May 1942, but Jews were being treated viciously in Poland from the beginning of the occupation there and word of it was filtering back. The practice of euthanasia had been reported. And Germany declared war on the United States.

Add all that up and it was not politically safe for Republicans to question the waging of war against Germany. But General MacArthur was a hero—the first hero cast up by the war. Thus it was politically safe to agitate publicly for more guns and men for MacArthur. It was not enough to cause a change in the prosecution of the war, but it gave Republicans something to fuss about and Washington reporters something to write about beyond the rising rate of production of guns and planes and speculation about where and when the next big push would come on the various war fronts.

All of this led on into a political love affair between the Republican party and General MacArthur that was to bloom later, in 1948, in an abortive presidential campaign. In 1942 the MacArthur campaign for more men and guns and ships for the Pacific war provided a touch of controversy in Washington. It relieved the prevailing atmosphere of harmony a little and kept a few writers busy until a new issue might develop.

But nothing else like it came along throughout the rest of the war. There were plenty of arguments inside the high command, but none of them were over the kind of issue the Republicans could seize upon for possible political advantage. Should the Western allies concentrate all their efforts on a cross-channel invasion of the continent in 1943, as the Soviets were demanding and General Marshall favored? Or should they approach the continent indirectly by first driving the Germans out of North Africa, then Sicily, then Italy, as the British favored? That was an argument over grand strategy. Republicans could see no gain for themselves by challenging the decisions made by Churchill and Roosevelt. No election was to be won by being for or against the cross-channel operation in 1943 or 1944.

Throughout the rest of the war there was really only one other issue that got itself into the public domain and became mildly controversial. That was the attitude toward Gen. Charles de Gaulle, the self-appointed leader of the Free French movement. Both Roosevelt and Churchill disliked the French general, and both held off recognizing him as the true leader of France. They snubbed him repeatedly in their war councils. They refused to tell him in advance of their plan to invade French North Africa. Instead they deliberately chose to deal with Adm. Jean Darlan (whom Admiral Leahy had known in Vichy and distrusted) as French leader for Algiers and Morocco until he was assassinated. Then they found a slightly known French general named Henri H. Giraud, who had distinguished himself in both World War I and World War II by being captured by the Germans, and named him as French leader, again ignoring General de Gaulle.

Much was written at the time about this matter of ignoring de Gaulle and trying to find some other French leader. General Eisenhower was directly responsible, and he was much criticized over the matter. But there was little mileage in this issue for the Republicans in Washington.

Of course they encouraged Admiral Kimmel, who had been made the scapegoat for the disaster at Pearl Harbor, to claim he had not been given all the information about Japanese plans that existed in Washington; in other words, that he had been the innocent victim of Roosevelt's alleged plan to get the United States into the war. A whispering campaign on this theme was kept going throughout the war. But it was thin picking for the Republicans. By and large, they were forced to support the war effort and even Roosevelt's leadership. The result was a wartime Washington almost free of partisan politics. The fact that the bombs that fell on the ships at Pearl Harbor came from Japan and by surprise made a difference in Washington. Politically, unnatural harmony prevailed from Pearl Harbor to Japan's surrender.

On the Crest of Victory

In early April 1945 I flew back to Europe to see the war end where I had seen it start. It was a marvelous adventure. It began in Paris. I was with a group of reporters. We checked in at the main press hotel, the Scribe. I had known it as a student tourist. It was old, from the turn of the century, but big enough for the whole press corps and located near the Opera and hence near the intersection of three grand boulevards. From the Scribe one could get anywhere in or around Paris easily. Buses, jeeps, and taxis were plentiful, and it was a short ride to Orly airport, where press courier planes ran a splendid, almost nonstop shuttle service around the great arc of the Allied command posts. One could board a courier flight at Orly and get off, at will, at any of the main command posts: Eisenhower in the center at Reims, "Monty" to the north, Patton to the south, and Mark Clark farther south still, near Naples. Distances were short. One could, if one wished, be back at the Scribe in Paris every night. Never before or since has the news coverage of a war been made so convenient and efficient for the reporters. For the next eight weeks I flew the courier shuttle at will and experienced a remarkable view of the many faces of the ending of the biggest war in all history. So many different things happened that I must tell the story in unrelated fragments, using for detail memory plus quotations from the articles I wrote at the time for the *Christian Science Monitor* and radio broadcast scripts done for CBS.

LUXEMBOURG, April 12. I was wakened in the middle of the night to see the black-bearded face of John Vandercook standing at the foot of the bed telling me I had to get up "because the president is dead." Our group was staying at a hotel in Luxembourg. We had gone there to visit an air force fighter base. We all knew that President Roosevelt had not been well during the conference at Yalta (February 4–11), but we did not know the seriousness of his condition. What John said hit me as being the impossible, the incredible. I felt numb. I struggled to comprehend the words, and then my reportorial training took over. I dressed, went out in the street, and began collecting reaction quotes from GIs. One of them said, "I feel as though I have just lost my father." I remember feeling chilly. It was dark. Around the corner came a big army vehicle with the narrow slits of hooded headlights barely showing, and another, and another. It was a convoy of what we called "dragon wagons," meaning heavy armored tractors pulling flat-bedded trailers carrying battle tanks. A steady stream of dragon wagons went by headed for the front. An armored unit was moving up. Roosevelt was dead, but the vast machinery of war was in motion and never missed a beat. I felt the power of that vast army as I had never felt it before. It was moving forward like the ocean tides. Roosevelt was gone, but the forces he had set in motion continued their forward momentum. Roosevelt was gone, but the war would go on to its destined end.

ALLIED HQ., REIMS, April 15. "Ike" had his headquarters in a big, modern, red-brick high school. We were greeted by the most beautifully tailored female officer I had yet seen. She was Kay Somersby, originally Ike's English chauffeur, later his receptionist, secretary, and frequent bridge partner in the evenings. She was as attractive as we had heard. We chatted pleasantly. We were ushered in. Our group included several, among them Lowell Thomas, who remembered World War I and its aftermath. U.S. troops had reached the Elbe on April 11. They were ordered to keep to the west bank. Our first question to Ike (remembering the failure to take Berlin in World War I) was "Why stop at the Elbe? Why don't you reach for Berlin?" His explanation went like this:

Berlin is a political, not a military objective.

The American zone of occupation, agreed at Yalta, ends at the Elbe. If my combat units go beyond we will have to move our supply line up with them, then have to take it all back after the surrender.

I have often worried about what would happen if our troops happened to run into Russians coming around a corner. I prefer to have a broad river between them when they meet.

We reporters knew that the British were unhappy and wanted Ike to push for Berlin. We pushed Ike a little, but he insisted that nothing was to be gained by going on to Berlin then. He wanted to clear his flanks first; besides there was talk of a German National Redoubt in the Bavarian Alps. He had already swung Patton from the direction of Prague toward the Bavarian mountains.

Gen. Omar Bradley in his book *A Soldier's Story*, published in 1951, said of this matter, "As soldiers we looked naively on this British inclination to complicate the war with political foresight and nonmilitary objectives."

DEATH CAMPS. Buchenwald was liberated on April 11 by General Patton's Third Army. When we visited it the bodies of German SS soldiers who had guarded the camp were still lying around where they fell when Allied troops overran the area. My reports included the following:

> I have visited Buchenwald . . . the gas furnaces of the crematorium consumed during the period of operation the total capacity of the camp of about 20,000 persons four times over . . . the inmates themselves say the majority of deaths were due to lack of food and clothing . . . the only possible explanation is that the camp was so operated and equipped as to produce through the semblance of natural causes as many deaths as possible—but to this single observer, the most horrible aspect of the matter was not the agonized faces and bodies piled like cordwood in the courtyard of the crematorium, but the degradation of those still living.
>
> These swarms of men and women had once been respectable and self-respecting persons. They had been so dehumanized by the treatment which they had received that it took considerable effort to see, behind their sallow skin, their furtive eyes and their external shoddiness, anything resembling what our western world regards as men.
>
> . . . the barbed wire fence separates by only a few yards the Buchenwald charnel house from the Buchenwald Zoological Garden, complete with simulated crags for sheep, and attractive animal signs pointing the way. Children were entertained by real animals while their parents were methodically converted into beasts.
>
> General Patton began the effort to reeducate Germany by sending 1500 citizens of Weimar into the Buchenwald concentration camp. I watched them come out. Some of the faces were white and drawn, Two are reported to have committed suicide afterwards. But I saw some laughing.

Later I went through the concentration camp at Dachau, near Munich, but several days after it had been "liberated" and been reported on in detail by others I wrote:

I merely want to confirm that I also have witnessed the long train of open gondola cars full of emaciated bodies, two rooms in the crematorium approximately 20 feet square piled about six feet high with more bodies, the usual incinerators, the poison-gas chamber, rooms inside the camp where the floor is covered with persons too ill to be moved. The whole camp, like Buchenwald, it is perfectly obvious, was designed and administered to produce maximum liquidation of humanity.

Violent Contrasts

Incidentally, Dachau itself is a typically pleasant south German city with a well-dressed, comfortable middle-class population whose tidy houses made a thoroughly respectable outer face for the camp. Attractive shrubbery and trees were well arranged around a harmless-looking wall, with only foliage visible on the other side. The external appearance is enhanced by the solid modern houses of the chief wardens which expressed the ultimate in propriety and correctness.

Here again are the same violent contrasts one finds everywhere in postwar Germany. The outward whiteness of this sepulchre, complete with its apparent innocence-protesting and probably innocence-intending average citizens against the organized viciousness within.

ZADAR (ZARA) YUGOSLAVIA. We flew over here one day from the huge Allied air base at Foggia in Italy, near Naples. The Yugoslavs had allowed (not eagerly since they still had a special relationship with the Soviets and communism) establishment of an American emergency landing field for the benefit of damaged and stragglers from the great bombing attacks still being staged into German-held areas from Foggia. The Yugoslavs were suspicious and anything but cordial. The troops guarding the field kept a close watch on us. One who spoke English did condescend to inform me that we Americans should be grateful to the Soviets for the jeeps. I protested that the jeeps all came from America. He would have none of it. He had seen jeeps before, from Russia, he said. He was sure that the jeeps our people had on the airfield here had come by courtesy of the Soviets. The name Willys on the front of the nearest jeep did not shake him, even after I told him that Willys was a factory in my own hometown, Toledo, Ohio, which had invented the jeep. The Titoist Yugoslavs of that era did not regard Americans as trustworthy friends or allies, largely because the United States was slow to accept Tito as the future leader of Yugoslavia. Washington's preference was for the anti-Communist Ustachi even though they had a record of alleged collaboration with the Germans.

On another flight out of Foggia we went up north in Italy looking for the front line, which at that time ran across the Italian peninsula north of Rome from one side to the other. We found the front line over the Po valley by a series of shocks to our passenger aircraft from antiaircraft fire uncomfortably close to us. The pilot did a sudden turn and clawed for altitude. We ended that flight safely back at Foggia.

SIXTH ARMY GROUP HEADQUARTERS, May 5. Field Marshal Karl Gerd von Runstedt was brought into the big briefing room and invited to submit himself to our group questionings. He had been in command on the German western front at the time of the Normandy invasion and had more recently planned and executed the Ardennes offensive. Eisenhower in *Crusade in Europe* refers to Von Runstedt as "the ablest of the German Generals." He seemed comfortable in front of our group of about twenty American reporters. His build was slender, his bearing soldierly, his uniform impeccable. He wore a monocle, spoke English easily, and answered our questions professionally. Here are excerpts from my report written that day.

> . . . Germany . . . never possessed either the equipment, the plan or the long-range preparation for the invasion of Britain . . . yes, they had a wish to cross the Channel. They experimented when they got there. They made several test tries when they got there . . . but it was done with "apple barges."
>
> He described the allied, pre-invasion air offensive as unheard of and "impossible." He spoke with awe and jealousy of allied landing craft, of naval guns which covered the Normandy landings.
>
> But most of all, he emphasized the importance of air power which paralyzed his counteroffensive in France, preventing him from ever bringing his reserves into action.

On the morning of May 6 I left Salzburg early as a passenger in a convoy of six jeeps and a signals (wireless) van complete with generator.

In command was Capt. Rhoman E. Clem, U.S. Army Third Division, Sixth Army Group. We had with us a German officer in dress uniform, including a greatcoat bearing the red lapels of the general staff. Each vehicle was equipped with a large white flag on a pole. We were headed for Zell-am-see, a mountain resort about fifty miles south of Salzburg and the headquarters of German field marshal Albert Kesselring, commander of the southern group of German armies. Our mission was to get his signature on the terms of surrender of his armies, said terms having already been agreed on by radio. When we neared the German front line, the staff officer stood up in the front of the lead jeep. We turned a corner and were face to face with the muzzle of a German antitank gun. It did not fire. We had entered German territory. At about twenty miles south of Salzburg the road had been blown. German soldiers were filling the hole. They were nearly finished when we heard a loud explosion further ahead around the next bend. The German officer explained that we were in SS country, where the officers had refused to recognize Kesslering's orders to let us pass. We went back to Salzburg for that night and started out again the next morning, this time taking a detour well to the west, through Kitzbühel, and reaching Zell-am-see without further incident. I was given a tidy room in a resort hotel on the edge of a long, narrow lake flanked by mountains. A prison camp must have been opened that day. About twenty British officers came strolling in, also several Yugoslavs, all in their own uniforms. A German sentry was posted at the hotel door, but allowed anyone who wished to enter. Suddenly the war was over. Sometime during the evening the radio announced that the armistice had been signed at Reims. Across the lake a single light went on, then some distance away a second, then a third. In about five minutes the whole lake was wearing a necklace of lights. The blackout was over.

The next morning we returned to Salzburg and I caught the press shuttle back to Paris, arriving in time to join the vast tide of humanity walking up from the Place de la Concorde to the great triumphal arch at the top of the Champs Elysée. The next afternoon I sat in the gardens of the Palais Royale with old friends while overhead the vast armada of Allied air power flew over Paris. Every plane in the British Isles and France that could fly came over that day. Never before or since have so many aircraft been over one city at one time.

How I Captured Albert Speer

Adolf Hitler committed suicide in his bunker underneath his Chancellery in Berlin on Thursday, April 30, 1945, after issuing a political testament naming Gross Admiral Karl Doenitz as his successor. At that time the admiral was at Flensburg, the most northern city in Germany, capital of the province of Schleswig-Holstein and located just south of the Danish border. It is on an estuary of the Baltic with a harbor deep enough for ocean-going vessels. A naval training station had been built along the estuary stretching for about four miles along the shore. As Allied armies burst into Germany from east, south, and west, the German high command had moved north to Flensburg and established itself in the barracks and hospitals of the naval station. The actual command post was on a passenger ship, the *Patria*. Doenitz had living quarters in the hospital compound and his office aboard the *Patria*. Enough stragglers and refugees from various departments of government in Berlin had joined him at Flensburg so that he had not only the operational high command, but also a skeleton government for a country that, of course, no longer existed. The surrender of the German armed forces had been signed at Reims on May 7, and all fighting ended forty-eight hours later. But the Anglo-American high command deliberately chose to leave the movement and dispositions of the German armed forces in German hands for the time being, and for practical reasons. Under international law a prisoner of war must be fed and sheltered by his captors. Until he is made a prisoner of war his food and shelter are the responsibility of his own government. The German government was allowed to continue to function for the practical purpose of getting the German army home, demobilized, and returned to civilian life as cheaply as possible for the victors.

On the day the German army surrendered there were thousands of

German troops still outside German territory. There were many to the south in Italy, Yugoslavia, and Austria. There were substantial numbers in the Netherlands, Norway, and Denmark. No organization could manage the orderly return of all these soldiers to their own homes as efficiently as the German high command itself. It was told to do so. It did so. On May 21, two weeks after the surrender, I flew from Paris to Copenhagen in the same plane with British general Sir Francis De Guingand, deputy to Field Marshal Montgomery, who was assigned to take the German surrender for Denmark and Norway. He had a platoon of British paratroopers with him. It was a very small force to control perhaps a quarter million German soldiers, but it was enough. German military discipline was still complete. We landed at Copenhagen in a sea of German soldiery, but all in perfect order. I had a happy reunion in Copenhagen with old friends. I was able to bring to Victor Rasmussen, one of the city's leading furriers, word that his son and daughter, both serving with the Allied forces, were well and happy, for which news I was tendered that night one of the great banquets of my life. Two days later I was off with a British army press officer, his driver, and his jeep on a return journey through Flensburg. From Copenhagen to Flensburg we drove along past an endless column of German troops marching home in perfect order.

Arrived at Flensburg we called upon the local British commanding officer, Brigadier Ford, who promptly invited us to lunch in the Rathaus, which he had taken over for his command post. During lunch an aide handed him a note. He read it, turned to me, and said, "My lads think they have bagged an important Nazi. His name is Rosenberg. Is he really important?" I replied that if it was named Alfred and if it was *the* Alfred Rosenberg he truly did have an important Nazi in his bag, the prime philosopher of nazism and one of Hitler's most trusted lieutenants. The brigadier asked, would I recognize him. I thought I would. He said, "He is in the cell below, let's go have a look." We went down into the basement, and there we saw a crumpled form on a cot behind prison bars who beyond doubt was *the* Alfred Rosenberg. An elderly woman was sitting in the corridor. The guard said it was his wife. They said they had taken away from her a pair of brass knuckles with inch–long spikes at the joints. We went back to lunch.

The brigadier then informed me that I would be having a good story the next day. He had been ordered to suppress the whole German government at ten o'clock the next morning. But, he added, a press plane was due in shortly from Paris with some thirty of my colleagues. For a moment I had thought I was going to have a marvelous exclusive story. I was the only war correspondent in Flensburg—until that press plane would come in. Then I would be one of many. But the brigadier tempered my lament by saying that there was another operation at eight o'clock that I could have to myself if I wished. My rule is to try not to go with the pack. I opted for the alternate project, which he did not identify. He merely told me to be at 7:30 at a certain point where I would find a jeep, driver, and British officer.

In the morning I was at the appointed place at the appointed hour. I climbed aboard the jeep and off we drove—one British captain, his driver, and myself—along a country road that paralleled the barbed-wire fence of the naval training station enclave. We drove along for about ten miles, seeing no other person or vehicle, then stopped at a simple gate in the wire fence and waited briefly while the captain consulted his watch. At exactly eight o'clock he told the driver to "gun it." We went in through the gate, followed a narrow winding track through sandy pine barrens, and emerged into a clearing in the middle of which stood a little Mother Goose castle, complete with turrets at the four corners, a drawbridge, and a moat. We clattered over the drawbridge and came to a screeching halt in the middle of honking, flapping geese. There was even a kitchen maid in starched cap and apron, screaming.

The captain jumped out of the jeep, drawn revolver in hand, and sprang up a broad staircase leading from the courtyard into the castle. I, being an unarmed war correspondent, kept as close to him as possible for my own safety. At the top of the stairs he turned left and pushed open the doors into a large room. It was a typical castle room, dark, low, heavy beams overhead, heavy furniture. A table was set for breakfast for two. A young German officer, neatly uniformed, stood by the table. The captain looked around and then said to the German officer, "Where is he?"

The German officer purported not to understand English. I found myself translating. There ensued the following three-cornered conversation:

Harsch: Wo ist er?
German: Er ist hier.
Harsch: He is here.
Captain: Where?
Harsch: Wo?
German: Hier.

Harsch: Here.

Captain (loud and firm): Where?

German: Da (pointing to a large, ancient, carved armoir against the wall).

Captain went to armoir, put hand on handle, was about to open.

German: Nein, nein, Sie müssen das nicht tun. Das ist privat, privat.

Harsch: He says you mustn't open it, it is private.

The captain snorted, pulled open the door, and disclosed a fully equipped modern bathroom, with an older man seated on the throne.

The captain hastily closed the door and the three of us waited outside, with no further conversation.

After a due interval, Albert Speer emerged from the closet.

The British captain told me to tell him to pack his bags. Speer asked how many. The captain said two. Speer began to pack. The captain told me to keep an eye on him and went off, leaving me unarmed with the man who had directed all of German industry during the latter phase of the war.

I watched him pack and remarked, "Well, it's over."

He replied, "Yes, thank God, and high time too."

I asked the obvious, "Why do you say that?"

For the next twenty minutes or so I was treated to what amounted to an outline of the book Speer later wrote during his years in Spandau prison. His claim was that he had known from Stalingrad on that the war was lost and so spent his time doing what he could to countermand and frustrate Hitler's orders to destroy everything in any retreat. Speer's argument was that he felt he must save all he could for the future of the German people. I was impressed by his argument then. I am satisfied by subsequent information that he did indeed persuade most German military commanders to ignore Hitler's orders for a Götterdämmerung. The German armies carried out very little destruction of bridges, buildings, and factories during the final weeks of the war.

I cannot now remember whether we took Speer in our jeep back to Flensburg or another car came to get him. I do remember next that I was standing in the hospital section of the German compound watching Admiral Doenitz come out of his quarters to be taken off in a command car. A British army sergeant was standing with me. We automatically went into the house Doenitz had just left. We emerged with various trophies of the event. I had a pair of dress epaulettes and a dress dagger.

(German officers of that era had given up swords and wore daggers instead.) I gave the Doenitz epaulettes and dagger to the Chapin Library at Williams College. They have since disappeared.

That is how Hitler's thousand-year Reich ended. There was no longer any German government. The continuity was broken. Germany became an area occupied by foreign armies.

I took the press plane back to Paris that afternoon. The war was over, the Third Reich was dissolved, the story was finished. There were new stories to be written now. I went back to Washington for the new beginning. Dean Acheson was later to write about it under the title *Present at the Creation*. A new world had to be created.

Present at the Creation

For me the events following the capture of Albert Speer in the little schloss at Glucksburg were at first anticlimactic. I flew back to Paris the next day. Paris is always Paris, and it was a pleasure to find it again at peace and "normal." But the excitement of war was gone. There was no longer a question of which part of the front to visit the next day. The press shuttle still ran, but now the only immediate question was which units would settle down for the occupation in Germany and which would be moved at once to the still unfinished war on the far side of the world. I was willing to fly back to Washington, rejoin my family, wait for the end of the Japanese war (which was obviously coming very soon), and begin to think about the problems of reorganizing the new world that would emerge from the wreckage of the old.

Dean Acheson described the early postwar era in a book appropriately titled *Present at the Creation*. Not many realized at the beginning of that process how strenuous, difficult, and long lasting it would be. The first part of the new creation was to salvage the economies of Western Europe. Alarming reports came in not only of near starvation in conquered Germany but of just plain exhaustion even in victorious Britain. Teddy White glimpsed the future in a book called *Fire in the Ashes*. But getting that fire going was a long and delicate task not made easier by Harry Truman's abrupt cancellation of Lend-Lease almost immediately after the German surrender. Britain was bankrupt. The others were at various stages of the same condition.

Looking back over the story from fifty years later it seems that Washington was marvelously wise and did at the right time all the right things to lay the foundations for the immensely prosperous Western Europe of today. A personal experience can illustrate how haphazard and accidental some of those steps actually were. The famous Marshall Plan, which turned the European economies around and began their climb back to economic health, was actually not a plan but an invitation to the Europeans to devise a plan, with the promise that the United States would support their efforts. The important thing was that the Europeans grab the opportunity Marshall was offering to them. The idea of U.S. support for a collective European economic program was first articulated in public in a speech Dean Acheson, then undersecretary of state, made at Cleveland, Mississippi, on May 8, 1947. Few noticed. In the back rooms of Washington the most urgent attention was given to further ways and means of prodding the Europeans into taking the necessary initiatives that could turn a desperately degenerative situation around. A second chance lay ahead. Secretary of State George Marshall was scheduled to make the commencement speech at Harvard on June 5.

June 5 was also the day I was flying to England in a Boeing bomber in the first postwar redeployment of the U.S. Air Force back to Europe. Add that June 5 was a regular day for my weekly American Commentary broadcast to Britain for the BBC. Since I could not on the same day both fly to England in a bomber and do a broadcast, I had asked Leonard Miall of the BBC if he would take over the broadcast for me. In preparation for that broadcast he stopped in at the British Embassy that morning and asked whether anything was going on that might be useful in his broadcast script. One of his embassy friends said Marshall was making a speech at Harvard that had some interesting ideas in it. He suggested that Miall get a copy. Miall went to the State Department, got a copy, decided that the speech was indeed extremely important, and added (based on the opinion of his embassy friends) that everyone in Europe should take note of it and that Washington would be waiting for the European reaction.

That night in London Ernest Bevin, Britain's foreign minister, heard the Miall broadcast. He was excited about it. The next morning he called his opposite number in France, Georges Bidault. Within two weeks, in Paris, Bevin and Bidault were discussing with Soviet foreign minister Vyacheslav Molotov what the Europeans might do. I like to think that I made a special contribution to the success of the Marshall Plan and history by handing my weekly commentary for the BBC over to Leonard Miall on June 5, 1947. Had I been writing the script that day I might not have known about the Marshall speech at Harvard.

That bomber flight to Britain on June 5 was a by-product of earlier events. The year 1947 was seminal. It had opened with Communist revolutions threatening in a number of countries, but particularly in Greece, where British troops were helping defend a weak government. Communist troops were on the outskirts of Athens. On February 21 the British government instructed its ambassador in Washington, Lord Inverchapel, to inform the State Department that all British aid to both Greece and Turkey would have to end "in six weeks." Would the United States take over?

News of the event broke in the following manner. On February 27 I received a call from "Mike" McDermott, press spokesman at the State Department, instructing me to go at once to a suite at the Statler Hotel. I was to go alone. I was not to mention where I was going to anyone else. If I saw other reporters going in the same direction, I was to say nothing to them. I obeyed instructions. I noticed as I approached the hotel that most of my colleagues who covered the State Department seemed to be going in the same direction. We ended up in a packed hotel room with McDermott, who first pledged us all to secrecy. He said the purpose of our being there was for us to be able to write the story more accurately when the official statement would be issued. Meanwhile, "here is General Marshall." The secretary of state then told us the details of the British notes, described the general situation in Greece and Turkey, and said congressional leaders had been informed and the president would soon be proposing to Congress measures intended to save Greece and Turkey. I went back to the office. The UP ticker was clattering out a story saying that the president would soon be asking Congress for funds to help Greece and Turkey. I learned later that a horrified junior aide to General Marshall saw the same report on the same UP wire and rushed into the general's office telling him that the UP had "broken the story." The general looked up and remarked, quietly, "High time." President Truman made his request to Congress on March 12 in a speech that laid out what came to be called the Truman Doctrine.

President Truman was later much criticized for having stated the case for aid to Greece and Turkey in broad and general terms. Walter Lippmann wrote a series of twelve columns arguing that to propose, as the Truman speech in effect did, to resist communism everywhere around the world would risk overcommitting the United States beyond its resources. The soundness of Lippmann's concern was confirmed by the Vietnam War, which was launched under the Truman Doctrine as being necessary to thwart the spread of communism. Vietnam was where, twenty-eight years later, the humiliating withdrawal of the last Americans from the roof of the U.S. embassy in Saigon in April 1975 testifies to the fact that Lyndon Johnson did commit the United States beyond its resources.

But back in 1947 the problem that George Marshall and Dean Acheson faced was how to get enough money out of a reluctant Congress to save Greece and Turkey from Communist insurrections. The Republicans had just won the 1946 midterm elections on a platform of cutting spending and opposing President Truman. The strongest influence in the party was Sen. Robert Taft of Ohio, a dedicated isolationist. Former president Herbert Hoover had just come back from a trip to Europe saying that it was on the verge of starvation but that the United States should "stop, look and listen" before plunging into any relief program. Truman, Marshall, and Acheson spent the first five days after the British notice of withdrawal from Greece and Turkey working out what they thought ought to be done, then summoned the leaders of Congress for a meeting at the White House.

That meeting in the White House on the morning of February 26 was the key moment in shaping the world of the next forty years. Would the Republican majority in Congress support an overseas effort to resist Soviet political and military expansion? According to Acheson's account in *Present at the Creation*, President Truman opened the presentation but "flubbed" it. Acheson asked permission to speak. Here follows his story:

> In the past eighteen months, I said, Soviet pressure on the Straits, on Iran and on northern Greece had brought the Balkans to the point where a highly possible breakthrough might open three continents to Soviet penetration. Like apples in a barrel infected by one rotten one, the corruption of Greece would infect Iran and all to the East. It would also carry infection to Africa through Asia Minor and Egypt, and to Europe through Italy and France, already threatened by the strongest domestic communist parties in Western Europe. The Soviet Union was playing one of the greatest gambles in history at minimal cost. It did not need to win all the possibilities. Even one or two offered immense gains. We and we alone were in a position to break up the play. These were the stakes that British withdrawal from the eastern Mediterranean offered to an eager and ruthless opponent.
>
> A long silence followed. Then Arthur Vandenberg said solemnly, "Mr. President, if you will say that to the Congress and the country, I will support you and I believe that most of its members will do the same."

Arthur Vandenberg was at that time chairman of the Senate Committee on Foreign Affairs and the accepted leader in the Republican party on foreign policy matters. His position at that moment was crucial. Had he refused to support the proposal to aid Greece and Turkey there would have been no Truman Doctrine, no Marshall Plan, and, probably, a sweep of Soviet influence through what we were beginning to call the Third World, which largely meant all those countries which had formerly been part of the several European empires. There would also have been no cold war, but there would have been a new Soviet Empire taking over the leading role in the world that had once belonged to Britain.

Lippmann was correct that the broad commitment to resisting communism on a worldwide basis carried the danger of an overcommitment of American resources, but it is also true that in February and March 1947 Congress would have turned down a simple request for aid to Greece and Turkey. Senator Vandenberg demanded a statement of a global threat calling for a global American response. That was the price he asked for his support. And that was the price the president paid.

There was no doubt in my mind then and none now that the price had to be paid to obtain the aid for Greece and Turkey. The news that the British were pulling out of the eastern Mediterranean broke on February 28 and automatically put into the public domain the question of whether the United States would pick up the burden. Enthusiasm for such a course was nonexistent. The Democrats in Congress held a conference and actually voted against supporting the Greek government or British policies in the Mediterranean. On March 4 the Senate voted to cut the president's current budget requests by $4.5 billion.

On March 10 the leaders of Congress were again called to the White House and given a rerun of the case originally presented to them on February 26. They listened and sat on their hands. No promises of support were made. On March 12 the president went to Congress and delivered his program for action in a speech that was an expansion of the Acheson theme, to which were added specific proposals, including $400 million in direct economic and military aid for the following year and economic and military teams for both Greece and Turkey.

The Truman Doctrine came out in the speech in the form of a few simple sentences, of which the following are the most important:

"I believe that it must be the policy of the United States to support free peoples who are resisting attempted subjugation by armed minorities or outside pressures."

"I believe that we must assist free peoples to work out their own destinies in their own way."

"Should we fail to aid Greece and Turkey in this fateful hour, the effect will be far-reaching to the West as well as to the East."

The formula required by Senator Vandenberg worked. The speech was accorded a standing ovation. Specific legislation was sent to the Hill, and the concerned committees of the two chambers went to work. There were a lot of questions and a lot of hesitation in both parties. The hearings lasted for two months. But public sentiment veered around to taking up the burden that the British were laying down. By the time the six weeks given in the British notice had run out, Washington, in anticipation of a favorable vote in Congress, was already sending people, supplies, and funds to both Greece and Turkey. The bills cleared Congress on May 12 by 67 to 23 votes in the Senate and by 287 to 107 in the House.

But even before Congress had agreed to aid Greece and Turkey and, by implication, had adopted the Truman Doctrine it was already obvious to most at the top levels of government that their problem was far larger than Greece and Turkey. As early as March 5 a joint committee from State, War, and Navy departments was at work appraising the general economic situation in Western Europe. Will Clayton, assistant secretary of commerce, was saying that there would have to be an emergency fund of $5 billion. The $400 million Congress voted for saving Greece and Turkey was already looking like a mere drop in the bucket of what would be needed. Acheson began a second job of public education by the speech he delivered in Cleveland, Mississippi, on May 8, which went largely unnoticed in Europe. It was followed by General Marshall's speech at Harvard on June 5, which did, as we have previously noted, reach its target, i.e., the ears of Britain's foreign minister Ernest Bevin, who got on the telephone the next morning to Georges Bidault, his opposite number in Paris.

At first it seemed possible that the Soviets would want to take advantage of the Marshall Plan, but Joseph Stalin in Moscow had no use for any such idea. He turned it down, news of which caused relief in Washington, London, and Paris. The Czechs wanted to join, but were brought quickly to heel from Moscow. The way was clear for the Western Europeans to work out their destiny by themselves. On July 3 Bevin and Bidault issued an invitation to twenty-two other countries to join them in Paris to consider a plan for the economic recovery of Western Europe.

Out of this finally grew the Foreign Assistance Act passed by Congress and signed by the president on April 3, 1948.

Thus were laid the foundations for the great new Europe of today. In the laying of them Acheson was the central figure. He was among the first to sense the danger that would come from the loss of Greece and Turkey to Moscow. He proposed the first practical steps to turn the tide. He was the first to think through the implications of a disastrous economic collapse of Western Europe and what was to be done about it. A word therefore about this man to whom today's world owes so much.

Dean Campion Acheson had a flair for the bold and dramatic. Tall, erect, with upswept mustache, often clad in tweeds and sporting a bright-colored bow tie, he was in dress and style as much the British Guards officer out of uniform as Anthony Eden (Lord Avon) ever was, perhaps more so. Eden was languid; Acheson was always alert, and quick in any situation, sometimes too quick and too sharp for his own good.

When Alger Hiss was convicted of perjury, there was no need for Dean Acheson to make a comment. Alger's brother, Donald, was a member of Acheson's law firm. Acheson had known Alger Hiss slightly, not intimately. The prudent thing for him to say was "The court has spoken." But that would not have done for Dean Acheson, whose father had been the Episcopal bishop of Connecticut. He had to cite Holy Writ—Matthew 25: 35, 36—and say, "The Church does not turn its back on the convicted criminal. I shall not turn my back on Alger Hiss." This was immediately taken, by all but theologians (in short supply in political Washington), as meaning that he challenged the verdict and denied the guilt. Not so. He accepted the verdict but, like the church, would not withdraw compassion when the friend was in trouble. There is no record that he ever saw Alger Hiss again. He had taken up a public stance that was beyond the comprehension of political Washington. It was used against him. It also accented the difference between Dean Acheson and his ultimate successor as secretary of state, John Foster Dulles. Dulles had recommended Hiss for the directorship of the Carnegie Endowment. When the verdict was announced, Dulles viewed the Hiss episode as a sad commentary on the decline of patriotism in the younger generation.

The two men found it difficult to speak civilly to each other. Their differences of manner and procedure were carryovers from the English civil wars. Acheson was the cavalier and king's man, Dulles was the pious Cromwellian roundhead. But they needed each other. Acheson told me that after the 1948 election he waited for what he thought was enough time for tempers to cool down and approached the unexpectably (by most but not by himself) reelected Harry Truman to seek permission to bring Dulles back into the State Department as an "adviser." Truman looked up and said, "Dean, I know what you want, and the answer is no." Acheson waited for a few more weeks and raised the subject again. Truman gave in. They had to have Dulles working with them to obtain needed Republican support for the great projects of that era.

The Texture of the Iron Curtain – 1947

The bomber that flew me back to England on June 5, 1947, launched me on a voyage of exploration into the unknown. I was headed for the lands beyond the iron curtain, the countries of Eastern Europe where political communism had come in with the luggage of the Soviet armies and was in the process of taking over the governments.

How extensive and effective was the takeover? Could the bulk of the people of a country such as Czechoslovakia, which before the war had been a successful liberal democracy, be converted to communism? Would such a conversion be superficial or lasting?

How solid was the curtain itself? Was it as impermeable as iron? If so, was war the only way to roll it back? Or was it made of some softer material permeable to the ideas and influences of the West?

Much turned on the answers. If the curtain was truly as impermeable as iron, then in all probability another dreadful war lay ahead. The West could scarcely reconcile itself to the permanent loss of Central Europe to Moscow and to Moscow's Communist ideology. The independence of Poland was what World War II had been all about. Britain and France declared war on Germany over Hitler's invasion of Poland. But if the curtain was made of softer material, then there might ultimately be a tolerable and peaceable relationship between Moscow and the West.

In the West in spring 1947 there were many questions about Eastern Europe and no sure answers. The enforced communization of the iron curtain countries was new in European experience. There had not been anything similar since the armies of Islam spread the teachings of Muhammed out from Arabia east and west until they dominated the middle world all the way from Gibraltar to the Philippines. Would the forced conversion to communism of the lands behind the iron curtain be as permanent as the forced conversion to Islam had been from the seventh to the fifteenth centuries?

I wanted to find the answers to those questions. Getting permission to visit those countries was difficult in 1947, but not impossible. Later it became much more difficult and for a time impossible. One man played an important role between East and West during that period.

Jozef Winiewicz was a prewar Polish journalist who at the end of the war in 1945 was sent to London as counselor of the Polish Embassy. He served there for two years, then was sent to Washington as Polish ambassador from 1947 to 1955.

He was the only diplomat from any iron curtain country who in those early cold war days deliberately sought regular meetings with Washington journalists. He gave a lunch once a month, regularly, over those eight years to a group of us who specialized in foreign affairs. He got me a Polish visa in 1947—and others later when he was back in Warsaw as deputy foreign minister. Once in Washington he asked me whether there was anyone at the West German Embassy who might be willing to meet with him privately and unofficially. I inquired at the German Embassy. As a result I invited the Polish ambassador and a German minister to lunch with me. They had a series of private meetings together after that. In time diplomatic relations were reopened between the two countries. I do not know whether those meetings paved the way.

But back to June 1947. When I stepped down from the bomber in England, I had visas in hand for Poland, Czechoslovakia, Hungary, and Yugoslavia. I went first to Frankfurt, West Germany, which was both headquarters and press center for U.S. occupation forces in all Europe. I was shocked to see how little in Frankfurt had been done to clear away the wreckage of war. The Truman Doctrine was two months old by that time, but Congress had so far voted funds only for aid to Greece and Turkey. No help for the Germans had yet been provided. I wrote that the Truman Doctrine "does not shield the German intellect from communist arguments—unless the Truman Doctrine is to mean food, coal, and reconstruction machinery." Another ten months would go by before Congress would vote the funds that would begin the economic revival of Western Europe. The need was great. My report from Frankfurt spoke of the appearance of the German people: "Two years ago they were shabby and pale, but their eyes sparkled with unconcealed distaste for their conquerers. Today they are also shabby and pale, but their eyes seem dull and apathetic, showing little trace of any emotion except hopelessness."

Water, electricity, and telephone services had been restored in Frankfurt and the trolley cars were running, but they were running through

Franklin Delano Roosevelt at Warm Springs, Georgia, January, 1933.
JCH is on the right, leaning against the fireplace. AP/Wide World Photos.

JCH and William L. Shirer, Berlin, 1940. Photograph by Tess Shirer.

Maginot Line, immediately after the French surrender, 1940. Photographs by the author.

Top: JCH with Sir Anthony Eden and Lady Eden at the Edens' country house in Wiltshire, 1968. Photo by Grenada TV.

Bottom: White House correspondent Tom Jarriel, JCH, King Hussein of Jordan, and Peg Wheaton, producer of "Issues and Answers." Photograph courtesy ABC News.

Facing page: JCH, January 1980. Photograph by Barth Falkenberg, courtesy The Christian Science Monitor.

Top: *Aboard the USS* Enterprise *en route to the Marianas for the first U.S. attack on the Japanese after Pearl Harbor, January 1942. U.S. Navy photograph.*
Bottom: *JCH behind Ike's right shoulder, Lowell Thomas on Ike's left, Rheims, France, April 16, 1945. U.S. Army photograph.*

Top: *JCH with his brother, Paul A. Harsch, Jr., Place Vendome, Paris, 1945.*
Bottom: *Raymond Gram Swing, JCH, and Edward R. Murrow at the Harsch home in Washington, D.C., 1947. Photograph by Janet Murrow.*

JCH in Whitehall, London, 1967. Photograph copyright National Broadcasting Company, Inc. All rights reserved.

the rubble of a destroyed city. The streets themselves had been cleared by piling the rubble along both sides. Riding along between those banks of rubble made much of Frankfurt seem like a wilderness through which, for some strange reason, a checkerboard of streets had been driven.

From Frankfurt I headed by U.S. Army courier plane for Warsaw. (There were in those military occupation days small American military units in each Soviet-occupied capital served by daily courier flights from Frankfurt; also Soviet military units in U.S.- and U.K.-occupied areas.) I was feeling much as Henry M. Stanley must have felt when he first set out for "darkest Africa" on his search for Dr. Livingstone.

True, the cold war was still new. Some historians date it from February 9, 1946, when Stalin made a bristling "guns not butter" speech, killing any serious prospect for easy and friendly East-West relations in the era ahead. Most people date it from Winston Churchill's speech at Fulton, Missouri, a month later (March 5), which coined both the "cold war" and "iron curtain" labels. In either case it was a new condition not more than fifteen months old.

The countries of Eastern Europe, however, had in fact been blocked off from easy and normal communication with the West for much longer. Beginning in 1938, first the Germans then the Soviets dominated the countries lying between Germany and the Soviet Union. By June 1967 they had receded from our consciousness in the West. They had grown to seem far away, unknown, and full of hidden dangers. And, which seems a bit surprising in retrospect, few American reporters were interested in them, which in one way was fortunate: amenities were sparse and Spartan.

Warsaw vied with Hamburg for the title of being the most destroyed city in Europe. The Germans had left Warsaw boasting that it could never be inhabited again. When I arrived in June 1947 there was only one hotel functioning and only two American journalists, both living in that one hotel, the Polonia, of which all of us who were there at that time have vivid memories and mixed feelings. It was a small hotel, probably built in the mid-twenties, about six or seven stories high, less wide than high, a flat, light gray, unornamented face, just across the street from the main railway station. The U.S. Embassy had one floor and each of the two resident American journalists, Larry Allen of the Associated Press and Sidney Gruson of the *New York Times*, had a small, single room lined from floor to ceiling with imported cans of food. The American Embassy people envied their British colleagues, whose embassy building, an elaborate high-Victorian wedding cake mansion, had miraculously escaped bombings and German demolition.

At the time of my arrival Poland was not yet a one-party Communist dictatorship. The Peasant party had been liquidated in January, but the Socialist party was still independent and trying to remain so. The Communists had been talking about a "merger." I obtained interviews with the heads of both Communist and Socialist parties and was assured by both that Poland would remain a plural democracy. I also had interviews with the foreign minister and the minister of industry, Hilary Minc. From the latter I learned why the Communists were delaying a full takeover. He had applied for a $600 million reconstruction loan from the World Bank in Washington. The consolidation of Communist power would immediately block the loan. Poland was in transition. The Communists had power but had not used it to the full yet. They hoped for the loan first.

Warsaw itself had regained about half of its prewar population, with many people living in makeshift temporary quarters. It was spring. The main streets were lined with temporary, one-story shops; flowers were everywhere; grass was showing again in plots cleared of rubble. Private enterprise was responsible, and citizens' love of their city. I wrote that "it is quite wrong to classify Poland at this stage as a country behind the iron curtain. The curtain may be dropping steadily, but it seems rather in momentary suspense."

Czechoslovakia too was in a state of momentary suspense. There was tension in the air. The Communists had been threatening a takeover, but had not yet dared strike. The Parliament was still plural with Communists in a minority. Justice was still evenhanded. Czech industry had been only lightly damaged during the war and the once-imperial glories of Prague—the Charles Bridge, the Hradicany Palace, the cathedral—were untouched, undamaged. There had been no fighting worth mentioning in Czechoslovakia. It was the least scarred of all and the most solidly democratic.

By the time I moved on from Prague to Budapest I was beginning to realize that each country was different. Czechoslovakia was the most Western, most modern, most bourgeois, and most resistant to communism. Its upper classes had been Austrian and German and largely went when the Germans left. The native Czechs and Slovaks left behind came close to being a democratic, self-reliant, one-class society. They expected nothing from Americans. They hoped to hold the Communists at bay by their own efforts.

Hungary was another matter. I arrived as the Communists were putting into operation a "three-year plan" that amounted in its practical application to a single-party dictatorship. The conservatives dreamed of British and American troops coming to their rescue and restoring their feudal lands and castles. The right wing in Hungary lived in a dream world that was being shattered that very week.

Then on to Yugoslavia, where more surprises awaited me. Here was communism with a vengeance. On the street outside my hotel, the Muskowa, was a row of boot blacks. So far as I could discover they were independent of any organization and definitely not a state enterprise. But also, as far as I could discover, they were the last and only relic of independent private enterprise. Everything else had been nationalized.

Also, unlike Poles, Czechs, and Hungarians, the Yugoslavs had no interest in talking to me, an American. The others wanted to persuade me that my country should be loaning money to them. They had a propaganda package to sell. The Yugoslavs couldn't care less. They had given me a visa and let me in. I was free to roam around at will. They offered me a ride on the Youth Railway, their stock window display for foreigners.

"But," I reported, "so far as making contact with government officials and political leaders was concerned I couldn't break through. I made my call at the press office. I was received by a young secretary dressed in Partisan Uniform. She took down the list of names of persons I wanted to see. She was all smiles and promises. She told me to come back the next day. I came back, and I was told to come again the next day. And that is how it went. The Yugoslavs were willing to admit a visiting correspondent from the West. But they weren't talking."

I was getting a taste of Tito's independence. Yugoslavia had liberated itself. Tito and his Partisans had driven the Germans out of their country before the Soviets could get there. He owed the Soviets nothing. He imposed his own brand of communism on his country at his own pace, but not on Soviet orders; nor was it a Soviet brand of communism, which is probably why Titoist communism proved more durable than the varieties imposed from Moscow on the other curtain countries. As this is being written, communism has been repudiated in all the others, even in Albania and in the Soviet Union itself. But in Belgrade the residue of the old central government still clings to Tito's variety.

I came out from the "curtain countries" by way of Vienna, Berlin, and Frankfurt trying to sort out a lot of unexpected and sometimes conflicting observations. The curtain was obviously closing down on Eastern Europe, but unevenly. Hungary and Yugoslavia had been communized, but the Czechs still expected to avoid it and the Poles were still resisting. Standards of living varied widely. High fashion, smartly dressed women, and moonlit dancing by the Danube in Budapest contrasted with barefooted men and women in Belgrade. Most surprising of all, to me at the time, was that there was plenty of food and faster reconstruction of bridges, highways, railways, and public services in the East than in the West.

"Fault Line" in the Curtain – 1949

I went back to Eastern Europe in 1949. I had to find out whether (and if so how much) it had changed since my visit two years before. I found it changed enormously. In terms of my own personal comfort the biggest single improvement was that in Warsaw I did not have to stay again in the cramped, flavorless Polonia Hotel. Instead I was able to stay at the once elegant Bristol, a turn-of-the-century, French beaux arts–style structure located conveniently on that broad avenue that marches southward along the ridge above the river from the Royal Castle, the cathedral, and the central square of the old city through the center of the later city and on to the embassies and main government buildings grouped near the Belvedere Palace and the once royal parks to the south.

The Bristol in June 1949 showed both her age and the scars of war. Her carpets were threadbare. The service and food were at best utilitarian. But the rooms were generous in size, the plumbing worked, and the lobby and dining room had become the political marketplace of Warsaw. Everyone came there—diplomats, journalists of all kinds, government officials. It was no surprise to find John Kenneth Galbraith at the next table, trying to find out just what did happen when communism took over a country that before had practiced a market economy. If you came out of the front door of the Bristol and turned right toward the castle you passed what had been the palaces of the high nobility—Radziwills, Esterhatzys, and such—which at that time had become offices of various government departments. If you turned left you would soon find yourself in the famous Nowy Swiat (Street of the New World), which was the cultural and intellectual center of the city. The main museums, the Institute of Science, much of the university were on or near the Nowy Swiat; so was the great Church of the Holy Cross, the largest church in Warsaw, from whose high pulpit the cardinal-archbishop's battle with the Communist state was frequently waged. If you walked by that church on a

Sunday the congregation spilled by hundreds out into the street, almost blocking it. Beyond that, on the left, was the new building housing the offices of the Polish Communist party. Beyond that were British and U.S. embassies, then the Foreign Office. Near there was a charming small palace in the park, which was later to be the scene of the first attempts of American and Chinese diplomats to get together after the Korean War. Warsaw was a crossroads of East and West. The Bristol Hotel was a convenient base of operations. You could learn a lot just by walking from the Bristol to the Foreign Office.

Poles have a deep love for their capital city, and justly so. Whether Communist or anti-Communist they all agreed on giving the rebuilding of Warsaw their first attention. In two years they had made marvelous progress. I found that in the Nowy Swiat—the midsection of the main north-south avenue—where in 1947 eighty houses were in ruins and only ten standing, there were now eighty standing and only ten remaining in ruins. In addition I noted that the reconstructions were an improvement on the prewar condition because they had been "restored from the original designs and therefore stand out in their original 18th Century unity and beauty, free from the encrustations of the Victorian period." Incidentally, where original designs were missing the architects found Canaletto paintings of enormous help because of their accuracy of detail, proportion, and color.

As remarkable as the physical reconstruction was the survival of Polish identity. The Polish soldier still wore the Polish eagle on his cap, not the Red Star. He marched to church in formation on Sundays as a regular military exercise. The churches, all of them Roman Catholic, flourished and were packed on Sundays. Many a priest was harassed or jailed, but they preached openly against communism and against the consolidation of Communist political power. The Polish people remained openly and obviously and devoutly Catholic and anti-Communist. In four years communism had made not a dent in the basic convictions and loyalties of the Polish people. Their hearts were in Rome, not in Moscow. Nevertheless, Moscow had consolidated its political control over Poland. Stanislaw Mikolajczyk, who had spent the war years in London with the Polish government in exile, came back in 1945 as head of the Peasant party and deputy prime minister. But by late 1947 his position had become impossible. Threatened with arrest, he escaped to the West.

Meanwhile the Communists seized power in Czechoslovakia in a coup d'état in February 1948. President Eduard Benes remained in office for a while in the hope of averting a civil war. Jan Masaryk, son of Thomas Masaryk, the founder of the Czech Republic, also stayed on as foreign minister in the hope of tempering the rush to Moscow and full communism. But on May 10 his body was found on the pavement below the window of his office in the Cernin Palace. President Benes finally resigned on June 7 and was replaced by Communist party chief Klement Gotwald.

The death of Jan Masaryk remains an unsolved mystery. Many think he was pushed from the window. The government reported his death as suicide. I had visited him in that same office on my 1947 trip. He was under no illusions at that time about the future. He knew the Communists would take over and both impose their own domestic policies on the country and put it into subordination to Moscow. My own feeling from the 1947 visit is that probably he had decided in his own mind that he should stay on as long as he could influence policy but when that time was over he would want to make a personal statement.

He could easily have escaped to the West. Either the American or the British embassy could and would have smuggled him out. He had a myriad of devoted friends in both countries. The Communists benefited from having his name associated with their government. I don't see that they had anything to gain by murdering him. I think his death was his last sacrificial contribution to the country his father founded and he loved.

By the time I got back in 1949 the fact that Jan Masaryk had died had in itself underlined the extent of the Communist takeover. Czechs and Slovaks were condemned to learn the hard way that communism was not good for them. Their story had been different from Poland's story. It is a little-known fact that much of the factory worker population in Czechoslovakia had voted in favor of the one-party slate that consolidated the Communist regime in 1948. It took from 1948 to 1968 (when Russian tanks suppressed the Prague Spring) for the bulk of the urban factory workers to turn against the regime. By then it was too late. Their rescue would be deferred until 1989.

Hungary was the first to fall under Communist control, partly because it had fought on Germany's side during the war. While Poland and Czechoslovakia were "conquered" by Hitler's armies and "liberated" by Soviet armies, Hungary, like Romania, had sent an army into Russia on the German side. Hungary was not "liberated" by the Soviets, it was "conquered," which made a difference. The Western allies showed less concern over Hungary's fate even though during the later phase of the war the regime had tried to break away from the German grip. Communization had gone fastest in Hungary, so fast that in 1949 they would not give me a visa. In an election in May, while I was in their neighborhood, the Communists rigged a single-list election by which, after two previous failures (1945 and 1947), they finally got an electoral majority to sanction the takeover that had already occurred.

Thus, when I reached Eastern Europe in May 1949 the curtain was settling down unmistakably on Poland, Czechoslovakia, and Hungary. The reverse had happened in Yugoslavia, but in a fashion for which Washington was mentally unprepared. Josip Broz, known as Tito, head of the Communist party of Yugoslavia, undoubted national hero, liberator of his country from Hitler, had broken with Moscow, but not with communism.

Make a note of the date of the break. On June 28, 1948, the Cominform (Communist Information Bureau), the central organization of the Communist world through which Moscow guided and controlled the policies and behavior of its allies, clients, and satellites, expelled Yugoslavia from its membership and declared against Yugoslavia an embargo that all Communist countries were required to observe. The expulsion was undoubtedly expected by Moscow to lead to a rebellion against Tito in the Communist party of Yugoslavia or at the very least to an economic squeeze that would force him and his country back into the Moscow fold. Probably what Moscow most hoped for, and perhaps expected, was that some loyal (to Moscow) Communist would assassinate Tito.

I had been at the State Department the day the news of the break arrived. The reporters present in the press room that day immediately rushed to Chip Bohlen's office. Chip (Charles E.) Bohlen was the State Department's top expert on Russia and the Communist world (along with George Kennan). What would happen next? Could Tito survive this pronunciation of anathema by Moscow? Chip said he would give Tito about six to eight weeks. He assumed, he said, that Moscow could not and would not tolerate the departure of Yugoslavia from the Communist fold. He expected that Moscow would find some means, either by external action or internal subversion, to bring Yugoslavia back to heel. He could not imagine Moscow letting Tito get away with independence.

This was the inconceivable happening. Washington had been assuming that communism and subservience to Moscow were one and the same thing. There was much talk in State Department circles of "the seamless cloak of communism." This break couldn't happen. If it did happen, it could not last. Such talk led to inaction. Washington did nothing to try to rescue Tito from whatever Moscow might try. But London was more willing to see a possible crack in the iron curtain. London did a simple, practical, and enormously helpful thing for Tito. It sent him a tanker ship of fuel oil and gasoline, which proved to be enough to keep his rail and highway transport running.

A year later when I got to Belgrade I found the main subject of conversation was still whether Tito could survive. He had survived for a year (eleven months to be precise), but for how much longer? There had been constant rumors of Soviet troops massing along the Yugoslav frontier. There had been plots. Tito's secret service had uncovered one plot and made two arrests. One man had been jailed, a second had been shot, Colonel General Arso Jovanovitch. There was economic trouble. Tito's trade had been largely with the Communist countries. He had lost his foreign markets overnight, and also the main source of machinery and spare parts.

This time I had no trouble getting appointments with officials of the Yugoslav government. They were eager to meet a Western journalist, and they were asking questions as well as giving answers. Officially, Yugoslavia was still very Communist. The new line was that true communism was to be found only in Yugoslavia. And their propaganda was still full of denunciation of "western, imperialist capitalism." But denunciations of Moscow's brand of communism rang with more feeling than the barbs hurled in our direction. For the first time on my two excursions behind the curtain, one Yugoslav official started asking me questions. One of them said, "Is it true that you still lynch negroes in the United States?" The question had the ring of a sincere interest in finding out whether their familiar propaganda line was true. He wanted to know the facts. The inquiring mind had revived in Yugoslavia.

That one single question had told me something of first importance. The curtain was not made of iron. It was permeable to ideas. Another question was in my mind when I arrived in Belgrade. How did it happen that Tito had been able to survive for a year? The people I talked to in Belgrade, both at the Western embassies and among Yugoslav officials and journalists, were all in agreement on the answer. He had never allowed the Soviets to penetrate his Communist party or his bureaucracy. In other countries they had moved into the local Communist party, also bureaucracy, at all levels, from top to bottom. In Yugoslavia Tito had built his own party and his own secret service. Moscow had contact in Yugoslavia not at all levels, but only at the top through Tito himself. Stalin could not give an order to underlings in the Tito apparatus in Belgrade. There was no substantial segment of the party that owed its loyalty to Moscow or took its orders from Moscow.

Behind the independence was the unusual fact that Tito and his Partisans had liberated Yugoslavia by their own efforts. Their country had not been "liberated" by Soviet armies. Its government had not been hand-picked in Moscow and imposed by Soviet troops. This was native local communism. It had done its own selection—and liberation.

Tito's survival was a major loss to Moscow. The whole world knew that he had been excommunicated and had survived. He was preaching the right of every Communist country to shape its own "separate road to socialism." What he had done had made him a hero in other Communist countries. I was in Prague on May Day, the traditional day for a big parade in every Communist or Socialist country. An enormous parade of "workers" was organized. It formed at the top of that great boulevard called the Wencesplatz, which starts in front of the National Museum and under the statue of King Wenceslaus on horseback on the top of the hill and runs straight down to the old city. At the bottom it dead-ends at a cross street. The Yugoslav information office occupied the showroom directly facing the boulevard. As the paraders came down the hill, they saw right in front at the bottom a huge picture poster of Tito. And as the paraders saw Tito they cheered and cheered again as they cheered for no one else. There were police around the window. I saw it repeatedly covered with paint or chalk or soap or something white. But as each major unit made its turn at the bottom of the hill somehow that white was wiped away and the paraders saw Tito's face again, and again cheered and cheered. On May Day 1949 the most popular person in Prague was Tito of Yugoslavia.

Chip Bohlen was correct in thinking that Moscow could not afford to let Tito survive independently. The example was contagious. And there is no doubt that the Soviets did what they could to bring Tito down. But he was fortunate in his geography. He had a long seacoast open to the West. From time immemorial there had been trade across the Adriatic. The West could reach him with aid through seaports used from Roman times and still usable today. They could reach him by more modern ways. He could not be blockaded from the Western world. Moscow's best weapon against Tito should have been the Yugoslav Communist party.

But defections were few. When tested it proved to be loyal to Tito, not to Moscow. There was no common Soviet-Yugoslav frontier for Soviet troops to cross. The economic blockade by Communist countries failed to work. The biggest danger was shortage of oil. Before the break Yugoslavia received most of its oil by barge up the Danube from Rumania. Yugoslavia's refineries were on the Danube for that reason, not on the coast. Once the oil problem was overcome it was possible to find sources in the West for Yugoslavia's other needs.

Much of Yugoslavia was still in a primitive state. A brilliant and sometimes wild colleague, Ed Corey of the UP, arrived from Paris in a big, open Renault car. He proposed a trip south to Skoplje, the capital of Macedonia, to find out how much, if any, disaffection there might be outside Belgrade and also to search for a new industrial city to be called Titograd that was said to be under construction near there. It was a wild trip often over wild terrain. I have in my memory glimpses of barefooted women pulling plows; of a wooden bridge with a missing plank, which Corey overrode at the highest possible speed; of a hotel in Skoplje with plumbing I try to forget; of streets of houses dating from the Turkish era; of my enormous relief when, having caught a raging cold (psychological reaction to Corey's driving?), I opted out of the further trip in search of Titograd and climbed aboard a modern railway car with sleeping compartments and retreated back to the luxury (by contrast) of the Moskowa Hotel in Belgrade.

Then back out of the curtain countries by way of Vienna, where friends were brimming with stories of how the Austrians were winning back control of their country in the Soviet zone of occupation. The Soviets had confiscated many a factory in their zone. The Austrians countered by building new factories making the same product but doing it better, thus taking the business away from the Soviet-operated plant. The Austrians were no longer afraid of the Russians. They were squeezing them out.

I made another detour to ride the airlift to Berlin. By that time it was routine. I simply showed up at one of the airfields from which American, British, and French planes were flying fuel and food to Berlin and boarded the next plane in line. It was being loaded with bags of coal. I sat in the cockpit with pilot and co-pilot. The flight was brief and uneventful. We were soon in a circle of planes over Tempelhof Field in Berlin, taking our turn to come down. I seem to remember (although I do not find this in my notes) that planes were being landed at the rate of one every two minutes. I do remember that after landing we got off the main runway as quickly as possible and over to an unloading area where trucks came alongside and a work crew came aboard as soon as the engines were cut off. That plane was back in line and ready to take off for another round trip in about half an hour. Never before or since has so much freight been moved by air so fast. But the important thing was that it kept the city of West Berlin fed and warmed through the winter of 1948–49 and the Soviets did not take hard action to stop it. The rest of Europe noted that the United States and its allies risked a military confrontation with the Soviets and won the hand. By spring when I rode the airlift the issue was no longer in doubt although Moscow did not lift the blockade until September. Moscow had been denied the capture of West Berlin.

By the time I got back to Washington I had the answers to my questions. The curtain was not made of iron. It was permeable. Ideas flowed through it. The minds of those who had already lived four years under Communist regimes had not been forever lost to the free world. The inquiring mind had survived and reasserted itself. George Orwell's *1984* was not based on valid reasoning. Moscow had conquered Poland, Czechoslovakia, and Hungary, true, but only because the Soviet army was upon them and had imposed the Stalinist system by force. There was no room for doubt that they would break away both from Soviet rule and from Stalinist-type communism if the Soviet army would go home. War was not necessary to "roll back" communism from Eastern Europe. Withdrawal of the Soviet army was necessary. If that could be achieved by methods other than war all would be better off. The West was winning the hearts and minds of all the "middle lands" that lie between Germany and the Soviet Union. The people of West Germany and all of Austria had watched events to the east and rejected communism. The Yugoslavs had made good their own escape from Stalin's grasp. I went to my typewriter and wrote the book that had emerged in my mind from my two trips to the curtain countries. I called it *The Curtain Isn't Iron.* Its conclusion read:

> The cause of the West has advanced in the cold-war struggle against Russian domination in eastern and central Europe. The Communist coup in Czechoslovakia was the high mark of Russian advance. Since that event the tide has turned decidedly in favor of the West. The victories have been dearly won and the progress has been slow. But there is no doubt that the advantage has gone to the West.

It would make poor sense to discard a winning technique as long as it is winning.

At the time I wrote the above, in 1949, there were still many in Washington who argued that the only way to roll back the iron curtain would be by war. It was assumed that without war Moscow would so impose its system upon the minds as well as the bodies of the subject peoples that they could never be reclaimed for the West. Such thinking led to reluctance to provide aid in any form to Marshall Tito's Yugoslavia. He was still an avowed and practicing Communist. His economic and social system was Communist. Many suspected that his break with Moscow was a ruse to fool us in the West. Others assumed that sooner or later he would patch up his differences with Moscow. The belief was persistent in Washington that the cloak of communism was seamless.

We date the break between Moscow and Tito as of June 28, 1948. Not until fourteen months later, on September 8, 1949, did the United States actually provide tangible help to Tito. On that date the Export-Import Bank in Washington announced that it had granted a $20 million loan to Yugoslavia. This followed by two weeks the lifting of the ban on sale of the U.S. weapons to Yugoslavia and also permission for the Yugoslavs to buy an American steel mill. It was difficult for Washington to bring itself to believe that a country still practicing a form of communism could actually be leaving the Moscow fold. Fortunately for Marshall Tito and his country, the British and French had moved faster.

I wrote at the time, "This is the first time since the war that an official agency of the United States Government has extended aid in any form to a communist government." It was a precedent which would be helpful later when China would also break with Moscow.

Postscript

The Tito break triggered a wave of purge trials through the "curtain" countries of Eastern Europe. Laszlo Rajk, foreign minister in Hungary, was executed in October 1949. Traicho Kostov, party leader in Bulgaria, was executed in December. The purge was slower in Czechoslovakia. There, the trial of Rudolf Slansky, secretary of the Communist party, dragged on into late 1952. He was executed on December 3. In Poland,

Wladyslaw Gomulka's trial was dragged out even longer. He was fortunate. He was still in jail awaiting trial when Stalin died in 1953. He was released from prison during Nikita Khrushchev's destalinization program and returned to power as head of the party in Poland in 1956.

Laszlo Rajk was the only one of the above whom I met on my travels. I interviewed him during my 1947 trip. I remember him as a tall, handsome man who impressed me as a sincere believer in communism. He knew and admired Tito. They had worked together recruiting for the International Brigade during the Spanish civil war. The charges against him were Titoism and nationalism. He probably was guilty, by Moscow standards, of both. In 1949 Stalin wanted no more Tito types in any country under Soviet control.

The China Story Begins

I came back to Washington in July 1949 full of optimism about Western progress in Europe. The high tide of Moscow's advance into Eastern and Central Europe had been the Communist coup d'état in Czechoslovakia in February 1948. That had been followed four months later on June 24 by the blockade of West Berlin, which was supposed to lead to the abandonment of West Berlin by the Western allies. On June 28 Tito was expelled from the Cominform, which was supposed to have brought him down and restored Yugoslavia to Soviet discipline.

But a year later, in June 1949, Tito was still in control of Yugoslavia and West Berlin was still alive, and still very Western.

Both of those major Soviet moves of early 1948 had failed. The blockade of Berlin had been countered, successfully, by the marvel of the great airlift and Tito had survived his expulsion from the Cominform and was in more solid control of his own country than before. Those two responses to Soviet action had turned the tide in Europe. By spring 1949 Moscow had already lost the hearts and minds of the peoples of Eastern and Central Europe. I was sure that it was only a matter of time before others would seek and ultimately regain their independence from Moscow. When I put my confidence down in a book, *The Curtain Isn't Iron*, I was accused of being wildly optimistic. In 1989 it read as prophecy fulfilled.

But on August 14, 1949, seismic instruments recorded a literal earthshaking event somewhere in the interior of the Soviet Union. Accumulating evidence soon disclosed the unwelcome fact that Moscow had succeeded in breaking the American monopoly in nuclear weapons. The Soviets had achieved their first A-bomb. More than that, in the same month of August, Chinese government forces armed and funded by the United States were in full retreat southward across the Yangtse River. Chiang Kai-shek had lost all the battles in the north of China. He fell back on Canton in the south and by December 8, 1949, fled to Taiwan (Formosa) with what could be salvaged of his army and his political following. Communist Mao Tse-tung was the new master of China and soon went to Moscow, where on February 14, 1950, he signed a treaty of alliance between China and the Soviet Union.

Those twin events, the loss of nuclear monopoly and the loss of China, made the second half of 1949 and all of 1950 a time of deepening anxiety in Washington. With completion of a Communist alliance between China and the Soviet Union, Stalin could control, certainly in theory, everything lying between the China Sea in Asia and the Elbe River in Europe. For the first time in history the bulk of the great Eurasian land mass was in the hands of one man, and that man, Joseph Stalin, was no friend of the United States or its allies. That combination of Soviet Union and China would have to be broken up before the West could breathe comfortably and safely again, all the more so now that the combination would soon be in possession of an arsenal of nuclear weapons.

Would Moscow be inclined to take advantage of its new power? The answer was not long in coming. On June 24, 1950, only four months after the signing of the Sino-Soviet alliance, the armies of a Communist North Korea surged over the truce line and headed for Seoul, the capital of South Korea. That left no room in Washington for doubt about Stalin's intentions. Obviously, his imperialism was on the march. He was going to take advantage of any and all opportunities that might open up. True, containment was working in Europe. Greece and Turkey had been bolstered and were on the way to safety, but the good news from Europe was overshadowed by the Soviet advances in Asia. Harry Truman did not hesitate. He decided almost without staff study that he would have to do whatever he could to save something of South Korea. And he did. The rest of that story you already know or can find in other places. I shall confine myself here to what I saw back in Washington of the choices, the decisions, and the bitter controversies over the choices that arose out of the Korean war.

I went to the Pentagon one day in October to see General Omar Bradley, who was then chairman of the Joint Chiefs of Staff. We chatted about the way the war was going. General MacArthur had begun his advance beyond the demilitarized zone that had separated South from North Korea. In the initial stages all went well. There was negligible North Korean resistance and no signs of any intrusion by either Soviet or Chinese troops. But General Bradley said he had one worry. He pulled down a map of Korea and showed me the two prongs of MacArthur's advance, the Eighth Army going up the west coast, the marines going up the east coast, and nothing in between. He was worried about the lack of communication between the two. He said that the Chinese could, if they chose, move into that great empty space between MacArthur's unconnected flanks. I asked him what he was going to do about it. He said it would be difficult to do anything because of MacArthur's enormous prestige both in Washington and around the country. He had to hope that MacArthur was correct in believing that the Chinese would not come into the war.

General Bradley was of course correct about public confidence in General MacArthur. He was getting high praise worldwide for his handling of the American occupation of Japan. In four years he had converted Japan from a military-dominated authoritarian monarchy to a modern, democratic, and constitutional monarchy. And beginning on September 15 he had conceived and executed brilliantly an astonishing reversal of the fortunes of war in Korea by his daring landing at Inchon far behind enemy lines. He was almost the only person involved who thought the Inchon operation could succeed. Only with utmost reluctance did the Joint Chiefs of Staff and the White House allow him to try it. And it had worked almost miraculously. Before the Inchon landing Allied forces were squeezed into a small perimeter at the southern tip of the Korean peninsula under constant pressure. Within two weeks that situation was transformed. Allied troops swept almost unopposed from Inchon to Seoul, recaptured the capital, and pushed on across the peninsula to cut the lines of supply from the north to the North Korean armies besieging the Pusan perimeter. The North Koreans were routed. Most of them were taken prisoner. Only scattered fragments—about thirty thousand out of four hundred thousand—of their original army made their way back to the north. The Inchon landing was the boldest, most brilliant, and most successful military operation since the Normandy landings. MacArthur's prestige as a military genius was at a new high. In Washington his military colleagues were reluctant to doubt his ability to handle whatever might happen in the mountainous spaces of North Korea. Perhaps he would be proved correct that the Chinese would not dare to challenge him.

But once again Douglas MacArthur spoiled brilliant success with a crashing blunder. In the Philippines just after Pearl Harbor, as we have noted before, he got highest marks for his redeployment of the Philippine army to the Bataan peninsula, but spoiled it by failing to stock the peninsula with sufficient food for that army. It was starved out. Now, once again, he capped a triumph with a blunder. He ignored the Chinese. He sent his troops to the Yalu River in willful disregard of the fact that on the day of the big offensive that was supposed to "get the boys home for Christmas" he was already outnumbered by the Chinese behind his own front line. His offensive was smothered at the opening moment and turned into sudden retreat. So important was that event to the next twenty years of history that we must examine just how it happened, determine if possible who shared in the blame, and draw some lessons from the debacle.

The spectacular success of the Inchon landing followed by the virtual destruction of the North Korean army opened up a new possibility. The United States had gone into the Korean War with the declared and limited purpose of repelling the aggression and restoring South Korea. There was no thought of doing anything more than just that, until Inchon. But suddenly there was nothing of military significance between General MacArthur's front, which by then was back on the 38th parallel, and the Yalu River frontier some two hundred miles farther to the north. To many at the White House in Washington, also some at the State Department and more at the Pentagon, here was a tempting situation. Why not go on ahead, take all of North Korea, and set up a new Korean government over the entire country? Militarily it would be easy, with one proviso. It would be easy provided neither Soviet nor Chinese armed forces were to intervene.

It is interesting in retrospect that two men whose opinions still weigh heavily in foreign policy councils in Washington, Paul Nitze and George Kennan, both said don't. Nitze at that time was chairman of the Policy and Planning staff at the State Department. Kennan was counselor of the department. I remember Kennan talking quietly about how sensitive the Chinese were to the approach of foreign armed forces toward their frontiers. Nitze spoke for the entire Policy and Planning group. Both argued that the wise and prudent course would be to be satisfied with the restoration of the status quo. They argued that to go north of the parallel might be regarded in both Moscow and Peking as an invasion of their area of influence won on the battlefields of World War II. Both would certainly regard it as an unfriendly move. One or both might well be inclined to send troops in to protect the Communist regime in North Korea.

There was strong contrary opinion. Secretary of State Dean Acheson could see no reason for stopping the pursuit of the defeated North Koreans at an arbitrary line such as the 38th parallel. He agreed to the drafting of instructions for General MacArthur that authorized him to seek the defeat of the remainder of the North Korean army north of the parallel, but with restrictions. He was to stop at once if Soviet or Chinese troops entered Korea. And he was to send only South Korean troops north of the "narrow waistline" about halfway from the 38th parallel to the Yalu River frontier. Also, he was forbidden to bomb near the frontier or across the frontier.

That authorization went to MacArthur on September 27 while the pursuit of the retreating North Koreans was in full cry. The limitations on his movements were watered down by a separate telegram from General Marshall, then secretary of defense, saying, "We want you to feel unhampered tactically and strategically to proceed north of the 38th parallel." All of official Washington was full of argument over how far MacArthur should be allowed to go beyond the parallel. General Bradley was most worried about the gap between the flanks. Admiral Leahy at the White House talked to me about the merits of the "narrow waist." He liked the fact that the navy could give artillery support at both ends of the line, leaving a narrower gap to be covered by air than anywhere else along the Korean peninsula.

By September 30 MacArthur had his permission to go north, and his troops were coming up from Pusan and getting organized along the line of the parallel and ready to resume the pursuit.

In Peking on October 3 China's foreign minister, Chou En-lai, summoned the Indian ambassador, K. M. Panikkar, to his office and told him that if the Americans crossed the 38th parallel China would enter the war.

(Between October 11 and 28 President Truman flew to Wake Island to meet General MacArthur. I went along on that trip. We of the press were put in a small hotel for transit airline passengers. From its porch we watched as General MacArthur got into an open car and rode to a hangar. The car stopped there out of sight of the incoming plane carrying the president. The car waited, hidden behind the hangar, until the plane had landed, engines were stopped, and the landing ramp was readied for the president. The car then sortied out from behind the hangar and sped to the ramp, where the general received his commander-in-chief.)

The warning of October 3 from Peking made no impression in Washington that I ever detected. I heard references to it. State Department people seemed inclined to treat Mr. Panikkar as a lightweight. I remember someone referring to him as Mr. Panic. Before, during, and after the president's trip to Wake Island General MacArthur continued to move his troops beyond the parallel and up to the "narrow waistline." By the time the president was back in Washington the general was ready to push north. At that point his troops were on the line beyond which he was supposed, according to his instructions of September 27, to send only South Korean troops. But in his own mind that restriction had been voided by the special telegram from General Marshall and probably, although this is not clear from the record, by whatever the president said to him on Wake Island when the two of them were alone together. Whatever the explanation, the fact is that on October 24 he ordered his commanders to "drive forward with all speed and with full utilization of their forces."

Then some very strange things happened. One Republic of Korea unit reached the Yalu on October 26 without incident, turned back, and was engulfed in a large Chinese force. On the next day two U.S. regiments brigaded with Korean units ran into another large mass of Chinese troops and were badly mauled. The survivors fell back to the next river line to their rear. At that point everyone seems to have halted to think things over. There was no more contact between Allied forces and the Chinese. No one on the Allied side seemed to know how many Chinese were actually in Korea or where. There were excited exchanges between MacArthur's headquarters and Washington. Acheson calls the period after those first encounters on the Yalu on October 26 and 27 a "last clear chance" and he faults himself for not having proposed during those days of lull on the battlefield a withdrawal to the "narrow waistline," where the Allied armies probably could have beaten off any attack on them. Neither Acheson nor anyone at the White House or Pentagon was willing to take the initiative in reining in the great General MacArthur. He was left to make his own decision. What he chose to do was to go ahead again. He informed Washington on November 17 that he would launch the drive to end the war on November 24. No one in Washington stepped forward to tell him not to go ahead.

So go ahead he did, on November 24. The Eighth Army on the western flank and the marines off on the east coast started and were immediately overwhelmed, smothered, and forced into retreat. It was one of the few big disasters in the history of American armed forces. Someone said it was the worst defeat since the first battle of Bull Run. President Truman declared a national emergency. Some expected war with Russia, and various people in Washington talked about using nuclear bombs.

In London, Prime Minister Attlee heard of such remarks and hurried to Washington to try to head off any such action. He was horrified at the idea. I know of no evidence that anyone in top place in Washington gave serious thought to using nuclear weapons, but the secretary of the navy, Francis P. Matthews, proposed a preventive war against the Soviets—and was reassigned to the American embassy in Ireland.

The essential fact was that the United States was at war with China and China at that time had a military alliance with the Soviet Union.

This was indeed a new and very dangerous situation. It had not been wanted in Washington. It need not have happened. It happened because the success of the Inchon landing and the collapse of the North Korean army opened up an opportunity to score a quick and perhaps cheap cold war success. The opportunity was tempting. The Chinese gave fair warning. Temptation overrode the warning. General MacArthur is blamed usually. It was certainly imprudent for him to discount the Chinese after those first two small-scale disasters on the Yalu on October 26 and 27 when two U.S. regiments, the Fifth and Eighth Cavalry, reported that they had been ambushed by "well organized and well trained units." And yet a month later General MacArthur still was confident that the Chinese would not interfere.

In Washington there were many who should have been more aware of the dangers of pushing deep into a position from which the United States could launch an invasion of either China or the Soviet Union or both. We Americans have been extremely sensitive to any approach of the armed forces of a major power to our shores. When the French put an army into Mexico during our own Civil War we could do nothing until that war was over, but the moment it was over we told the French to get out; since we then had the world's biggest army, they did. The Monroe Doctrine was intended for just that purpose, to keep others away from our neighborhood. The Cuban missile crisis was a case in point. Everyone in Washington in 1950 should have realized that neither the Chinese nor the Soviets would accept passively a U.S. advance to the Yalu any more than we would at that time, or any time, accept a similar Soviet or Chinese advance toward our frontiers. The president and the secretary of state surely shared the blame with General MacArthur for a military advance in November 1950 that launched the United States into an unnecessary state of hostility with China that would last for twenty-two years.

We usually speak of the Korean and the Vietnam wars as two separate stories, but in a larger sense both were phases of a basic hostility between the United States and China, which in turn was based on the assumption in Washington that Mao Tse-tung's China was an instrument of Soviet purpose aimed at dominating the entire world. It was ended only when China broke so openly and unmistakably with Moscow that Washington was finally, reluctantly, almost resentfully, forced to accept the fact of an open break. The reluctance which we saw in regard to the Tito break was repeated with the Chinese break.

The state of hostility between the United States and China, which was begun on November 24, 1950, by the unwise and unnecessary march to the Yalu, would continue in various forms until the day Richard Nixon arrived in Peking in 1972.

Looking back over that entire episode one of the many surprises to me is the role played or rather not played by the British ambassador of that time, Sir Oliver Franks. Few British ambassadors in Washington have ever been so much respected and so much attended as he. He was consulted constantly by top people in Washington on all subjects, including even domestic American affairs. Had he advised strongly against the fatal march to the Yalu he might easily have headed it off. He did not. After it was all over I asked him why he had not done all he could to prevent it. He replied that he thought a successful march to the Yalu would give the West some "situations of strength." He said he saw no reason not to reach for them, if available, as he assumed they were.

Defeat on the Yalu set off a wide-ranging debate over national policy that cut through party lines. General MacArthur wanted to bomb mainland China in retaliation for China's entry into the Korean War. This idea was picked up enthusiastically on the hawk side of the Republican party, inhabited at that time by the China Lobby, a collection of businessmen with Chinese connections, and by members of the missionary movement. A major advocate of a policy of carrying Chiang Kai-shek back to the mainland with an American army was Congressman Walter Judd of Minnesota, who had been born in China to a missionary family. But against those who wanted a great U.S. military offensive against the Communists in China and Russia too (some said) was former president Herbert Hoover, who favored a retreat from both Europe and Asia to "this Western Hemisphere Gibraltar of Western Civilization." This came to be called the Fortress America policy. Hoover was supported by Joseph P. Kennedy, who favored withdrawal from Europe on the ground that our policies there were "politically and morally bankrupt."

The immediate and practical question was whether to allow General

MacArthur to start bombing inside China. He had been arguing that we should either pull out of Korea entirely or take the offensive against China. It was widely suspected in government circles in Washington that his real objective was to start a big war against both China and Russia. The problem was resolved by relieving him of his command. This brought down on President Truman's head a thunderstorm of abuse from Republicans, but it also put an end to serious talk of going to war then and there against Communist China and Russia. General Matthew B. Ridgeway, already in command of the Eighth Army, was given the entire Far East Command and proceeded to revive American forces in Korea, stabilize the front, and carry out a gradual forward movement that before long had American troops back on a well-organized and well-fortified line across the peninsula more or less on the 38th parallel, where the dividing line between North and South Korea remains to this day.

The Power of Ideology

It took the British government three months to accept and recognize the reality of the changes that took place in China in late 1949. It took the United States government twenty-two years to do the same. The difference contains a lesson in power politics and provides an example of how foreign policy in Washington is often a by-product of domestic politics rather than the result of cool calculation of the national interest. It is also an example of why often there is so much friction between Capitol Hill and the Department of State. The Hill is motivated largely by domestic political considerations. The State Department tries to base policies on an objective calculation of long-term national interest. Let us, therefore, examine the story of U.S.-Chinese relations from 1949 to 1972 to see what it can tell us.

During the year 1949 the government of Nationalist China, headed by Chiang Kai-shek, disintegrated. At the beginning of the year it controlled most of China with armies outnumbering its rival Communist armies by about two and a half to one. The Nationalist armies had been generously supplied between 1945 and 1949 with American weapons and American economic aid at a total cost to the American taxpayer of about $2 billion, yet the Nationalist armies were defeated and finally routed by the superior morale of and popular support for the Communist armies. On October 1 Mao Tse-tung proclaimed the People's Republic of China and set up the new Communist government in Peking. On December 8 Chiang Kai-shek fled to Taiwan. On January 5, 1950, the British announced diplomatic recognition of the new People's Republic and reopened their embassy in Peking. On February 14 Mao Tse-tung was in Moscow, where he signed a treaty of mutual aid and military alliance with the Soviet Union. On June 14 the United States withdrew all its consular officials from China. From then until 1972 the United States continued to treat the Nationalist regime on Taiwan as the government of all of China.

In the years following those events I spent many an hour trying to answer the question frequently put to me by British Embassy friends about American hostility to China. They could never understand why the American government was so devoted to the Chiang Kai-shek regime and why it was so unrealistic as to pretend that his regime could possibly represent the hundreds of millions of people in mainland China.

The first and probably the weightiest reason was the same one that explains American delay the year before in recognizing and taking advantage of the breach between Tito's Yugoslavia and the Soviet Union, that is, the belief in the seamless cloak of communism. Communism in those days was still a powerful emotional force in the minds of many peoples in many countries. It had the emotional force of a religion. Emotional religions breed rival religions. Anticommunism became a powerful emotional force in the United States in the postwar era. A basic tenet, almost a sacred dogma, among anti-Communists was the assumption of a worldwide Communist conspiracy controlled from Moscow to take over the world. It was simply axiomatic among them that any Communist was an agent of Soviet power. For a Communist to be anti-Soviet was deemed inconceivable. Many Americans, including James Jesus Angleton, head of clandestine operations at CIA, regarded the breaks between Moscow and Tito and between Moscow and Peking as clever ruses intended to deceive us in the West.

There was an added quality in the American reaction to communism in China arising out of an unusual national experience. China was the main object of the great Protestant missionary movement that from the middle of the previous century had sent thousands of American missionaries to China. As a child in a small midwestern town, I was taken frequently to hear somebody's Aunt Sophie or Aunt Agatha, back from a Methodist or Baptist or Congregational mission in China, tell about the progress of Christianity in China. Both my grandmothers collected old clothes to be sent to the China missions and funds to found universities and hospitals in China. China was the favorite American national charity. Our diplomacy in earlier times had reflected this by trying, not with much success, to protect China from exploitation by the European empires and later against the Japanese when they invaded China before World War II. For China to go Communist was, in popular American eyes, an act of monstrous ingratitude. The hand we fed was turned against us.

Add to the above that Chiang Kai-shek had married Mei-Ling Soong, who was not only a Methodist but also a graduate of Wellesley College in Massachusetts. Chiang himself officially was a convert to Christianity. Mme. Chiang was beautiful in her youth and extremely persuasive and popular on the American lecture platform in maturity. She became the prize exhibit of the China lobby that came into existence with the downfall of Chiang in China and whose first goal was to prevent U.S. recognition of Communist China. Walter Judd, the son of a missionary family, born in China, led the pro–Chiang Kai-shek forces in Congress. Henry Luce, founder and publisher of *Time* magazine and its influential siblings *Life* and *Fortune*, also born in China of missionary parents, gave constant support. The constituency of the China lobby consisted of literally millions of Protestant families throughout the country. A colleague remembers that, in his youth in a southern Methodist family, every Methodist in his local church knew and personally corresponded with someone in one of the Methodist universities or hospitals in China.

The influence of Henry Luce's magazines backed by the missionary constituency was easily sufficient to prevent the government in Washington from following the British lead and recognizing the new Communist regime in China. Chinese intervention in Korea took care of the next goal of the China lobby, military protection for Taiwan. Previous to the intervention Mr. Truman declared total U.S. neutrality between the two Chinese governments. In theory at least, the United States would have sat on the sidelines had the mainland Communists attempted to invade Taiwan or vice versa. But once the Chinese had intervened with major force in Korea, driven American armed forces back down the Korean peninsula, and retaken Seoul, Washington policy toward Taiwan was reversed. The president ordered the U.S. Navy to patrol the straits and prevent either Chinese faction from crossing the straits. The effect was to put a protective American military arm around Taiwan. Chiang's regime was no longer under danger from the mainland. The U.S. Seventh Fleet stood between them and the Communists.

At this point it is timely to step back and notice that the original Communist initiative in Korea, which soon brought the United States into actual war with Chinese armies, also triggered American intervention in a second Asian theater of war, Vietnam. North Korea invaded South Korea on June 25, 1950. On June 26 President Truman decided to send American forces to the rescue of the South Korean regime that we Americans had set up in Seoul under Syngman Rhee. On June 27, when he ordered General MacArthur to send American forces to Korea, he also signed orders sending thirty-five U.S. military advisers to Vietnam and authorized a subsidy of $15 million in military aid to the French to help them sustain their colonial regime in Indochina, which included the country we came to know as Vietnam.

The major American involvement in Vietnam, which ultimately reached half a million troops, came under Pres. Lyndon Johnson in 1965, fifteen years later, but its genesis is from the same day, June 27, 1950, which saw the beginning of the Korean War.

For the next four years the United States steadily increased its military aid to the French while the French military effort steadily lost ground to the Communists led by Ho Chi Minh. The French effort came to a disastrous climax at Dien Bien Phu in 1954. Beginning on March 13, Communist forces began their bombardment of the French army of some thirteen thousand men trapped inside that jungle fortress. American pilots were able to airdrop enough supplies to keep the French garrison alive through March and April. But the Communists were able to bring up enough antiaircraft artillery to put an end to the air supply. On May 7 the white flag went up. The United States had spent roughly $3 billion in sustaining the French attempt to defeat the Communists in Vietnam. At the end there was nothing left to show for the investment. The Chinese had not put their own troops into the battle in Vietnam. In that phase of the twenty-two-year war the United States and China fought with proxies, the United States using the French, the Chinese using the Vietnamese Communists, but the sinews of war were supplied by mainland China versus the United States.

That was the second act in the series of Chinese-American wars. It ended in Geneva at a conference where the French agreed to leave Southeast Asia. The conferees divided the former French colony as Korea had been divided between north and south. John Foster Dulles, who by that time had finally taken over the State Department in Washington from Dean Acheson, was there as an observer. He declined to sign the documents reached by the other participants. I watched as he also refused to shake hands with China's prime minister, Chou En-lai.

That gesture of the refusal to shake hands with a Communist, albeit the prime minister of the most populous country on earth, was an indication of how intense were ideological emotions in those days. It was a symptom of the mental framework within which American foreign policy was operating. It was a by-product of the underlying assumption of a Communist world conspiracy controlled and directed from Moscow.

Back in Washington after the fall of Dien Bien Phu and after the division of Vietnam into a North and South, I began to wonder how seamless was that seamless cloak of communism. Stalin died on March 5, 1953, just after Dwight D. Eisenhower was inaugurated as president of the United States. That was three years after the military alliance between China and the Soviet Union had been signed. During those three years I had never detected any outwardly visible strain in that alliance. Nor do I recall anyone else pointing a finger at some event or remark and identifying it as a sign of disagreement between Moscow and Peking. But it was not long after Stalin died that unusual things began to happen. First, it was the withdrawal of Soviet troops from Dairen and Port Arthur, the two main seaports at the southern end of the Manchurian railway system. Next it was Soviet withdrawal from all of Manchuria. Finally, the Soviets pulled out of Sinkiang and gave up their share in joint stock companies in both Sinkiang and Tibet.

These were immensely valuable properties, both economically and strategically. Russia had long wanted Manchuria. Control over it was the main single issue in the Russo-Japanese war of 1904–5. It was amazing that within two years of Stalin's death his successors had given away an empire, plus the railway line that linked Soviet Central Asia most directly to ice-free seaports at Dairen and Port Arthur. I wrote then that there must be strains in the alliance. What I wrote was noticed by Mike Mansfield of Montana, a newly elected senator who in his youth had been a U.S. Marine in China. He and I from then on kept up a sort of China-watch of our own. Both of us believed that China would sooner or later break itself free from Soviet influence. He opened his own line of communication to China and argued for U.S. recognition of China.

By 1956 others were beginning to notice signs of strain in the Sino-Soviet relationship. Con O'Neil, a British Foreign Service officer, came back from a tour of duty in Peking in 1957 declaring that a break was inevitable. He said it might be years away, but that it was bound to come sooner or later. He was reprimanded for having entertained such an unorthodox idea.

Victor Zorza, a Russian expert writing for the *London Observer*, specialized in reading local provincial Russian newspapers. He deduced the break from obscure items such as an obituary for a soldier who had "died for his country" on the "far eastern front." But as late as 1968 Richard Allen, doing foreign policy on the Nixon campaign team and later in the Nixon White House, dismissed all such signs as being the result of either Western wishful thinking or Soviet disinformation aimed at lulling us into complacency.

In 1972 Richard Nixon recognized the reality of the Sino-Soviet break and went to China to capitalize upon it. But it was a long-delayed recognition of the known fact. The decisive moment probably came in 1958, when the Soviets refused nuclear weapons to the Chinese during the Quemoy-Matsu affair. The United States seemed to threaten to reinvade the Chinese mainland from the two offshore islands, which were still in Chinese Nationalist (Chiang Kai-shek) hands. The Chinese apparently wanted, and expected, both nuclear weapons for the Quemoy-Matsu battle and the technology for making their own nuclear weapons. The Soviets were not happy about having China become another nuclear power. They not only refused the technical information the Chinese needed but also, according to the Nixon White House, sounded out the Nixon administration on the idea of a preemptive Soviet strike against the Chinese nuclear test center at Lop Nor in Sinkiang.

Clear and public evidence of the Sino-Soviet break came in the winter of 1959–60, when the Soviets pulled their technicians out of China by the trainload, taking the factory blueprints along with them. But not until 1972 did American diplomacy recognize the opportunity and act to exploit it. Thus, it took twelve years from the actual break for American diplomacy to take advantage of the chance to help China escape from the Soviet embrace (by giving it an alternate source of modern technology). The Nixon trip, the first to China by an American president, left Russia without a single willing, major ally. By that time it had only Cuba and Vietnam left.

That long delay in doing something so obviously to American advantage was the result of that emotional anticommunism that was general in the West at the time and acute in the United States. To many people in Washington, particularly in high places, it was still unbelievable that a country calling its system Communist could be anything but an enemy of the United States and an ally of the Soviet Union.

That doctrine was irrational, as emotional feelings often are, but powerful. It was both fostered and exploited by the China lobby, which yearned for a reinvasion of China aimed at overthrowing the Mao Tse-tung regime and returning the Chiang Kai-shek dynasty. In their eyes anyone favoring relations with the Mao regime must be a Communist. The allegation was tossed about freely as the debate raged in Washington over whether to recognize the mainland regime.

The Nixon visit to China ended both the myth and the danger to the United States of "monolithic communism." China became a free agent in world affairs, independent of Moscow. Washington could cut back on its military burden. When Richard Nixon took office in 1969 the United States maintained a military establishment of three and a half million men to sustain a "two and a half war strategy." It was assumed in those days that the United States needed to be able to fight Russia, China, and Cuba all at the same time. After the Nixon trip to China Washington dropped down to a "one and a half war" concept and allowed U.S. armed forces to drop during the remaining Nixon years from the pre-Nixon level of three and a half million down to two and a half million.

The United States lost thirty-four thousand men killed in the Korean War and fifty-eight thousand in the Vietnam War. Were those wars necessary?

At the end of World War II the Communists in French Indochina led by Ho Chi Minh collaborated with the American forces. The OSS (forerunner of CIA) supplied them with funds and weapons. In return they rescued American pilots shot down in their area and provided information about Japanese forces and movements. It was the opinion of the OSS people who worked with them and also of State Department experts on Southeast Asia that the Ho Chi Minh forces were bona fide nationalists who would probably win the civil war that would follow inevitably the end of World War II. In the early postwar era Abbot Moffat, head of the Southeast Asia desk, recommended that the United States maintain friendly and supportive relations with Ho, who had asked for American help. Moffat recommended supporting Ho and refusing to let the French attempt to reclaim their former colonies. Moffat was overruled. The European desk needed French commitment to the new Western Europe that was the priority aim of postwar American diplomacy. Above all we sought to heal the ancient hostility between French and Germans. The French, in effect, made the recapture of their lost colonies the price for cooperation in Europe. We let them go back to Indochina, and we funded their long, bloody, and losing war against Ho Chi Minh. And when the

French lost we put our own troops in, all on the assumption that it was necessary if we were to prevent international communism from capturing all of Asia and sweeping out from Asia to contaminate other regions of the world.

The first part of the Korean War was unavoidable. The North Koreans invaded South Korea as blatantly as Saddam Hussein invaded Kuwait. They were certainly authorized by the Soviets to do it. We know that from Nikita Khrushchev's memoirs. Whether Moscow actually planned it is another matter, but at the very least the invasion was authorized, not discouraged, by Moscow. This posed a test of American willingness to sustain a policy of containment of Soviet imperialism. But that reasoning only applies up to the point where, after the Inchon landing, American armed forces had reliberated South Korea and reestablished a frontier along the 38th parallel.

The advance of American troops to the Yalu River in violation of Washington's orders to General MacArthur and in spite of an explicit warning from China brought on an actual war between the United States and China and helped to solidify the atmosphere in which the United States supported the French in Indochina and took over the burden there when the French failed. The United States in turn failed to overcome Ho Chi Minh's armies. The last gasp of American intervention was a helicopter lifting the American ambassador off the roof of his embassy in Saigon in 1975. Four years later a Chinese Communist army attacked Communist Vietnam. There has been continuing friction along the Chinese-Vietnam border ever since. And China itself, still Communist, long ago turned to the United States for protection against the Soviet Union.

One lesson to emerge from the Korean War certainly should not have needed learning. Big countries are sensitive to the approach of other countries' armies to their frontiers. MacArthur should never have been allowed to march north of the 38th parallel, and certainly not right on to the Yalu River—unless the United States deliberately sought a war with China, which no one in a responsible position in Washington consciously wanted. Observance of the Golden Rule (Do unto others as you would have them do unto you) would have spared the United States an unwanted war with China.

Another less obvious lesson is that ideology is a treacherous basis for national policy. In Washington the basic belief behind the twenty-two-year war with China was in the unity of the Communist world. There was a deep and widespread fear (called the domino theory) that if communism won in Vietnam it would sweep on through all of Southeast Asia and then spread north through the island chains, the Philippines and even Japan, and southwest to Africa. A speech by Lin Piao, Mao's principal deputy in China through the Great Cultural Revolution, talked about communism spreading out from Africa and Latin America and surrounding and choking the industrial democracies. It was taken seriously by many in Washington. It was part of the rationale behind the commitment of half a million American troops to the Vietnam War in 1965.

Since then China has invaded Vietnam and was beaten back with heavy casualties and there have been several battles along the Issuri River between Communist China and Communist Soviet Union.

Ideology influences the foreign policy of nations at times and in varying degrees, yet usually national interests take precedence over ideological interests. The classic case in point is the story of the religious wars of the seventeenth century. When those wars began in Germany in 1618, the German states divided into a Catholic League versus a grouping of the Protestant states. Protestant Sweden sent powerful armies to Germany in support of the Protestants against the Catholics and the Hapsburg Empire. Yet long before the end of those wars Catholic France joined with the Protestant Swedes in support of the Protestant Germans.

In the case of China and the Soviet Union, the common ideology of communism and a shared hostility toward the United States brought them together in the first instance. But the alliance was uneasy from the outset and began coming apart as soon as Stalin died in 1953. It was not in China's national interest to have the Soviets planted firmly in Manchuria, Sinkiang, and Tibet, all three being border provinces that the Chinese had long claimed as part of their natural sphere of influence. Mao began pushing the Soviets out of those provinces as soon as Stalin was replaced by lesser creatures in Moscow. There still remains Outer Mongolia, which in Chinese eyes belongs to China's national heritage but continued to 1990 as the most highly subsidized client state of the Soviet Union, favored even above Cuba. Someday the Chinese will probably manage to reclaim it.

It is a reasonable proposition that General MacArthur's unauthorized drive to the Yalu in 1950 delayed the break between Moscow and Peking by some five years, and thus by that amount of time the day when the

Chinese would turn away from Moscow and look to Washington for protection from Moscow. If Washington had been able to foresee the inevitability of the ultimate break, it might have avoided taking the actions that delayed it. Washington's own ideological myopia obscured that prospect.

NATO, a Limited Alliance

From the founding of the NATO alliance in 1949 and the rival Warsaw Pact in 1953 down to the breakup of the outer Soviet empire in 1989 the main story in the news and in the minds of all world leaders was of course the rivalry between the two great blocks of power, the one centered in Washington and the other in Moscow. The danger that a cold war would turn into a hot war was never far from the consciousness of everyone, high and low. This tended to obscure another story running through the history of those times and lasting as long.

That other story is about the troubles within the NATO alliance itself, which could easily have torn it apart.

Something of the flavor and intensity and danger in that story of events inside the alliance is conveyed by a personal experience. Step back mentally with me to 1956. The Israelis invaded Egypt first, on October 29; the British and French followed six days later. The United States voted in the United Nations to condemn these actions and to call for the immediate withdrawal of the invading forces. Here was the United States voting against its two closest allies, Britain and France, and against its special client, Israel.

That was the climax of the Suez crisis, which had been precipitated when Egypt's new, bold, and fiercely nationalist leader, Gamal Abdel Nasser, had seized and nationalized the Suez Canal. The British and French wanted it back and were in collusion with Israel to that end. But President Eisenhower was determined that they should not get it back.

My efforts as a reporter to get at the inside of this amazing story of a fractured alliance were hampered by the fact that most of the people I had known at the British Embassy had been recalled or posted elsewhere during the weeks immediately preceding these events. The ambassador, Roger Makins, whom I had known from wartime, was gone and replaced temporarily by one John Coulson, who had never been on post in Washington before and had no high-level personal connections in Washington. I had known him as a fellow student at Corpus Christi, Cambridge, but not well. Besides, it turned out that he was in total ignorance of what his country was doing.

Only one person of high British rank and with many friends in high places in Washington, Lord Harcourt, was left at the British Embassy and he was the Treasury representative, not a member of the Foreign Service. We happened to meet, by chance, at the Metropolitan Club, which was frequented in those days by State Department and friendly foreign embassy diplomats. He looked like a troubled and unhappy person. I did not need to ask a question. He volunteered the information I needed most to know. "Do you realize," he said, "that there is not a single person in your government today who will discuss money or oil with me?"

He went on to say that his friends, of whom he had many, were extremely polite. But when he mentioned money or oil the response was social, such as "Please give my regards to Lady Harcourt" or "Are you planning a holiday this winter?"

This was the roughest moment between allies in a series of difficulties inside the alliance. From the beginning NATO was organized to defend the countries on both sides of the North Atlantic. It had no other agreed function. But most of the members had interests outside their home territories. Did the alliance cover only the United Kingdom in its British islands off the coast of Europe or Britain with its vast overseas empire?

The problem of the alliance and the colonial empires of the various members of the alliance was present before the alliance was formed. Let us review the earlier examples and then return to the Suez affair, which was to be the most dramatic and wrenching test of the range of the alliance.

As World War II ended, the Dutch, French, and British went back as best they could to such colonies of theirs as had been overrun by the Japanese in Asia.

The Dutch mounted an immediate military campaign in the East Indies to suppress a native independence movement. They mounted a parallel propaganda campaign in the United States for U.S. support for their colonial effort. Part of the propaganda campaign was a free trip to the islands for a group of American journalists, including Charles Gratke, the foreign editor of my newspaper. The plane crashed near New Delhi on the return flight on July 15, 1949. All aboard were lost. Washington declined to provide support to the Dutch. They finally gave up and ceded sovereignty over most of the islands on December 27 of that year.

The turn of the French came next. Like the Dutch they wanted to get back their lost colonies. As related in the previous chapter, Abbot Moffat, who headed the Southeast Asia desk at the State Department, recommended against letting them come back. The United States had the decision; the U.S. Navy, having defeated Japan, held effective control of the entire Pacific basin. The French could not come back without our consent. Moffat favored withholding consent on the ground that the Viet Minh represented native nationalism and would ultimately be the winning local political force in the country. Moffat believed that it would be wise for the United States to associate with the ultimate winning side in what became Vietnam.

History proved Moffat to have been correct. The Viet Minh eventually won out over the French, over local rivals, and over the United States. We could have been spared the Vietnam War had Moffat's advice been accepted. It was not.

The French were allowed to send more troops to Vietnam and recapture control of the seaports and major cities. Washington helped with money and weapons. From 1946 to 1954 the French, with U.S. permission and support, waged a losing effort to regain effective control of what was still called Indochina.

The end of that story was painful for the French and for U.S. relations with the French. When the French army at Dien Bien Phu was hopelessly surrounded and running out of food and ammunition a U.S. naval force stood within aircraft range off shore. Its carriers were armed with nuclear weapons. The French asked for help. American weapons could, at least in theory, have saved Dien Bien Phu and spared the French the humiliation of the surrender. President Eisenhower said no.

French feelings were not soothed by the sequel. France agreed at a conference at Geneva to take all of its troops from the area and give up its prewar stake in Indochina. But the United States refused to recognize the division of the country into two Vietnams, a Communist north and a non-Communist south. Having let the French down, the Eisenhower administration then proceeded to back the non-Communist regime in the south headed by the Emperor Bao Dai, later by Ngo Dinh Diem. The pattern was set that led the United States into the longest war in its history and its first military defeat.

If, back in 1945 and 1946, more attention had been paid to Abbot Moffat and the OSS, much loss of life and treasure would have been avoided.

The United States had given the Dutch four years before letting them go down to defeat in Indonesia. They had given the French far greater support for twice as long, but then refused to accept the outcome intended by the others present at the Geneva conference. Ten years later, under Lyndon Johnson, the Americans plunged back in with arms and half a million American troops and tried to do what the French had failed to do. They also were unsuccessful.

Meanwhile the British had their turn at trying to salvage a remnant of their Victorian empire. The story began on April 6, 1955, when an ailing Winston Churchill finally, and reluctantly, surrendered the prime ministry of Great Britain to his longtime understudy, Anthony Eden. Churchill had done his best to "not preside over the dissolution of the British Empire" but even during his term as prime minister that process had gone on. On October 19, 1954, he had allowed the signing of an agreement with the new ruler of Egypt, Col. Gamal Abdel Nasser, providing for the withdrawal of all British military forces from Egypt by 1956. Eden had negotiated and signed the agreement as foreign minister. During the first months of his own tenure at 10 Downing Street he continued the policy of seeking friendly relations with Egypt. The United States and the United Kingdom together proposed substantial economic aid for Egypt and funding for the great high dam at Aswan that had long been an Egyptian dream. British troops would leave the vast military base that stretched ninety miles along the Suez Canal and that they had occupied for seventy-four years. In return Egypt would be friend, partner, and client.

That was not to be. The last British soldiers hauled down the Union Jack from the base at Suez on June 13, 1956, but by that time Colonel Nasser had become suspicious that Western economic aid could turn into a new form of Western colonialism. Further, his willingness to go ahead with the full terms of the 1954 project was decisively undermined when both the United States and United Kingdom declined to sell him anything like the quantity of modern weapons he wanted.

Israel was a key factor. Israel was deeply disturbed by withdrawal of British troops from Suez, where they had shielded Israel from Egypt. Removal of the troops ended security for Israel on its southern flank. The last thing Israel wanted was the new unshielded Egypt to be armed by the United States and United Kingdom. Every influence Israel could bring to bear in London and Washington was used to break up the emergence of a happy triangular relationship between the United States, the United Kingdom, and Mr. Nasser's Egypt.

How early and how hard the Israelis tried is illustrated by one particularly wild scheme ending in fiasco. In July 1954 Israeli military intelligence, Aman, planted a sabotage team in Egypt to attack both British and American properties in Cairo and Alexandria with fire bombs. The attacks took place on July 14 and 23 and might have caused trouble between Cairo and the British and Americans except that Egyptian police caught one of the Israeli agents when his phosphorus bomb exploded prematurely. The agent's apartment was full of sabotage equipment and Israeli training manuals. That was known as the Lavon Affair because Pinkas Lavon was Israeli minister of defense at the time. An investigation was unable to decide whether Lavon was personally guilty.

More effective than the bungled fire bombing was Israeli political influence in London and Washington blocking from Colonel Nasser the weapons his pride and his exuberant nationalism required. That in turn caused Colonel Nasser to think about cutting loose from U.S. and U.K. patronage and looking for his weapons elsewhere. A remarkable conference had been scheduled for April in Bandung, the summer capital of Indonesia. It was to be the first gathering of the nonaligned. It was a forum for all those countries with an inclination to keep out of the East-West rivalry of the great powers. It appealed to many who were emerging from nineteenth-century imperialism. Colonel Nasser attended. He met China's Chou En-lai. He asked Chou whether he might be able to get weapons from Russia. Chou agreed to pass the inquiry along. By September Nasser had a deal with Moscow for the weapons.

Back in London die-hard Tories were pushing at Eden to reverse course on dismantling the empire. They particularly resented the withdrawal from the great military base along the canal. The hauling down of the Union Jack for the last time on June 13, 1956, almost lit a fuse. A month later, on July 26, Colonel Nasser did light that fuse by seizing and nationalizing the canal. On the Tory side in Parliament it created an almost irresistible demand for getting back the canal. To Tories it was barely tolerable to have British troops leave while the canal continued to belong to an international company in which Britain was the largest stockholder. To have Colonel Nasser seize it outright and plant his troops along it, on both sides, was too much.

Add that on May 26, just two months before Nasser nationalized the canal, the Tories had won a general election with a significantly improved majority. They had won in 1951 by a majority of seventeen seats. In 1955, led by Eden taking over from the sadly faltering Churchill, they won a broad majority of sixty seats. The Tories could think of a possible reversal, or at least of halting the retreat from empire.

Add a third element to this powder magazine. The French were deep in their own crisis over Algeria. Half the people of France were determined to keep it. They claimed it as part of France. Half were ready to let the Algerians have their freedom. Passions were at a white heat. In Paris, on the Champs Elysée, mobs were shouting, "Algérie Française" and "De Gaulle au pouvoir." In the Place de la Bastille equally angry mobs were screaming, "De Gaulle au poteau" (De Gaulle to the gallows). Both groups were acting on the mistaken assumption that if De Gaulle were to come to power Algeria would remain French forever.

Colonel Nasser had been encouraging and helping the Algerians.

By July 26, when Nasser took the canal away from the Suez Canal Company, in which the British held a majority of the stock, there were thus three important powers in a mood to do unpleasant things to him. The Israelis wanted the British back on the canal and the whole of the Sinai Peninsula and the Gaza Strip in their own hands. The French wanted pressure on Nasser to force him to stop encouraging the Algerians. And half of the British, reliving their memories of "the thin red line" that, running through Suez, had bound Kipling's Victorian empire together, wanted the canal back.

The stage was set for the next phase in the great Suez crisis. Inevitably, Britain, France, and Israel began talking to each other about taking collective action.

The details of the fighting that emerged from this extraordinary conjunction of purposes is told sufficiently in other places. It is necessary here only to note that Israel's forces surged into the Sinai Peninsula on October 29 in secret collusion with the French and British. On the following day, in accordance with the secret plan, Eden announced an ultimatum to Israel and Egypt demanding a withdrawal of *both* their forces from the Canal Zone. (That would have left Israel in possession of the entire Sinai Peninsula up to the Canal Zone, and Britain and France free to take back the canal itself.) Nasser defied the ultimatum.

The British and French bombed Nasser's airfields on the evening of October 31, their paratroopers landed at the entrance to the canal on November 5, and their main invasion fleet arrived off Suez before dawn of November 6. That delay of six days between the bombing on October 31 and the arrival of the ground landing force on November 6 was fatal to the project. It was during those days that Bill Harcourt in Washington was trying to talk about oil and money and getting polite, social remarks in return. The British and French troops stormed ashore at dawn on the sixth after a forty-five minute preliminary artillery bombardment and more bombing. But on that same morning in London at a cabinet meeting Harold Macmillan, then chancellor of the exchequer, reported a disastrous run on the pound. Britain's gold reserve had dropped by a hundred million pounds. And there would soon have to be oil rationing if the fighting continued.

The landing and the ground fighting began early on the sixth. Before the day was over Eden had agreed to a cease-fire to begin at midnight London time—two o'clock in the morning of the seventh at the canal. It was one of history's shortest wars. The swift end had been imposed by many factors in the situation, including threatening noises from Moscow. But the decisive action was the quiet order passed down from the White House to all officials of the U.S. government in Washington that any question from any British official about oil or money was to be met by a polite social response.

It was an awesome example of the power of the American presidency to act in unseen ways. There was no official embargo, no public boycott, no proclamation. There was just a quiet evasion when anyone from the British Embassy tried to raise the two matters which were vital to the survival of the British government. Unseen by the public, Britain was literally being choked.

The unseen and silent choking did not end with the ceasefire. President Eisenhower had no intention of letting the British regain the canal or the Israelis keep the Sinai Peninsula. Money and oil would be available, but only if and when they had taken their troops off Egyptian soil. Eden was reluctant, and that is when Sir Harold Caccia arrived to rebuild the British Embassy staff in Washington and his country's relations with the United States.

Eden's preparations for the Suez venture had included, as we noted earlier, stripping the embassy in Washington of its top people who had personal connections in Washington. This had made it impossible for anyone in the embassy to leak Eden's intentions, but it also complicated his damage control during the heat of the venture.

The new ambassador, Harold Caccia, who did have excellent Washington connections, arrived on November 7. A few days later I was invited to a small dinner for him. Present also were Supreme Court Justice Felix Frankfurter and Walter Lippmann and James R. Reston of the *New York Times*. Mr. Caccia told us he too was finding no one ready to talk about oil and money. What was he to do? He turned first to Frankfurter. Then to the others. Each in turn gave an opinion. When we had finished he said, "Do you people realize what you have said? Do you realize that in effect you are telling me that to get relations between our two countries back on track I must tell my prime minister to resign?" We agreed that that was the case.

One thing that neither Anthony Eden nor Israel's leaders had considered in their planning for the Suez affair was that Washington would actually take physical steps to block their purposes. They expected raised eyebrows and a "tut tut," but not what happened. Golda Meir visited Washington after the dust had settled. I was present in a group of reporters invited for a postmortem. She asked us collectively whether we thought Eisenhower actually would have cut off private as well as public aid to Israel if the Israelis had refused to take their troops out of the Sinai Peninsula and Gaza. She found it difficult to believe that he would really have done so. Most of us were, on the contrary, very sure that he meant business.

To me the pressure on Israel was less surprising than the pressure on Britain. Ike had little use for Israel. He probably had no qualms about forcing it to go back. But it was hard for him to take such strong measures against a Britain whose troops had served under his command in World War II and that still was his close and most important ally. It was also hard for me. This was one of the times in my journalistic career when I got it wrong. At the time it never occurred to me that Eden was lying when he pretended that he was not a party to the Israeli invasion of the Sinai. It took me weeks to begin to realize and accept that it had all been a collusive plot.

Partly my naiveté about Eden and Suez was left over from school days. My generation grew up on English heroes from King Arthur through Drake and Raleigh to Nelson and Wellington. Partly it was also due to the remarkable closeness between the two countries during World War II. Winston Churchill remarked after Pearl Harbor that the two countries were bound to get mixed up together during the course of the war. As a war correspondent my accreditation was as good with a British unit as with an American. We wore identical markings and uniforms. We traveled as much with one army or navy as with another. I felt as free to ask questions and seek information from a British headquarters as from an American. In my own general attitude toward the two governments distinctions became blurred. We were more than allies. The relationship was very close. I could not at the time of Suez really believe that the British government could deliberately deceive the American government.

The Netherlands, France, and Britain were not the only countries to discover that the NATO alliance did not work outside the North Atlantic basin. The first outbreak of real war to emerge from East-West rivalry was in Korea. One evening in Washington shortly after the North Koreans had surged across the frontier and driven Americans and South Koreans down into the perimeter at Pusan, and when the fighting was getting uncomfortably serious, there was a gathering of State Department people with several from the British Embassy and a few journalists. During a lull in the general conversation I, with normal journalistic brashness, asked of a Britisher, "When are you going to send some troops over there to help us." Dead silence for half a minute. Then H. Freeman Matthews, who at that time was undersecretary of state for political affairs, said: "I didn't hear the answer." There was no answer.

Washington greatly wanted its allies to join in the fight for South Korea. The British eventually sent a Commonwealth Division with a battalion of the Yorkshires which performed heroically during the rout of the U.S. Second Division. The "Yorks" were largely responsible for keeping the escape route open for the "Seconds." Most of the men of that division escaped, although leaving their heavy equipment behind. The Turks also sent fighting troops, who performed well. But mostly, the war in Korea was an American show. The reluctance of the others to get involved was symptomatic of the attitude of all members of the alliance to anything happening outside Western Europe and North America. The security of those two parts of the world is what the NATO alliance was all about.

And that also gives us the essential clue to what the long tension of the cold war was really all about.

World War II was a profoundly unsettling event. It unsettled most of the long established centers and frontiers of power. Germany and Japan were mighty powers at the beginning of the war. They were nothing at its end. The British Empire reached its utmost expanse immediately after the war, but its fabric was overstretched by the war. Its dissolution was coming. The phrase *third world* crept into our vocabulary. What was the third world? It was a collection of countries or areas all of which had belonged to some European power before World War I. Suddenly after World War II they were unanchored. They floated loose in uncharted seas.

It is impossible today to convey to anyone born since the Korean War the sense of anxiety that pervaded Washington on June 25, 1950, when the news came in that the armies of North Korea, backed, we presumed, by the might of Russia and the manpower of China, had invaded South Korea. "Communism" (meaning Soviet imperialism) was on the march. Was this the beginning of the big push intended to overwhelm all of those floating third world countries that for so long had belonged to Europe and to the Western economic community?

Only three years before, in 1947, Dean Acheson thought that "we were met at Armageddon." He believed that Soviet pressure on Iran, Turkey, and Greece "had brought the Balkans to the point where a highly possible Soviet breakthrough might open three continents to Soviet penetration."

That crisis had been averted by the Marshall Plan, the Truman Doctrine, and the NATO alliance. But now, only three years later, here was an actual military offensive aimed at seizing South Korea, which, militarily, is vital to the security of Japan. Only the year before, in midsummer in China, the pro-Western regime of Chiang Kai-shek had collapsed. Chiang fled to Taiwan, taking a remnant of his army with him. Now all of mainland China was united under Communist rule and allied with Moscow. Within the same month, the Soviets enjoyed their first successful nuclear missile test. Then Communists invaded South Korea.

In Washington's minds the meaning of the sequence was unavoidable. Communism had won China. It now ruled everything from the Elbe River in Europe to the China Sea. It had achieved the nuclear deterrent. It was in a position to launch a major offensive safe from the American nuclear monopoly. Never had Moscow been so powerful or in such a position for launching a broad offensive aimed at control over most of the third world. Some of the more enthusiastic Chinese leaders began talking about communism sweeping out through Southeast Asia, capturing Africa and Latin America, and isolating the last bastions of capitalism in Western Europe and North America. There was plenty of Communist rhetoric to stimulate Washington's worst fears.

There was a sequel to the Suez story for me in London. In July 1957, six months after the painful experiences Lord Harcourt and Sir Harold

Caccia had in Washington, I arrived in London on assignment for NBC. A chance acquaintance invited me for a drink at White's Club. White's, for the uninitiated, is the heartland of high Torydom. The building on the outside is a fine, restrained, gentleman's Georgian town house a few doors up St. James's Street from Boodle's, where the country gentry tend to gather, and across the street from Brooks's, which once was the London center for the great Whig aristocrats. White's was something else again. Country gentry and Whig aristocrats would be equally uncomfortable at White's. It is unlikely that any member of White's could have entertained a shadow of doubt about the desirability and propriety of Eden's attempt to regain the Suez Canal. If one had, he would have kept his doubts to himself. The word must have been passed before I arrived at White's that a "Yank" was coming in. I arrived, was backed into a corner of the bar, and was immediately assailed verbally by a good dozen members, who proceeded to accuse my country of trying to destroy the British Empire. The exercise was known as Yank baiting. It was practiced by those present as vigorously and relentlessly as the same persons would chase a fox or tramp the grouse moors in season. It was the roughest debate I was ever pushed into. I defended myself well enough to earn an invitation to join the St. James's Club, which was frequented more by diplomats than by those who rode to hounds. But I had learned the hard way that the British felt we Americans had let them down badly over the Suez affair. The boundaries around the NATO alliance had been identified for all to see. It did not apply to the prewar colonies of its members.

Postscript

Shortly after my ordeal at the bar at White's, William Clark invited me to do a weekend of grouse shooting with him at his brother's castle in Northumberland. I had never before been on a grouse moor, nor had I ever even held a shotgun in my hands, much less pulled the trigger, but the idea of going "grouse shooting" on a north country moor was irresistible. I accepted in cheerful ignorance of what lay ahead. I had known William Clark in Washington, where he had been a correspondent for the *Manchester Guardian*. When Eden took over Number 10 Downing Street from Churchill he invited William to join him as his press officer. During the Suez crisis William found himself trying to justify to his former journalistic friends and colleagues a policy with which he was in profound disagreement. He could not resign while British troops were under fire (part of the unwritten British code of the gentleman), but he could, and did, resign as soon as Eden agreed to the cease-fire. This, it turned out, was regarded by his brothers up in Northumberland as virtually treasonable. William had not visited his family in Northumberland from the moment of his resignation. The grouse-shooting weekend was to be an attempted moment of reconciliation with his family. I was being taken along to provide a cushion between William and the brothers. They would hardly be as rough on him with an American foreigner present as would otherwise be the case.

William's older brother, John, lived in the country near Hexham, which is the main town along the Roman wall between Carlisle and Newcastle. John did live in a castle, but it was not a castle in the sense of Windsor or the Tower of London or Dover castle. It was actually a peel tower, meaning a single tower with a walled enclosure big enough to take in the local cattle when the wild Scots came down over the border in a cattle-raiding expedition. The tower itself was open on the ground level for feeding the cattle; kitchen and dining room were one flight up, bedrooms up two more flights. It was a single family dwelling built in the fourteenth or fifteenth century when the Scots still practiced cattle raiding as a way of life. And it did have a moor just outside. In the morning William, brother John, and I went off to the moor with a single dog to rouse the grouse. I was attired in waterproof trousers and jacket, which I soon had to shed as we tramped through hip-high grass. I shot several times in the general direction of a grouse, but hit nothing, which probably was just as well because William actually brought down two or three grouse. This gave him a slight improvement in his stature in the eyes of his brother. At least he could shoot better than the Yank. Thanks to my presence at all family gatherings over the weekend there was consistent civility between William and his two brothers. My presence was justified, and I had all I would ever need of tramping across a grouse moor. My advice to anyone invited for a similar shoot (as distinct from the kind where beaters drive the birds to stationary shooters) is to dress light, not heavy. It is hard and hot work just getting through that heavy grass. (Incidentally, a peel tower has only space for one bathroom and, in that case, only enough hot water for a single tub. I got first use, but was warned to use as little soap as possible for the benefit of the two others who would be using the same water after me.)

William never returned to government work in England. He went to India for a while, "to let things settle down in London," returned to head an institute set up to aid former British colonies, then went to the World Bank in Washington, where he wrote speeches for Robert McNamara.

The Delights of London

The verbal battle at White's was my initiation to London club life. It was also the beginning of a happy, if perhaps unwise, interlude in my career. Walter Lippmann urged me to stay in Washington. He said London would be a detour in my career. He was probably correct. It was a seven-year detour, during which I lost my place in the line of Washington journalists. Once one steps out of that line he seldom, if ever, comes back. Add that there are few lateral entries. David Schoenbrun of CBS tried it and came to early grief. He announced as he left Paris for Washington that he was going to show the corps of Washington correspondents how to cover Washington. They saw to it, collectively, that he never made the grade. His career in Paris had been a spectacular success. It went straight downhill from the moment he hit Washington.

On several occasions before my decision to go to London Walter Lippmann had talked about the possibility of having me share in writing his illustrious newspaper column. At one time he talked of having me write once a week under his title "Today and Tomorrow." At other times he spoke of collaboration and a joint byline on the column. In spite of that prospect, I found that I couldn't refuse when Bill McAndrew, head of news at NBC, offered me the post of NBC senior European correspondent based in London. I loved London from my occasional visits to it during my student days at Cambridge. I love England: its climate, its food, its traditions, its style of life. The two happiest years of my early life were those spent at Cambridge steeping myself in history between afternoons on the river pulling an oar through water in the company of seven other hearty young men. I can still feel the thrill of the moment when, on a raw, rainy day with fingers numb from the cold, we eight suddenly found ourselves rowing in perfect rhythm. The boat leapt forward. From the day I came down from Cambridge I yearned to go back to England. When offered a chance I could not resist.

Walter Lippmann remained a friend. When he and Helen made their annual progression to Europe, Anne and I would be informed in advance of their schedule in London and we would be offered "a day." That meant a dinner party at our house at Number 12 Hanover Terrace. I had noticed Hanover Terrace in my student days. I had dreamed of living there sometime. We had driven by it on Sunday mornings when I was visiting the Olliers for a weekend. Louis Ollier was an American businessman in London, vice-president for Europe of the Studebaker Corporation of South Bend, Indiana. He had a wife and two daughters whom he hoped someday to present at court. They lived in elegance in a house at Mill Hill that had once been a hunting lodge for King Charles I. There were butlers and chauffeurs at Bittacy House, and the household on Sunday always drove into town, men wearing morning coats and top hats, to church (they were Christian Scientists) by way of Regent's Park and Hanover Terrace, which is a row of houses all together in a single harmonious unit that looks like a palace and in fact belongs to the Crown. All persons living at Hanover Terrace are tenants of the Crown. It is a pleasant feeling being a Crown tenant. As we drove by that terrace I resolved that someday I would live there, and the day came when I did. It took some doing. I first bought a sublease to the three middle floors, then another sublease to the top floor, finally the actual Crown lease from a Dr. Choyce who lived in the basement. I could call the whole house my own. Once a year the Lippmanns came to dine, and we had among our guests many a politician (once a deputy prime minister) and on one occasion even royalty, Prince William of Gloucester, whom we seated next to Helen Lippmann, who obviously enjoyed his company. He was an extremely attractive young man, who sadly and most unfortunately flew an airplane into the ground soon thereafter. The Lippmanns came to dinner every year while we were in London, but Walter never again mentioned collaboration on his column. I had declined his advice and taken myself away from Washington, which was the main source for the material of his columns.

Thus I gave up a possible chance (never made specific) to be Walter Lippmann's journalistic associate in Washington in return for my seven years in London. What did I get for it and was it worth it?

Just living at 12 Hanover Terrace was a plus. It was half the width of the Bellamy house in *Upstairs, Downstairs*, but in other respects similar. There was a below-ground entrance for tradesmen and servants and a green baize cover over the door that separated the Upstairs from the Downstairs. During much of our tenure at Number 12 a Mrs. Baker presided over the Downstairs as firmly as Mr. Hudson ever did in the Bellamy household. The house was five stories high. There was a basement with kitchen below, then the main floor with dining room in front and small reception room behind. The drawing room was a flight up in front with french doors opening on a balcony that looked out over Regent's Park. There were two floors of bedrooms and baths above, a total of five bedrooms. Guests arrived at the front door, which was sheltered under an arcade running the entire length of the terrace. The arcade supported the balcony, which also ran the full length of the building, making it look like a single, harmonious structure. The first time my top boss, David Sarnoff, came to dinner after we had settled into Hanover Terrace he expressed surprise to discover his London correspondent living in "a palace." He was visibly impressed. Howard K. Smith, my opposite number at CBS, lived in similar quarters at Clarence Terrace a half mile away, also on the park. The location was convenient for both of us because our respective offices were located near Broadcasting House, home of the BBC, whose facilities we both used frequently. Those terrace houses around Regent's Park had been built by King George IV's favorite architect, John Nash, sometime between 1810 and 1820. To live in one was to catch something of the flavor of English upper-class life in the prosperous and expansive era that followed immediately after the Napoleonic wars, when Britain was the first true superpower of the modern world.

There were many other pluses for me and my family from those seven years in London. For one year we had all three of our sons with us. Our oldest, William, was then a student at Williams College in Massachusetts. I managed to arrange an exchange for him with a student at my former college at Cambridge, Corpus Christi. Our second son, Jonathan, spent that same year at Westminster School, which occupies much of the close of Westminster Abbey. We brought our youngest, Paul, with us and he spent most of our London years at a boarding school near Oxford. Family memories include both Bill and Jonathan rowing at Henly, Bill in the Corpus First Boat and Jonathan for Westminster. I visited Bill at Cambridge shortly after he started his year there. As we were walking back from tea at a don's house, where one of his children was lugging a cello on his way to a string quartet rehearsal and another was just in from a rehearsal for a Restoration drama titled " 'Tis a Pity She's a Whore," Bill remarked, "Gee, Pop, there's a lot of culture here." Jonathan came home usually for weekends. On one I asked him, "Precisely where is the chapel at your school?" He looked down on me from his superior six-foot height and informed me, "We don't go to chapel, we go to abbey." Literally, his chapel service each morning was in the choir stalls of Westminster Abbey, with the helm and shield of Edward, the Black Prince, hanging overhead. Paul's school was near Oxford in a Jacobean manor house surrounded by woods, pastures, and playing fields. On one occasion when Anne and I drove there for a weekend visit he came running toward the car to meet us, beaming with obvious pride, and breathlessly informed us that "I had six-of-the-best and didn't cry once. Sykes cried." Six-of-the-best meant a caning at the hand of the headmaster. The lad who could take it without crying was admired by his peers. Paul was often applauded on the rugger field and called "the best fly half the side ever had." Mrs. Baker at 12 Hanover Terrace was always happiest when one or more of the boys came home for a holiday or weekend. After a particularly lively weekend I found her a day or so later in a real sulk. "What in the world is the matter with you?" I asked. She snapped back at me, "Insufficient male companionship, of course." There was always chocolate cake "Downstairs" when the boys were at home.

There was plenty of news in and from London during those seven years. London is a major hub on the airlines of the world. When Nehru died in India I was able to get to New Delhi from London quicker than any other NBC correspondent. Getting to Geneva was still quicker. One year I spent roughly a third of my time in Geneva at one conference after another having to do with trying to resettle the world after the vast upheaval of World War II. I also managed several more trips to Eastern Europe. I was back in Warsaw in December 1956, a month after the Hungarian rising and its vicious suppression by Russian tanks, when without advance warning the foreign minister of China, Chou En-lai, appeared at a diplomatic reception. A veteran Austrian ambassador who had had his training in the days of the Hapsburg Empire remarked that China had chosen to play a role in Europe again "for the first time since Genghis Khan." China did not like what Moscow had done to Hungary. It put a protective arm around Poland's shoulder by sending Chou En-lai to Warsaw. It also fortified my conviction that strains were developing between Peking and Moscow.

Following the collapse of Anthony Eden's Suez venture in late 1956, and under Washington pressure, Eden did resign and the prime ministry of Britain was handed over to Harold Macmillan partly because he had been a political adviser to General Eisenhower during the war and was supposed to have good personal relations with the man who by then was president of the United States. It worked. The relationship was quickly patched up. American credits and American-controlled oil were released to Britain, and Mr. Macmillan proceeded with a favorite Tory project: decontrol of rents. Freshets of new money welled up as though out of the streets all over England but, particularly, in London where rents had long been frozen, during the war as a wartime measure and after the war by Socialist dogma. The result of the unfreeing was spectacular. London spruced itself up. Buildings were cleaned. Flower boxes appeared in windows. New restaurants opened. Women's clothes became livelier in style and in color—and Christine Keeler was noticed in the swimming pool at Cliveden by John Profumo.

London in those days was having its first taste of high living since before the Great Depression of the thirties. There was plenty of money. It was spent freely and in the spending gave the Fleet Street press a feast of boisterous scandals. John Profumo was both a prominent social personality with a Hollywood actress wife, Valerie Hobson, and also secretary of state at the War Office. Somehow word leaked out that a Soviet military attaché had been an acquaintance of Miss Keeler before her unadorned figure in the Cliveden swimming pool caught the attention of Mr. Profumo. Add that Cliveden was the country estate of the Astor family. Here were the makings of a story that dominated the popular press for a good year and provided Britain with welcome light diversions after years of war followed by Socialist austerity. I came to London in 1957 to find a replay of what London must have been like when the civil wars ended and the austerity of Oliver Cromwell and his Puritans was swept aside as King Charles II reclaimed the throne for the Stuart family and launched the social and cultural permissiveness of the Restoration.

As at the time of the Restoration the theater flourished and incidentally solved a dangerous dilemma for me. When I had my instructions for my behavior in my new post from Bill McAndrew, he warned that General Sarnoff would be making an annual visit to London and that my first duty in London would be the proper care of the General, who at that time was chairman of the board of RCA, which wholly owned NBC. At NBC he was referred to as the General in a tone of voice that implied virtual equation with the Deity. He had acquired his military title during the war when he had served as a top communications officer for the Allied High Command. He was well known in London and was given red carpet treatment by old friends and acquaintances when he came.

On the General's first visit after my arrival my office staff, knowing the routine, arranged for the best river-view suite at the Savoy, his favorite hotel, and also a Rolls Royce to meet him at the pier in Southampton. (He always came by ship, which meant one of the two queens, Queen Mary or Queen Elizabeth.) I went down with the Rolls to Southampton and stood deferentially at the foot of the gangplank when the General and Mrs. Sarnoff descended. Meanwhile a man from the Savoy Hotel had extracted the Sarnoff luggage from the ship and we were quickly on our way to London. Mrs. Sarnoff, whom I met for the first time, was of French background, highly educated, and of cultured and gracious manners. The General was keenly interested in the latest news of cold war events, which was my specialty. We had a pleasant trip, and all went well until the last moment at the hotel when the luggage had arrived and been stowed and the General said, "Now, we want to go to the theater tonight." I said, "Very good, sir, what would you like to see?" He replied, "A leg show." I started to say, "Very good, sir," but Mrs. Sarnoff interrupted and said, "I do not want a leg show." I looked from one to the other, gulped inwardly, and was not helped out of the quandary by the General telling me to "pick something." Back at the office I called Anne and related the problem. She replied that it was no problem. We would take them to see *Irma La Douce*, then newly opened and the latest hit on the London stage. It had one pair of lovely and well-displayed female legs, but set in such a sophisticated French context that no person of French culture could be offended. The General was delighted by the legs, Mrs. Sarnoff was delighted by the context, and my tenure as NBC's London Bureau chief was confirmed.

The Sarnoffs usually dined with us at Hanover Terrace on their visits. On one such evening the General told of his first visit to London as a child with his mother, on their way from a village "somewhere between Minsk and Pinsk" to New York where the father had gone ahead to find a home for them. His family had walked from their village in Russia to Danzig, taken ship to London, stayed with relatives in East London in the dock area, and gone on by train to Liverpool, by ship to Montreal, by train to Albany, and by a Hudson River steamboat down to New York, where they arrived in midsummer wearing their heavy Russian clothes. The father was ill. David was peddling newspapers the next day, to help support the family.

Many another amenity came my way during the years in London. Hanover Terrace itself was redolent of English history. H. G. Wells had lived next door at Number 13. The composer Ralph Vaughan Williams lived down the other way at Number 9. Lovely paths wandered through the woods and dells of Regent's Park across the street. The whole of the island of Great Britain (England, Scotland, and Wales) was within a weekend range of London. We traveled widely, both in the British Isles and farther afield—winter skiing in Austria, a summer holiday with full family in Brittany, a group tour of the Middle East to see "the rose red city" of Petra, which someone said was "twice as old as time."

Add to the above the sheer joy of some of the journalistic assignments. The great funeral for Winston Churchill was, I suppose, the most moving human drama in which I ever had a part. I did a voice-over for NBC during much of the ceremony. At one point I did a guest performance for British Independent Television that gave me my one and only presence on the same stage with the great Lawrence Olivier. My part was to read a passage from one of Lincoln's speeches for which they wanted an American accent. Several other people were reading other documents appropriate to the occasion. Each had a lighted lecturn on a darkened stage. Next to me was Olivier. I came in ready to read without doing more than scan my part. I found Olivier repeating a word or a phrase over and over again to get the intonation just right. I learned from watching him something of how hard a great actor actually does work over his delivery of words and phrases.

And one day I went to the palace to have lunch with the queen. It was customary then, and perhaps still is, for an American correspondent long in London to be included occasionally in one of the queen's Thursday luncheons. These were arranged to include eight guests. The queen and Prince Philip sit opposite each other. A gentleman-in-waiting takes one end of the table and a lady-in-waiting takes the other. Then, with eight guests, each is seated next to at least one member of the household. I drew a seat to the left of the gentleman-in-waiting. To my left was Dame Barbara Salt, first British woman ambassador, who was seated on Prince Philip's right. The table was too large for general conversation, but we all kept an eye on the queen. As she turned from the guest on her right to the one on her left all the rest of us turned also from side to side. I can report that the food was excellent and the service perfect. The best hotel in London in my day there was the Connaught, and the best restaurant in terms of prestige as well as quality of food and service was the grill at the Connaught. The service at the palace was even better, largely because the ratio of staff to guests was higher. If I recall correctly there were four full butlers plus four footmen. No plate was ever left empty.

Of the conversation I remember only overhearing Prince Philip discussing with a yachtsman guest on his left the possibility of England putting a worthy challenger into the next race off Newport, Rhode Island, for the America's Cup. Affairs of state were not settled, or even mentioned, at that luncheon, but it was extremely pleasant to have lunched with the queen.

Another happy experience occurred on my last day in London. When I came into the office Flo Peart, our highly competent office manager, informed me that the Foreign Office had called and she had taken the liberty of making an appointment for me with Sir Paul Gore-Booth, who at that time held the top career post in the Foreign Office, that of permanent undersecretary. I had known Paul well from long before when he held a lower post at the British Embassy in Washington. I knew him so well that I walked to the nearest chair and started to sit down without waiting to be invited. Paul stiffened in a most formal manner and said, "Joe, first, Her Majesty. . . ." I blinked and stood up. He completed the sentence, "has instructed me to inquire whether you would accept a CBE." By that time I gurgled incoherently something like "Gosh, golly, gee whiz." Paul thought I was hesitating and added, "Joe, you would be two pips up on the Beatles." I replied, "Oh, that doesn't matter, I would be one pip up on Drew Middleton."

All of the above of course calls for an explanation. The Order of the British Empire (OBE) was instituted by King George V during World War I largely for use with colonials and assorted foreigners. It comes in four ranks: Member, Officer, Commander, Knight. The Beatles are Members, which is indicated by the initials MBE. Drew Middleton was the chief London correspondent of the *New York Times* during my time in London. His behavior pattern showed an overtone of assumption of being therefore the first American correspondent in London—or so it seemed to the rest of us. Drew had long since been awarded the OBE. My CBE would outrank him by, in the English vernacular, "one pip." I was vain enough to be delighted at the prospect of being "one pip up" on Drew, who I knew would feel that someone on Her Majesty's staff had made a crashing blunder by giving me the CBE over his OBE. Needless to say, I assured Paul that I would be happy to accept my CBE, which is a very pretty medal in the shape of a Maltese cross with the faces of George V and Queen Mary in the center in enamel, the same to be worn with white tie and tails hanging from a fine pink ribbon. I find I have few occasions for wearing it, but it's pleasant to have in my bureau drawer and is one compensation for having missed the chance, if it ever existed, to have been Walter Lippmann's journalistic collaborator.

Incidentally, Anne doubts that Walter ever would have brought himself actually to share his column with me or anyone else.

The Communist Alliance

On an early visit to Warsaw I was impressed by the apparent sincerity of one of the young editors I met at a gathering of Polish and Western journalists. I am not going to use his name lest it might still embarrass him at home. As a matter of fact I was careful for his protection never to put his name in writing in my notes. Hence, at this later day I am not even sure of his full name. Our acquaintance started with a brisk debate over the merits of communism versus a free-market economy. I found him intelligent and not dogmatic. He argued the case for the Communist system with conviction but also with objectivity. He recognized the extent to which it had been abused in some Communist countries and turned into a mere excuse for a brutal dictatorship. He recognized that the theoretical goals of a Communist system might prove to be impractical and unworkable in a sophisticated modern society. In other words, he could think objectively. I sought him out always as soon as I reached Warsaw. Our conversational repertoire soon left communism-versus-capitalism behind and went on to the future of Soviet relations with the other countries in the Communist community. The biggest single question in the minds of both of us was the prospective life of the Chinese-Soviet relationship. He insisted that it was durable for the simple reason that each needed the other. Moscow's interest in that relationship was obvious. Having China on its side was an enormous advantage in the world's balance of power. So long as a working military alliance lasted Moscow enjoyed effective control over everything lying between the Elbe River, in Central Europe, and the China Sea. For China the relationship offered weapons, access to modern technology, assistance in rebuilding industry, and protection against any capitalist state's attempt to regain a prewar position in China. It made sense and it worked for a while. Years later, in 1988, as tourists, my wife and I stayed for a night in Sian (pronounced She-ahn), the city famous for the buried ceramic army, in a hotel built by Soviet architects during the Soviet-alliance era. We were most grateful when a mistake by the local tourist agency was discovered and we were moved to the modern Golden Chain Hotel, which had been built and was being run by a Swedish hotel company. The change was a blissful relief. The Golden Chain Hotel in Sian is attractive, light in tone, comfortable, and efficient in all respects. I have been in many of the world's finest hotels. You can't find a better hotel, with better equipment or better service or better food, than the Golden Chain in Sian. The Soviet-era hotel from which we escaped was by contrast a sort of medieval dungeon. It was dank, heavy, dingy, and dull; the food was as uninteresting as only an official Chinese government restaurant can produce. The hotel was adequate. The equipment worked, even a TV set, but it was so marvelously dreary! There are similar hotels dating from the Soviet-alliance era in all the main cities of China. The Soviets came to China in large numbers during the alliance period from 1949 to 1960, and they built hotels and factories, but the buildings were not what any Westerner would consider modern. Architecturally they are from the early Stalin era.

Does the very obsoleteness of Moscow's contributions to China during the alliance era give us a clue as to why the Sino-Soviet relationship ended so quickly and decisively and produced one of the most intractable hostilities in this world? Even Mikhail Gorbachev, the Great Peacemaker, was unable to woo the Chinese back into a reasonably friendly relationship. To this day there is more friction and less collaboration in the Sino-Soviet relationship than in China's relations with Japan, the United States, or Western Europe.

According to the common wisdom the break between Moscow and Peking started during the Quemoy-Matsu affair of 1958–59 with the refusal of Moscow to give the Chinese nuclear weapons. Nikita Khrushchev compounded that failure by seeking easier relations with the Americans. The word *appeaser* began appearing in Chinese comments on Soviet policy. By 1964 both Soviets and Chinese were building up their troop levels along their common frontier and the Chinese had built a rival network of pro-Chinese Communist parties around the world. In almost every country they either captured the local Communist party from the pro-Soviet element or built a new and rival Communist party. Ideologically, a schism had split the Communist world.

How does a Western reporter learn about such things? My anonymous Polish editor came to me one day in Warsaw in 1959 and said, "Joe, I have so often told you it could not happen that I feel I must tell you now that it has happened. There is a split. It is real." But how and why did it happen? His version is clearly not the whole story but a fragment of the story. He himself was a member of the Central Committee of the Polish Communist party. He told me he and his colleagues had been summoned hastily to a special meeting the previous day at party headquarters. His party leader, Vladislav Gomulka, had just come back from a trip to Moscow. He and the other satellite leaders had been summoned by Nikita Khrushchev. Khrushchev himself had been to Peking (his last trip there) to try to learn what was going on there. Mao Tse-tung had launched what he called the Great Leap Forward. I was told that Khrushchev had been horrified. He thought the Chinese had gone mad. Perhaps most important, they were trying to gain their modern industrialization on their own, not through help from Moscow. I was not clear myself at the time just what the Chinese were doing that allegedly shocked Khrushchev. But he had come back from Peking, summoned his own satellite leaders, and conveyed to them his concern over the course of events in China. It was passed on to me by a member of the Polish Central Committee. The fraternity of journalists was working. I had my confirmation of the breach that would later take the form of the open Great Schism of the Communist world.

That episode in Warsaw was followed shortly by the withdrawal of the Soviet technicians from China. During the winter of 1959–60 they were taken home by the trainload. They were pulled out from all over China, where they had been building the factories and the dour, dank hotels my wife and I remember with a shudder from our night in one of them in Sian. The Soviets were modernizing China with obsolete technologies. The Great Leap Forward was a characteristic Chinese try at doing the job on their own, relying on China's greatest asset: its own manpower and the willingness of that mass of humanity to work, even by hand. Chairman Mao was going to make steel in backyard smelters instead of in the big mills the Soviets were intending.

Chairman Mao was also declaring his independence of the Soviet Union. He didn't need the Soviet architects and engineers. He didn't need big steel mills. He didn't need the Soviet army. We in the West did not realize what was happening at the time. It was one of those moments in history when power passes from one pair of hands to another. The decline of the British Empire proceeded so gradually, on the surface, and so peaceably that few realize that in fact Britain ceased to be one of the great powers of the world on one single day, August 15, 1947, the day India was declared to be free and independent.

Britain was a great world power so long as it could command the enormous manpower of the Indian army. Someday if you are in or near the Belgian city of Ypres go to the Menin Gate and notice the names of soldiers from India who fought and fell for Britain in the mud of Flanders just beyond that gate in World War I. It is a forerunner of the famous wall in Washington with the names of those Americans who died in the Vietnam War. At the Menin Gate are carved in white stone hundreds and hundreds of names, names of men who never heard the sound of the bells of Bow in London. These men came mostly from India and Pakistan, some from other former British colonies. Britain was a mighty world power until August 15, 1947, the day when it gave up command of the Indian army.

We do not know the precise day on which Moscow lost control of the Chinese army. It must have been sometime in 1956 or 1957 when Nikita Khrushchev came to realize that China was no longer willing to honor his wishes. Just as Britain was a true world power so long as it controlled the Indian army and could use it, so the Soviet Union was a true world power so long as it could control and put to its own purpose the enormous military manpower of China. From that unknown moment when it lost that control, the Soviet Union ceased to be a true world power. The greater Soviet Empire was in truth short-lived, only from 1949 to probably 1956 or 1957. It continued to be an extremely important regional power until recent times, but its span of true world power stature was less than ten years. And now its status as a major regional power is uncertain. It has lost the conquests of the Communist era. The question now is whether it will be able to hold the territories and peoples conquered under the czars. It was not so long ago when Sweden was a greater power than Russia. It could happen again. We are a long way from knowing how far the Soviet Union will decline and disintegrate.

I find it particularly interesting that I had my first solid confirmation of the break between the Soviet Union and China from a Polish journalist who happened to be a member of the Central Committee of the Polish Communist party. Poland and China had much in common and were of special interest to each other. Poland was the keystone in Stalin's empire in Eastern Europe. It lies on the main line of communication between Moscow and both East Germany and Czechoslovakia. Without Poland the whole Stalin conquest in Eastern Europe would come apart.

It did come apart from the time Solidarity came to power in Poland. As for China, it was Stalin's empire in Asia. Without China there is no Soviet world empire. My mind goes back to that wise old Austrian diplomat who watched Chou En-lai at the big reception in Warsaw just after Moscow had savaged Hungary in late 1956 and was apparently thinking seriously of doing the same to Poland. The Chinese had put a protective arm around Poland. The Austrian was correct. It was the first time China had played a role in Europe since Genghis Khan.

George Kennan, in his famous Mr. X article in the *Atlantic* magazine, said that Stalin's empire contained the seeds of its own dissolution. Not for the first or the last time, George Kennan was correct.

Arabs and Israelis

Since the end of World War II in 1945, I have probably written more columns and news reports about Israel and its Arab neighbors than on any one other subject except possibly East-West relations. Other important stories have come and gone. The Cuban missile crisis absorbed all our attention for about six months, if that long. There was the story of the Prague Spring and its pathetic denouement under the treads of Soviet tanks. The Suez crisis nearly broke up the NATO alliance. South Africa has demanded and received much attention. China has been a major player on the world stage. But those subjects come and go. The story of Israel and the Arabs does not. It is always there, the unsettled problem in the Middle East, sometimes getting mixed up at the fringes of the larger story of U.S.-Soviet relations, but always there, a running sore, causing one war after another—five in all. The only international problem that has been with us longer and has proved equally impervious to settlement is the story of Northern Ireland. But there is a difference. The Northern Ireland problem is between the Irish and the English (and Scots). The rest of the world watches with remote dismay but keeps out. It does not really touch or concern the bulk of the outside world. The problem of Israel does touch and does concern the interests of large parts of the same outside world. There are some 840 million Muslims living mostly in a broad belt stretching from Gibraltar to the Philippines. They are the second largest religious group in the world, second only to the Christians, who are approximately double their number. To the Muslims the second most holy place in the world is the Dome of the Rock on the Temple Mount in Jerusalem. Devout Muslims believe that the Prophet Muhammed ascended to Heaven from that rock. It was in Muslim hands for some fourteen centuries before the 1967 war. It seems intolerable to Muslims that it is now under Jewish control.

To the more numerous Christian community Jerusalem, the scene of the crucifixion of Christ, is, along with Bethlehem, the place of Christ's birth, the holiest place on earth. Muslims and Christians care enormously what happens in and around Jerusalem. But Jerusalem is equally important to the much smaller (eighteen million worldwide) but politically important Jewish community. Jerusalem is the ancient capital of the Jews, the center of their early history as a nation, and the locus of their original temple, which housed their national treasures, the Ark of the Covenant, the Seven Golden Candlesticks, and their sacred records concentrated in the Torah. To Jews, not having Jerusalem in their hands can seem as intolerable as having it in Jewish hands can seem to Muslims and Christians. Millions of people in the outside world care enormously about what happens in the Holy Land of three great religions with often conflicting interests. The problem seems as intractable of solution as is the issue between Catholics and Protestants in Northern Ireland, but of immensely more concern to the outside world. Over half of the world's population is either Christian or Muslim.

The problem arises out of rival claims to the land of Palestine. The Jews, who had all of it in biblical times, would like to have all or most of it today. The Arabs, who have lived in it from time immemorial, often under alien rulers, down to our own time, would like also to have all of it, but particularly those areas that are largely inhabited by Arabs and that were granted to them in the partition plan voted by the United Nations after World War II on November 19, 1947.

The Christians, who owned all of Palestine for a brief hundred years during the age of the Crusades, no longer complicate the problem by any claim beyond control of their own holy places: the Holy Sepulchre and the scene of the Nativity, which they have. However, Christians do care very much about continued free access to those places, and most concerned Christians would prefer to have Jerusalem and its surroundings, including Bethlehem, placed under an international authority as intended and provided under the 1947 UN partition plan. But the serious issue is between Jews and Arabs, to each of whom the whole has at various times been promised. The issue has become particularly acute since World War II because of the Holocaust and, subsequently, a revival of anti-Semitism in the Soviet Union.

My own contact with the problem began in 1939, as related earlier in this book. Jews were being pushed out of Nazi Germany in particular and indeed out of all of Eastern Europe in general. Many of them would have liked to go to Palestine, but that was not considered by the Western governments of the time to be a possible solution to the problem. When I reported for duty in spring 1939 at the office of the Intergovernmental Committee on Political Refugees in London, I found that the secretariat of the committee had been operating from the beginning on the assumption that there was not sufficient space in Palestine to accommodate a significant number of Jews. President Roosevelt's instructions to Myron Taylor at the Evian conference had specified Angola as the place for a new homeland for the Jews, never Palestine. (See appendix B.) The three principal Western governments—Britain, France, and the United States—all took it as axiomatic that it would be impossible to put any substantial number of Jews into Palestine without disastrously offending the entire Arab community and most of Islam. The three operated in the work of the committee on the assumption that Arab and Muslim good will was of first importance. Moreover, so far as I could tell at the time, it never crossed the mind of anyone in high place in Britain that Palestine would ever be anything but a part of the British Empire. We never made a move in the committee secretariat without the approval of the British Foreign Office. On the occasions when Pell was out of the office and I was in charge I cleared anything I proposed to do with Sir Herbert Emerson, who remained physically at the Foreign Office. Pell at one time thought we might be able to place a few Jewish refugees from Germany in various British colonies. No such proposal ever got beyond the British Foreign Office.

It is to be noted in this connection that other territorial mandates granted by the Old League of Nations had provided for the ultimate independence of the mandated territory. Only the British mandate over Palestine lacked such specific provisions. Add that in 1939 a British White Paper had set seventy-five thousand as the limit on the number of Jews who would be allowed to enter Palestine over the next five years. After that there would be no more migration of Jews into Palestine without the consent of the Arabs, who would be unlikely ever to give such consent.

Nor at that time was there great pressure among the Jews for Palestine as their future homeland. The Zionist movement originally called for a homeland for Jews somewhere, but not necessarily in Palestine. Theodor Herzl, founder of the Zionist movement, was not in the beginning specific about Palestine. He asked for "a portion of the globe large enough to satisfy the rightful requirements of a nation . . . Shall we take Palestine or Argentina? We shall take what is given us and what is selected by Jewish public opinion." That was said in 1896. True, a year later the First

World Zionist Congress in Basle committed itself to Palestine as the target area, but the Jewish leaders with whom we dealt during the work of the Intergovernmental Committee in 1939 did not push us to change our minds. They agreed that Angola was a realistic choice as the place for the resettlement of large numbers of European Jews. I never heard a single demand for Palestine in place of Angola as our committee goal. The Jewish community itself was fragmented on the subject of Zionism. We dealt in the committee daily with the top leaders of both the London and New York Jewish communities. The fact is that in 1939 they agreed to finance a major program for moving large numbers of Jews out of Central and Eastern Europe to what would be a new Jewish homeland in Angola.

Then there was a hiatus in the Palestine story. The war came and absorbed the energies of the nations. When the war was finished, the problem of the Jews of Central and Eastern Europe had been transformed by the horror of the Holocaust. I followed the combat troops into the concentration camps. I saw in those camps the emaciated remnants of what had once been Europe's marvelously productive Jewish population of some 7 million persons. How many survived? At the end, after as many as possible were sent back to their own places of origin, there were about one hundred thousand in refugee camps yearning, understandably, to leave Europe forever behind and to find a new homeland where they could regain a life of human dignity and security. There is where I picked up the story in Washington.

Before the war we who had chronicled and worked on the problem of Jewish migration were not working under any great sense of urgency. At the Intergovernmental Committee we assumed that taking 160,000 Jews a year out of the heart of Europe would ease the problem by steadily reducing the friction between the Jews and other communities. Now there was urgency. Life in the refugee camps set up by the Allied military commanders was infinitely better than life had been in the concentration camps but was not endurable indefinitely. Most of the survivors had to be settled somewhere out of Europe. Where to send them?

The Angola option still existed in theory. The files of the Intergovernmental Committee still contained the signed commitments of leaders of the Jewish communities. There was still more than ample space in Angola for the one hundred thousand refugees. But the Holocaust had transformed attitudes within the Jewish community. Out of the Holocaust there welled up an enormous emotional urge among the survivors to go to Palestine. In their own minds Palestine was once more the Promised

Land where they could find not only "milk and honey" but friends and self-respect and dignity and government by Jews and for Jews; could, that is, if the British would honor the first part of the Balfour Declaration.

That declaration is a marvel of self-contradicting ambiguity (see appendix E). The first clause promises a homeland in Palestine for the Jews, but the second clause says that "nothing shall be done which may prejudice the civil and religious rights of existing non-Jewish communities in Palestine."

It is impossible to reconcile those two commitments. A true homeland for Jews could be set up in Palestine only by taking land from Arabs, which would "prejudice" Arab interests. To understand this awesome contradiction we must take a step back in time to 1917 when the Balfour Declaration was issued. At that time in Europe the great war was raging to its bloody climax with the issue still in doubt there, and in the Middle East combined German and Turkish armies were holding the British at bay. The British needed the good will of the Jewish community in Europe and of the Arabs in the Middle East. Clause one of the Balfour Declaration was aimed at the Jews in Europe, clause two at the Arabs in the Middle East.

Here it should be noted that in World War I the world Jewish community was mixed and divided in its sympathies toward Germany and Britain. Among the Jews their perceived enemy was Czarist Russia, not Germany. Russian Jews cheered as liberators the German soldiers who surged into Russia after the German victory at Tannenberg. Britain in 1917 wanted Jewish goodwill and the pool of technical knowledge which could come with that goodwill. Hence the promise of a homeland for Jews in Palestine after the war.

But how valid was that promise by 1945? It had never been implemented seriously. A modest wave of Jews flowed into Palestine immediately after World War I, but it soon led to violent Arab rioting all over Palestine. The British brought troops from as far as Malta to quell the rioting and immediately slowed down on more Jewish immigration. After the fighting ended in 1945 the British began admitting Jews to Palestine at the rate of fifteen hundred a month but they considered the 1939 White Paper as still in force and intended to stop all further Jewish immigration when the seventy-five thousand limit provided for in that paper would be reached. They set up a military blockade and rigidly enforced their quotas.

Jews in Europe were soon chartering ships to run the British blockade, sometimes coming to grief as Cuban and Haitian and Vietnamese refugees today often drown in their desperate effort to reach safety. Inside Palestine the Jewish Executive Authority decided to attack the blockade and the quotas by attacking British forces. In September 1945, they authorized terrorist attacks on those forces. Their most spectacular operation, on July 22, 1946, was the blowing up of a wing of the King David Hotel, which housed the British military command. The death toll was ninety-one British and Arabs. Other episodes that the British have not forgotten to this day included the hanging of two British sergeants and the booby-trapping of their bodies. Savage warfare of this type continued through 1946 and 1947 and down to the British withdrawal in May 1948.

In the United States the Jewish communities united in an appeal to the White House to break the British quota system and the blockade. Whatever differences there had been before the war in the Jewish community about Palestine as a Jewish homeland had been largely smothered by the Holocaust. Jews of most groups united in urging the government in Washington to get those hundred thousand refugees to Palestine.

Washington itself was sharply, even bitterly, divided on the issue. The plight of the refugees had aroused widespread sympathy in American public opinion. Sentiment built up in Congress on behalf of the refugees. The White House listened attentively and sympathetically. But the State Department was adamant. Its reasoning is well expressed by Dean Acheson, then undersecretary of state, in his book *Present at the Creation* as follows:

> I did not share the President's views on the Palestine solution to the pressing and desperate plight of great numbers of displaced Jews in Eastern Europe, for whom the British and American commanders in Germany were temporarily attempting to provide. The number that could be absorbed by Arab Palestine without creating a grave political problem would be inadequate, and to transform the country into a Jewish state capable of receiving a million or more immigrants would vastly exacerbate the political problem and imperil not only American but all Western interests in the Near East. (p. 169)

I heard the same case made at far greater length and in full detail from Loy Henderson, head of the Near East division of the State Department at the time. I heard it also directly from Mr. Acheson and from others in the State Department. I never found a dissenting voice at the State Department, which I was covering daily as a reporter at the time.

The professional diplomat whose job it is to think in terms of the long-term national interest could only see that "the Palestine solution" to the refugee problem would inflame Arab resentment and also, incidentally, violate a promise made by President Franklin Delano Roosevelt to King Ibn Saud of Saudi Arabia in a letter written on April 5, 1945, just seven days before the president died: "Your Majesty will doubtless recall that during our recent conversation I assured you that I would take no action, in my capacity as Chief of the Executive branch of this Government, which might prove hostile to the Arab people."

There is doubt about the policies President Roosevelt would have pursued toward the Palestine issue had he lived to deal decisively with it. As on a number of other matters his position was ambiguous. He wrote a letter to Sen. Robert Wagner of New York on October 15, 1944, on the eve of the 1944 presidential elections and just before the senator was to attend the annual convention of the Zionist Organization of America, in which Mr. Roosevelt promised that if reelected he would "help to bring about" the realization of the Zionist hope for "the establishment of Palestine as a free and democratic Jewish commonwealth."

But the promise to Senator Wagner was made both before a presidential election day and before the president had gone to Yalta and on his return from there had had a remarkable meeting with King Ibn Saud aboard the U.S. cruiser *Quincy* in Great Bitter Lake in the Suez Canal. Not until then had Mr. Roosevelt apparently realized how deeply the Arabs felt about the idea of any large-scale movement of Jews into Palestine. After that meeting he told his interpreter for Arabic, Lt. Col. Harold B. Hopkins, that he "fully agreed that a Jewish state in Palestine could be installed and maintained only by force." And some four months later, after he had had a further chance to study the Palestine problem, he wrote the April 5 letter to King Ibn Saud.

The letters to Senator Wagner and King Ibn Saud are as irreconcilable as the clauses of the Balfour Declaration. In the first Mr. Roosevelt virtually promised all of Palestine to the Zionists. In the second he virtually promised no further Jewish migration to Palestine. How would he have resolved the conflict had he lived? David K. Niles, who served as the White House contact for Jews during both the Roosevelt and Truman administrations, was quoted later as doubting that Roosevelt would ever have agreed to a Jewish state in Palestine.

After Roosevelt died on April 12, 1945, there ceased to be any doubt on this matter. Harry S. Truman took over the presidential office with a solid personal commitment to Zionism. He promptly wrote to British prime minister Clement Attlee urging the immediate transfer of the hundred thousand Jewish refugees to Palestine. This led to a series of Anglo-American conferences groping toward some kind of agreed plan of action, all of which ended in frustration. By autumn 1946, with a midterm election coming up, Mr. Truman became impatient. He was informed by the Democratic National Committee that his expected opponent in the next presidential election, Gov. Thomas E. Dewey of New York, was going to come out on October 6 in favor of the immediate admission of the "hundred thousand" to Palestine. Mr. Truman made his public move on October 4. Governor Dewey did as predicted on October 6. With both American presidential contenders demanding, publicly, early action on the "hundred thousand" the British government gave up.

The British Empire was under pressure all around the world. The British cabinet faced the realization that Britain could not afford the cost of enforcing peace between Arabs and Jews in Palestine without U.S. support. The cabinet decided to surrender the mandate and turn the problem of Palestine over to the United Nations. In January 1947 they began to pull British dependents and nonessential officials out of Palestine. On February 18 Britain's foreign minister, Ernest Bevin, told the House of Commons of the decision to withdraw from Palestine. He knew then, and so did everyone else, that this was one of those decisive turns in history. It was in fact the first step down the road to liquidation of the British Empire.

From then also begins the condition in Palestine with which we are faced today. The United Nations debated long and in anguish over what to do. That ended in a vote on November 29, 1947, to partition Palestine between Jews and Arabs under a plan worked out in a UN committee. Under that plan the Jews were to get 53 percent of the land in spite of the fact that at that time the population of Palestine consisted of 1.2 million Arabs and 650,000 Jews and Jews at that time owned only 7 percent of the land in the part of Palestine to be allocated to them. The Jews were to have the coastal plain stretching south from just below Acre to the Gaza Strip, including the cities of Haifa and Tel Aviv but not Jaffa, which was set aside as a small Arab enclave. The Jews were also to have the province of Galilee and most of the Negev. The city of Jerusalem with surrounding land, including Bethlehem, was to be under international control.

The decision to partition Palestine according to the above plan was approved by a vote of thirty-three in favor with thirteen opposed and ten abstentions. All Muslim states voted against the partition plan, also Cuba and Greece. Britain and China were among the abstentions. The Canadian delegate was said to have voted for partition "with tears in his eyes." In Washington the State Department headed by Gen. George C. Marshall opposed the partition plan on the grounds that the establishment of a Jewish state in Palestine would destabilize the Middle East indefinitely to the long-term disadvantage of the United States and its allies. General Marshall nearly resigned in protest. The Department of Defense, then headed by James Forrestal, also opposed both partition and the setting up of a Jewish state in Palestine, but the White House headed by President Truman strongly supported partition and organized energetic and clandestine lobbying at the United Nations for votes for partition. The official U.S. delegation, taking orders from the State Department, worked to the last moment for a trusteeship, not for partition.

The first fighting was a local Arab guerrilla attack on Jews near Tel Aviv on the day after the partition vote in the UN General Assembly. Guerrilla-type warfare between local Arabs and Jews built up gradually inside Palestine throughout the waiting period between the UN vote on November 29, 1947, and the date set for final British withdrawal, May 18 of the following year. The fighting reached a climax in mid-April 1948 when (on April 9) a combined force of Jewish Irgun and Stern Gang fighters massacred 254 Arab residents, mostly women and children, in the village of Deir Yassin just west of Jerusalem. Four other Arab villages were similarly attacked on the same day, but their fate never received the same attention as did the killing at Deir Yassin. The Arabs retaliated on April 13 by bombing a convoy on the way to the Hadassah Hospital on Mount Scopus, killing thirty-four Jews and wounding twenty-one. The massacre at Deir Yassin triggered a mass flight of over seven hundred thousand Arabs out of lands assigned to Israel. Later Prime Minister Ben-Gurion was quoted as saying that "without Deir Yassin there would be no Israel." Dr. Chaim Weizmann, president of the World Zionist Organization, referred to the flight of Arabs after Deir Yassin as "a miraculous simplification of Israel's tasks."

The state of Israel was proclaimed by a group of Zionist leaders meeting in the Tel Aviv Art Museum on May 14, 1948, to take effect at midnight. Arab armies from outside Palestine invaded Israel the next day. Heavy fighting continued into 1949, during which Israel won most of the battles and gained additional land including the cities of Jaffa and Acre, a corridor from the coast up to Jerusalem, and the new west side of Jerusalem itself, but not the old, inner walled city. At the end of the fighting, Israel's holdings in Palestine west of the river had gone up from 53 percent to 78 percent.

Meanwhile an extra dimension had been added to the problems of the Middle East. The United Nations had sent Count Folke Bernadotte of Sweden to Jerusalem as UN mediator. He attempted to work out a cease-fire and a peace on terms to include the return of Arab refugees to their original homes or payment to them of reparations. On September 16 he signed a memorandum recommending to the United Nations that restitution or reparations be included in any peace. On September 17 he was assassinated in an alley in Jerusalem near his office. Israel never agreed to either restitution or reparations for the refugees. The bulk of them and their descendants still live to this day in the camps where they found shelter in September 1948, to be joined later by refugees from subsequent Arab-Israeli wars.

The Israeli conquests during the 1948–49 fighting plus the original UN proposed territories make up what the world in general thinks of as being the territory of the state of Israel. The boundaries set up by armistice agreements with Israel's Arab neighbors in 1949 have remained the generally recognized boundaries ever since. Israel captured the whole of the Sinai Peninsula during the 1956 war, but was persuaded by President Eisenhower to withdraw afterward on threat of blocking the transfer of funds from the United States to Israel. Israel again conquered the Sinai Peninsula during the 1967 six-day war, lost part of it and regained it during the 1973 Yom Kippur war, then gave it up in a peace treaty with Egypt after Camp David in 1979. It also captured the whole of the West Bank and the Golan Heights during the 1967 war and has controlled a slice of southern Lebanon as a "security zone" since the 1978 war. But in the eyes of the world community the boundaries that prevailed from 1949 to 1967 remain the accepted boundaries of Israel. Israel has announced the annexation of all of Jerusalem and of the Golan Heights, but such annexation is not recognized as valid under international law by the world community. The United States still places its embassy officially in Tel Aviv in deference to the legal view that Jerusalem is not inside the recognized territory of the state of Israel. Most other countries do the same.

Ever since the six-day war of 1967, peace plans and talks and negotiations have all taken place within the framework of UN Resolution 242 (see appendix F), which was drafted and approved at the United

Nations in New York following that war and which calls for recognition of the state of Israel by the Arabs in return for Israeli withdrawal from "occupied territories." The phrase *occupied territories* has repeatedly been interpreted by various Western and American diplomats, including U.S. secretaries of state, as meaning the substantial portions of those lands taken by Israel during and since the 1967 war with only "minor modifications" of the boundaries. That is, down to this day the world community, expressing its opinions through various debates and resolutions in the councils of the United Nations, still regards the acceptable boundaries of the state of Israel to be those that prevailed between 1949 and 1967 and expects Israel someday to give up occupied territories lying beyond those boundaries with only "minor modifications."

There lies the heart of the problem of peace in the Middle East.

The Israelis originally accepted the UN 242 Resolution formula of trading territory for peace. U.S. Ambassador to the UN Arthur Goldberg, a Jew, shared in the drafting of that resolution and was proud of having deleted from the English text the definite article *the* at the passage referring to "occupied territories." It had originally read that Israel would withdraw from "the occupied territories." In the Goldberg draft it appeared less specifically as "occupied territories." In that earlier period the Arabs refused to accept any negotiation. Their declared goal, stated in the charter of the Palestine Liberation Organization, called for the liquidation of Israel. Not until 1988 did the PLO concede the right of the state of Israel to exist.

Many Arabs still claim the whole of Palestine and still cling to the hope of someday driving the Jews into the sea. But with the passage of time responsible Arab leadership has come to accept the reality of a Jewish state in Palestine and is more or less mentally ready now to think in terms of an Israel within its pre-1967 borders. Meanwhile, however, Israel, under the leadership of the Likud party, pulled away from UN Resolution 242. The recent Likud government avowedly wished and intended to keep all or most of the occupied territories. Prime Minister Yitzhak Shamir in August 1991 pledged to his party that he would trade "peace for peace," not peace for territory.

American diplomacy in the wake of the 1991 Gulf War again set out to draw both Arabs and the Israeli government back toward a settlement within the UN 242 formula. The hope was that by gradual persuasion the Arabs could accept the pre-1967 boundaries with "minor modifications," which in diplomatic discussions usually means for Israel a little more width for the corridor from the coastal plain up to West Jerusalem and perhaps a little more width for the coastal plain itself at its narrower points. But it is unlikely, indeed almost inconceivable, that the Arabs would accept much less than the 22 percent of West Bank Palestine left in Arab hands after the original war ended in 1949. They also feel that they must have East Jerusalem, which is still a predominantly Arab community and includes much of importance to the Christian community. It includes St. George's Cathedral, the central Anglican establishment in Palestine, and also several important Roman Catholic convents, monasteries, and other institutions. It is frequently overlooked in the West that a substantial number of Palestine Arabs are Christians—Orthodox, Protestant, and Catholic. Beir Zeit University, a main center of Palestinian nationalism, is an Anglican establishment and many of its students are Christian Arabs. In Israel the Likud party insists that Jerusalem is indivisible and must remain entirely in Israel.

The future of the ancient city of Jerusalem may be the last issue to be resolved. It is in fact, and has been since the time of the Crusades, an international city with its four distinct quarters: one for Jews, one for Muslims, one for Greek and Latin Christians, another for Armenian Christians. The 1948 partition plan called for the whole of greater Jerusalem to be under international rule. Some features of that plan need changing. West Jerusalem, outside the walled city, is overwhelmingly a Jewish community and is tied physically and culturally to Israel, just as East Jerusalem is overwhelmingly Arab and tied physically and culturally to the Arab part of Palestine. A practical solution conceivably acceptable someday to all would be a UN commission in charge of the walls and all within the walls while Israel came up to the walls on the West and Arabs on the East. In that event Muslims could visit the Dome of the Rock without passing through Israeli police lines, and Jews could visit the site of the original temple and the Wailing Wall without passing through Arab police lines. The Israeli capital could be in West Jerusalem and the Arab capital in East Jerusalem.

In the dreams of many who are working toward a permanent conclusion of the differences between Arabs and Israelis there is, someday, to be a restructuring of the whole of Palestine, both East and West banks. There would be three separate communities: Israel, the Kingdom of Jordan, and a Palestinian state. The three would form an economic common market as the Netherlands, Belgium, and Luxembourg have done in Europe. This three-part community could, in theory at least, be prosperous and economically self-sustaining.

But there is one essential final step toward such a dream. It can happen only if Israel will give up political control over the bulk of the occupied territories. That is the main hurdle to be overcome; and there are two reasons, one ideological and one practical, why this hurdle is high and why it is proving to be so difficult to persuade Israel to jump over it. The ideological reason is the emotional unwillingness to give up what Jews call Judea and Samaria. The practical reason is that Israel can afford *not* to give up the occupied territories because the United States pays to make it possible.

Since the 1967 war the United States has subsidized Israel at an official rate that, from a small beginning, has gradually risen to about $3.7 billion a year. The actual subsidy, if all forms of U.S. support to Israel are counted, runs much higher; it includes such items as U.S. help with the cost of moving Jewish migrants from the Soviet Union to Israel, of building housing for those immigrants in Israel, of treating the interest on Israeli government bonds and contributions to Israeli charities as tax exempt under U.S. tax laws, of tariff exemption for Israeli goods entering the United States, and of paying for some Israeli weapons built in Israel. Add to this the $2 billion a year the United States pays to Egypt to be at peace with Israel. Financial support for Israel takes many forms and since 1967 amounts in fact to the United States paying what it costs Israel to *not* make peace with the neighboring Arabs by refusing to surrender the occupied territories.

In very rough terms the United States provides more than one thousand dollars a year to every Jew in Israel; this is about three times more generous to Israel than the Soviet Union was toward Cuba at the height of the cold war.

The net conclusion from all of the above is that under present conditions Israel has little incentive to take the final step necessary for a lasting peace with its Arab neighbors. It holds both the land that its government and many of its people want to keep and also a sufficient American subsidy to cover the costs of remaining in a state of suspended hostility with the Arabs. The subsidy is not in danger so long as the condition of suspended hostility continues. The subsidy would probably be reduced gradually after a successful peace settlement since there would be a declining rationalization for the subsidy.

This is a dilemma for Israel. Most of its people would undoubtedly prefer a reliable peace to indefinite hostility, but the realistic choice may well be between subsidized hostility with the occupied lands or a peaceful life minus both the lands and the subsidy.

There was a time at Camp David in 1979, when Jimmy Carter was president and Anwar Sadat of Egypt was the effective leader of the Arab community, that peace came almost within grasp. Menachem Begin of Israel signed his name to a plan that would have started the Arabs of Palestine on the road to local self-determination. They turned it down. They were as adamant then about a homeland of their own, at once, as the Jews had been in the days after 1945.

Several elements in the equation were favorable to peace at that time. The demographic equation was running against Israel. Its citizens who could get American visas were moving to New York. There was actually a net outflow of Jews from Israel while the Arab birthrate was higher than the Israeli birthrate. Since then much has changed. The Jewish population of Israel has been replenished first by black Jews from Ethiopia and now by large numbers from the Soviet Union. Add that the United States has just "defanged" Iraq, the most belligerent of the Arab states and the only one possessing strategic weapons capable of neutralizing Israel's own arsenal of nuclear warheads. The odds for peace were better at Camp David than they are now.

It is hardly more than a footnote to history that during the Gulf crisis, after Saddam Hussein invaded Kuwait in August 1990, he asserted that he would withdraw his troops from Kuwait if the Israelis would withdraw theirs from the occupied territories in Palestine. Was it a mere propaganda gesture or did he mean it? The government of the United States ignored the suggestion, never tried to find out whether it could have been a serious offer, for the obvious reason that such an exchange could not have been implemented. Israel would not give up the occupied territories for the sake of Kuwait, nor would the administration in Washington have been willing or politically able to force Israel to do so.

Covering this story has had its difficulties for reporters. My own first brush with the pro-Israel lobby came in 1949 during the first Arab-Israeli war. I went one day to the Department of Defense in Washington and asked for a briefing on how the war was going in Palestine. On the basis of the information I was given, I wrote a news report saying that while the fighting would probably go on a little longer the Israelis were in fact already the winners. I was then called "anti-Semitic" in the local Jewish press. Sometime later I asked a Jewish friend what I had done to win that label. He replied, "You announced our victory prematurely. You announced it before the annual fund drive for Israel."

Kiryat Arba is an Israeli settlement just outside the ancient city of Hebron. First it was an Israeli army post. Then Israeli settlers clustered around it and built themselves a modern town with high-rise apartments. It towers over the low buildings of the neighboring Arab city. On a trip there in 1979 I was looking at it from a little distance. In my memory I also seemed to see a Norman castle somewhere in England overshadowing an Anglo-Saxon village. The Israeli settlers sometimes sortie forth from Kiryat Arba to cut down Arab vineyards and olive trees. Arabs throw stones at Israeli cars. Each retaliates against the other.

Kiryat Arba was the base from which a group of settlers reestablished a small Jewish community in the center of Hebron. Shootings and killings have occurred between the settlers at Kiryat Arba and the Arabs of Hebron.

On the same 1979 trip I spent a day at Beir Zeit University. It lay in a small town near the city of Ramallah, which itself is more or less in the middle of West Bank Palestine. It was in pleasant, hilly country. It reminded me of some small hill town in Tuscany. There was tension in the air. The students who talked with me had a recent episode on their minds. One of their fellows had been sitting on a bench outside a girls' dormitory, waiting for his date. A car loaded with Israelis went by at high speed. A shot from the car hit the student. The Israeli authorities promised to investigate. I never learned the outcome of the investigation. The students were eager to tell me of their own personal experiences at the hands of the Israeli armed forces and police. It was a story of constant harassment, of being stopped and searched, of interrogations with humiliating treatment, of being kept from school, and, of course, of the long periods when their university was closed down as punishment for such things as flying a Palestinian flag or stone throwing or demonstrating. They were attractive young men and women dressed much like American students at any American college or university. They spoke excellent English. Most of the faculty members I met were Americans who were spending their sabbaticals from their American universities at Beir Zeit. What I heard there and what I saw of the way the Israeli police and soldiers treated Arabs in Jerusalem and the West Bank brought back old memories of how I saw Jews treated by German police in Berlin in 1939. (That was before the Holocaust and when there were still Jews on the streets of Berlin.) The similarity is unavoidable to anyone who has been a witness to both of those conditions.

It is a bitter irony of history that it was the persecution of Jews in Hitler's Germany, climaxing in the horror of the Holocaust, that fueled in the Jewish community an irresistible demand for a homeland of their own in Palestine. The dispossessed Arabs of Palestine are the ultimate victims of German anti-Semitism.

Had there been no Holocaust the Jewish homeland today would probably be in Angola, not in Palestine. Angola is where they were wanted, where there was ample empty space, where the Jewish diaspora could have been accommodated without displacing large numbers of long-term residents, and which in 1939 was regarded by most of the outside world as the most suitable and available place for them.

In the Broadcasting Jungle

I was in news broadcasting for thirty years and found it mostly a rewarding experience, both financially and professionally. I owe to it a considerable improvement in my writing style. During the later years of my career I have been commended frequently for simplicity and clarity of style. This I owe largely to the fact that in news broadcasting one must use words that the ear accepts easily. The long, involved sentence and the heavy word that proves erudition are equally fatal in news broadcasting. Edward R. Murrow was one of the greatest and most successful of news broadcasters. He wrote for the ear. His words and sentences came out in a staccato beat. He was a master of color, but always achieved it in short, simple words. The classic was his description of incendiary bombs falling on Berlin "like a fistful of white rice . . . on black velvet." My newspaper writing done after several years of broadcasting experience is simpler, more direct, more understandable than what I wrote before I made the acquaintance of a microphone.

As previously related, I got started in broadcasting at the beginning of the war in Berlin as a substitute at CBS for Bill (William L.) Shirer.

Back in Washington during the middle of the war Raymond Gram Swing was the voice of wisdom on the evening news broadcasts over the Blue Network of NBC, later ABC. "Well informed people" used to read Walter Lippmann three times a week in a column widely syndicated by the *New York Herald Tribune* and listen to Raymond Gram Swing five nights a week for his fifteen-minute analytical commentary. Swing also did a twice-weekly commentary for the BBC. Poor health at one point forced him to cut back to once a week for the BBC. I fell heir to the broadcast he had to give up. For fifteen years I did a weekly commentary for the BBC. In 1943 CBS invited me to come over to them on staff and do a regular five-minute evening commentary sponsored by the B. F. Goodrich Company.

From then until 1971 my primary employment was in broadcasting: first at CBS, then at a short-lived network called Liberty Broadcasting, then to NBC, finally at ABC. However, I never broke my connection with the *Christian Science Monitor*. During my nearly thirty years in broadcasting I always continued writing as a regular contributor to the *Monitor*. In each successive contract with the broadcasting networks I insisted on a clause specifically permitting me to continue writing regularly for the *Monitor*. I did this partly out of loyalty to my journalistic home, which the *Monitor* always was, partly out of financial prudence because employment in news broadcasting was then, and still is, notoriously transitory. Many others, like myself, wandered from one to another of the networks. Then there was a third reason. While it is true that much of the public now gets its news first from radio and/or television and frequently forms its opinions from material heard over those vehicles of communication, the newspaper remains important in the shaping of national policy. My broadcasts on television got me many a flattering glance of recognition on the street and sometimes a sharp word of disapproval from a total stranger, but the opinions I expressed in my columns in the *Monitor* reached into the White House and Congress. One of my best friends on the White House staff, Bromley Smith, followed my thinking on current affairs from the daily White House news summary. He said he never read the *Monitor* itself, but he was always current in what I was saying in my columns from reading the morning news report that is prepared in the White House during the night and circulated to everyone, beginning with the president, first thing in the morning.

The White House cares about the newspaper columns. Many a national issue is fought out on the op-ed page columns before the decision is made at the White House. A classic recent example was the almost daily barrage of prowar columns in the *New York Times* and *Washington Post* that preceded the president's choice of war over sanctions in the Gulf. There were also antiwar columns. The exchange brought out clearly that, while sanctions could liberate Kuwait, only war could "defang" Saddam Hussein's nuclear and other weapons of mass destruction. The choice of war was obviously made for that reason, that is, to delete from the military balance in Arabia the chemical weapons Saddam had and the nuclear weapons he might someday be able to have. The choice of war protected and protracted Israel's position as the only nuclear power in the Middle East.

In other words I kept up my column writing during my broadcasting years and at the end went back full-time to editorial and column writing at the *Monitor*, partly to keep my springboard into national policymaking. To have someone at the White House telephone to discuss a column you have written is heady stuff.

In the meantime I had the remarkable experience of living through the coming first of radio, then television, into the pattern of public life, causing many a change in how people get their information and form their opinions on public affairs.

The coming of the new is not always welcomed by the old. I remember the treatment we newspaper reporters accorded NBC's Frank Burgholtzer on the Truman campaign train in 1948. Frank had a big box, a mystery to the rest of us, in one end of the press car. He was always talking into it, sometimes when we were trying to listen to briefings from the news office. We treated him as though he were some kind of a telephone repair man getting in our way. The importance accorded today to a TV anchorperson was achieved only slowly and granted grudgingly by the "regular press."

The influence radio and television have had on public opinion is particularly noticeable in American politics. In 1948 Harry Truman won his unexpected election largely by his lively (usually called spunky at the time) speeches from the open back platform of his campaign train. Sometimes the stop would be as short as ten minutes. Harry was there with some local reference followed by his favorite excoriation of the "do-nothing Congress." "Give 'em hell, Harry!" rose from the audience. He was admired for his pluck and for keeping on campaigning when everyone knew that Governor Dewey would be the winner. But then Governor Dewey wasn't the winner.

It was the last time a presidential election was won from the back platform of a campaign train. With the coming of Dwight D. Eisenhower to the presidential scene everything changed. Not only was he the successful leader of the Allied armies in the greatest war of all time, hence a truly national hero, there was also a masculine assurance in his manner and style that captured the confidence of a majority of American men and women. Once that confident assurance appeared on the television screens "Ike" was unbeatable. To many an American he was the very image of the kind of man who can be counted on to knock down the wolf outside the cabin door and come back with a plump deer over his shoulder. You would feel safe with Ike. Adlai Stevenson's intellectual speeches on the great issues of the day did not play on television against that reassuring Eisenhower manner. From that election onward candidates were to be judged by how they looked and sounded on television—sometimes disastrously.

Television can be merciless. George Romney of Michigan was once a leading contender for a Republican nomination. Then in answer to a question about changing his position on the Vietnam War from pro to anti, he replied that in the beginning of the war he had been "brainwashed." That was the end of the Romney boom. George Bush came to instant disaster when he ran against Ronald Reagan for the Republican nomination in 1980. Do you remember the high school auditorium in Nashua, New Hampshire? All the Republican candidates were there expecting to take part in a group appearance. "No," said George Bush. He said it was to be a debate only between himself and Reagan, whereupon Mr. Reagan said he wanted everyone to be in the affair and added as a clincher, "After all, I am paying for this." That was the end for George Bush in the 1980 campaign. He came over on television as mean-spirited. Mr. Reagan came over as generous and friendly. The Reagan nomination in 1980 was sewed up in about two minutes of drama on that high school stage. And in New Hampshire eight years later, when the primary returns showed Bush ahead of Dole after a heated campaign, a television reporter asked Dole whether he had anything to say to Bush and Dole replied: "Tell him to stop telling lies about me." That flare-up of anger ended the Dole campaign for the Republican nomination. His temper was too quick and sharp. Once it was seen on national television there was no undoing that one fatal remark. Candidates must use television, but it can destroy a candidacy as well as make one.

We had a wonderful sense of being pioneers in those early days of both radio and television. I did a voice-over (narration) for the combined networks on the first time television was ever admitted to the halls of Congress. I remember having to spot the various dignitaries as they entered the chamber of the House of Representatives and the climactic moment when I could identify Fishbait Miller, the House doorkeeper, as he came to his own biggest line, "Mr. Speaker, the President of the United States." It's always a great television show when the president addresses the assembled members of both Houses of the Congress, with the Supreme Court in a front row and the diplomatic corps just behind. Unfortunately, not since television began has a British ambassador shown up at one of these occasions as I once saw one, dressed in the kilted uniform of one of the King's Scottish Archers. Since the ambassador in question, Sir Ronald Lindsey, was six feet, seven inches in height that uniform belonged in the television age.

I had one particularly painful experience during my broadcasting years. Bill Shirer, as previously related, launched me on my career in broadcasting in 1940 in Berlin. In 1947 in New York, Edward R. Murrow, then vice-president for CBS News, asked me to take over Bill Shirer's regular Sunday evening spot, which had, until then, been sponsored by the J. B. Williams Shaving Soap Company. That put me in the middle between my original sponsor in broadcasting and my boss, both of whom I greatly admired. I found myself walking into the CBS building, then on Madison Avenue, through a picket line that was chanting:

> Joseph Harsch is Murrow's choice,
> We want William Shirer's voice.

At that uncomfortable moment I did not yet know what was going on. To this day there is controversy over facts and interpretation. Shirer had been dropped by his sponsor, and so informed by the advertising agency that handled the account. It was said that it was because he was "too liberal." Frank Stanton, then CBS president, confirmed recently that the agency did consider him too liberal and chose to drop him.

The charge of liberalism against Shirer has always puzzled me. He was, generally speaking, "liberal" in his viewpoint on current affairs, but so also was everyone else at CBS, myself included. The J. B. Williams Company did not ask for a "conservative" to replace Shirer. They dropped news entirely and went over to other vehicles for their advertising. Differing versions of the Shirer-Murrow controversy are told in Shirer's own autobiography, *A Native's Return*, and in two biographies of Murrow, *Murrow: His Life and Times* by A. M. Sperber and *Edward R. Murrow, An American Original* by Joseph E. Persico. To the enormous detail in those three accounts I need add only the following from memory about my own part in the affair.

After being greeted by that chant at the entrance to the CBS building on Madison Avenue on Monday, March 24, 1947, I went to Shirer's office on the seventeenth floor and said, "Bill, what the hell is going on." Bill started to give me his explanation. He was interrupted by a deputation led by Freda Kirchway, editor and publisher of the *Nation*, who had been upstairs protesting to CBS chairman of the board William Paley against Shirer's loss of his program. She seemed surprised to see me there and said, somewhat sharply, "Joe Harsch, you are making it difficult for us to present this as a liberal issue." I backed out and went on up to Murrow's office on the next floor. My recollection of what happened next—from memory since I made no notes at the time—is as follows.

Murrow told me that he had ordered Shirer to take a leave of absence in order to have an operation and time for convalescence. He said Shirer had proposed to keep up his broadcasting during the convalescence by having a news ticker and microphone in his hospital room at Lake Placid. Murrow said that he considered this to be poor journalism and had insisted that Shirer instead should take a leave of absence, go to Lake Placid, and have his operation and his convalescence at leisure and in comfort; there would be a new time slot for him at CBS when he was ready to come back to work. He said there was going to be a general reorganization of the whole CBS news schedule at the end of the summer. He then asked me to take over the Shirer program in the meantime.

The above account conflicts with Shirer's records. In a letter to me dated March 14, 1991, Shirer says:

> The year before, in the summer of 1946, I did broadcast from Lake Placid. I had not yet fully recovered from an emergency operation in January and was very tired. My doctor insisted I take the summer off to get back my health. So I had gone to Murrow and the sponsor and explained that I'd like to take the summer off. In those days many major programs went off the air for 13 weeks during the summer. Both the sponsor and CBS asked me to continue broadcasting the Sunday show even if I had to do it from Lake Placid. But in early March, 1947 the situation was different. It was too early to make plans for the summer and I had none—certainly none to have an operation and broadcast from a hospital in Lake Placid.

In Murrow's office on that critical day in March 1947, I understood that Murrow was telling me what was just happening, that a second Shirer operation supplementary to the 1946 operation was due shortly. He presented it to me as the explanation of why CBS needed a substitute for Shirer pending the revamping of the whole news schedule to come in the autumn.

The upshot of it all for myself was that I took over the Sunday 5:45 P.M. fifteen-minute time slot, unsponsored (with Shirer's generous personal consent to me after he had in fact left CBS). Technically, the affair ended for Shirer with his resignation. Factually, he was pushed out. He had a brief twilight in radio broadcasting at the Mutual network, but his broadcasting career was essentially over. Later he had a new career. The end of broadcasting forced him to go back to his typewriter and write for publication. He tried novels and plays with mediocre results. Finally, he did what he could do best; he started writing the full story of Hitler's Germany. The end result was *The Rise and Fall of the Third Reich*, a superb achievement that stands today as the classic one-volume account of that amazing historical tragedy.

My own association with CBS eroded. B. F. Goodrich dropped news and went back to entertainment. The former Shirer program was closed out at the end of the summer. I did unsponsored broadcasting for CBS for a while, but like many others who failed to attract sponsors, my contract was not renewed. The date of my last CBS broadcast was March 1, 1949. I had become redundant at CBS but was immediately picked up, beginning April 1, by the struggling new Liberty radio network. After it folded in 1953 I went to NBC, which, having trimmed down its wartime news staff, was building it up again in a serious effort to compete with CBS for prestige in news.

In the formative years of broadcasting, NBC under David Sarnoff specialized in entertainment, both high-class and popular. NBC is the only network that ever owned its own symphony orchestra headed by the Maestro, Arturo Toscanini. But not before and not even during the war did NBC seriously try to challenge CBS's primacy in news. CBS had specialized in news as much as NBC had in entertainment. CBS was the premier news network from the day CBS News Director Paul White, at the time of Hitler's annexation of Austria, conceived of putting the live voices of Edward R. Murrow and William L. Shirer on the air together. That was the first time any network had used its own correspondents live on the air with eyewitness news coverage. It was the birth of modern news broadcasting, and it was done at CBS. Not until about five years after the war did NBC decide to try to catch up. I was one of several former CBS news people picked up by NBC at that time, in my case in 1953. This led into a fourteen-year experience at NBC, of which seven years (from 1957 to 1965) were spent in London.

One episode during the London years fits into this chapter on broadcasting. It is an example of the sort of thing that should not happen in the news business but has happened in television news because of the star or anchor system.

The Russian poet Yevgeny Yevtushenko made his first trip out of the Soviet Union and to London during my tour as NBC bureau chief in London. He was coming as a guest of the BBC. The New York office cabled me to get an interview with him. I applied through the BBC and was told that he was doing no interviews for anyone except the BBC. The BBC presented him to the press the day after his arrival in London. I attended and noticed that before the press conference began he was in lively conversation in Russian with a French colleague, Michael Gorday of *Le Soir*. Also, during the conference he frequently turned to Gorday for a whispered exchange before answering a question. Obviously, they were best of friends. After returning to my office I telephoned Gorday and asked if he could get an interview with Yevtushenko for NBC. He said he was sure "Yev" would refuse. I said, "It's a hundred pounds for each of you." He said, "I'll try." He soon called me back and said Yev had agreed. I reported to New York that NBC could have Michael Gorday interviewing Yevtushenko. They expressed delight and said to go ahead with plans. A day or two later they phoned and said to ask whether Gorday and Yevtushenko would be willing to have Chet Huntley, then NBC's anchor on their evening news program, sit in on the interview and ask one question. They agreed, although reluctantly. New York then sent over a producer to handle the interview. The interview was taken out of my control.

In due time the interview took place. Gorday started off by posing one question "on behalf of my colleague Chet Huntley." Then he went ahead and did the interview, in Russian, on camera. After it was finished Yevtushenko was paid off and dismissed. Then they turned the camera on Gorday, who translated the entire interview, his own questions and then the answers, into English. When it was finished he too was paid off and left. And that was that, except that after Gorday had left they sat Chet down in front of the camera and Chet repeated all of Gorday's questions. You can guess the rest. When the interview was presented on NBC the audience saw Huntley asking all the questions. Gorday's voice came in translating the answers, but he was never seen asking a single question. It was presented as a Huntley interview. Jack Gould, TV critic of the *New York Times*, wrote a column in praise of Chet Huntley for his enterprise in obtaining the first ever interview in the West with Russia's most famous living poet. Various prizes were later awarded Huntley for his remarkable enterprise. In television of that era the star anchor had to be made to look good. I like to think that this kind of plain fakery could not exist today.

NBC had another problem with Huntley a little later after Bob Kint-ner had become president of NBC. Huntley did a program one night on the nutritional merits of "nature-fed beef." Then it was learned that he had bought a feedlot for beef in New Jersey and started marketing "Chet Huntley's nature-fed beef" on the New York market. Bob Kint-ner told me that he informed Huntley that he must never again promote "nature-fed beef" on an NBC news program and that he would either have to stop news broadcasting or sell his feedlot. Kintner said he ex-plained to Huntley that doing both constituted a conflict of interest. He said Huntley never seemed to understand why what he had done was unethical, but he finally consented to sell the feedlot and go out of the business of marketing beef.

One of my happiest broadcasting memories is of the 1960 Demo-cratic convention. NBC assigned me to cover Adlai Stevenson. Most of the time that meant that I sat with a camera crew in the stairwell out-side Adlai's hotel suite. He had led the Democratic party twice against Dwight D. Eisenhower. He had campaigned gallantly and honorably and had done as well as anyone possibly could with the odds stacked against him. He had developed a large and devoted following in the party who yearned to nominate him a third time when, running against Richard Nixon, he would have an excellent chance of winning. There had been an enormous, supposedly spontaneous demonstraton for him on the con-vention floor before the nominating speeches were to begin. The floor was packed with Stevenson supporters. My own son, Jonathan, was an enthusiastic Stevenson worker and found himself "running" uncreden-tialed Stevenson people into the hall. He would collect a batch of door passes from those already inside, take them out, bring in a second batch, and so on. The pro-Stevenson machine was formidable. About the time the nominating speeches were beginning Adlai stuck his head out of the door to see what was outside. He saw me and invited me inside. I joined him there seated in front of a television set surrounded by his closest friends including his sister, Marietta Tree, and his chief political adviser, George Ball. We all watched the beginning of the nominating speeches for John F. Kennedy. George Ball came in from a telephone call in an adjoin-ing room, went up to Adlai, and said, "Governor, it isn't too late. Please let me pass the word that if nominated you would run." Adlai happened to look at me and said, "What do you think I should do?" Automatically I backed George Ball. I said I thought it was his duty to run. (Bear in mind here that I was brought up in a staunch Protestant family that had an inherited fear of the pope and "romanism.") I said he had to run to "protect the Protestant Succession." He said, "Joe, you're not serious, are you?" "Yes, of course I am," I said. I added that I had all my life been brought up to believe that our liberties depended on the Protestant Succession, that the president, like the king or queen in England, had to be a Protestant. I said such things as that I could still "hear the guns of the Spanish Armada," and "no Catholic must ever become president." He looked at me for a moment, then said, "Joe, you are serious, aren't you? I think you better come with me." He led me into the next room. He shut the door on the nominating speeches for Kennedy. He sat me down and for the next half hour gave me a lecture on religious tolerance that was brilliant and totally convincing. When he had finished I was able to vote for a Catholic for president, as I did on election day. He had washed my inherited prejudice about the pope and "romanism" out of my political thinking. And he did it while his own last chance to be president was running out. Probably he still could have had the nomination up to the moment he took me into the back room for the lecture. By the time we went out to join the others in front of the television the convention'had been stampeded to Kennedy.

One might say that Adlai Stevenson wasted his last chance for the presidency of the United States to teach religious tolerance to a reporter. My guess is that more probably he wanted to escape from George Ball's importunings since his mind was already made up firmly against running a third time. My out-of-date prejudice provided an easy escape from any further discussions of the matter.

Would that I had a tape recording of that lecture.

The George Polk Affair

Every year, in March, an American journalist is given the George Polk Award "for courage and resourcefulness in gathering information and skill in relating the story."

I met George Polk several times in 1945 in the *New York Herald Tribune* office in Washington. In early 1946 he was hired away from the Trib by Edward R. Murrow, at that time head of CBS News. Ed was proud of adding George Polk to his CBS staff. George had had a heroic war record as a U.S. Navy pilot, with much publicized adventures, particularly on Guadalcanal. He had nightmares the rest of his life from an encounter with a live Japanese in a foxhole on that island. After his discharge from a Navy hospital, George had gone back to journalism. He was tall, handsome, companionable, good at storytelling, and eager for more adventure. Ed thought George would make an ideal foreign correspondent. CBS assigned him first to the Middle East, where he was based for a while in Cairo; then, after President Truman decided in March 1947 to save Greece from a Communist insurgency, he went to Athens to cover the civil war raging there. By early May 1948 George was due for home leave but hoped to score one more journalistic coup before coming home. Leaving his new, young Greek wife in Athens, he flew to Salonika in hope of establishing a contact there that would give him a chance to cross the line and visit the commanding general of the Greek rebel forces, General Markos Vafiadis, in the mountains just beyond Salonika. Like many another good journalist, George wanted to find out what it was like "over on the other side." Another American journalist in Greece at the time had the same idea. Homer Bigart of the *New York Herald Tribune* carried the idea out successfully by going first to Yugoslavia. But George didn't have time for that roundabout route. He had only two weeks left before heading for home and a prospective Nieman fellowship at Harvard. For him the only available route to General "Markos" was the quick one, clandestinely, probably by boat, along the coast from Salonika, then directly up into the mountains.

To this day there is no sure knowledge of what happened to George Polk on his presumed way to meet General Markos. He flew from Athens to Salonika on an early morning flight on May 7. He checked in at the Hotel Astoria, then went to the American Consulate, after which he visited the press office of a United Nations special commission on the Balkans that was functioning in Salonika. He had lunch with the press officer of that organization, and later met Helen Mamas, a stringer for the Associated Press. During the afternoon he was in his hotel room, apparently expecting some visitor who never showed up as far as the hotel staff knew. By 7:30 he was in the bar of the Mediterranean Hotel with a group of colleagues including Helen Mamas and, later, a Greek journalist named Gregory Staktopoulos, a correspondent for the British News Agency, Reuters.

The next morning George visited the British consulate, where he asked, unsuccessfully, the British said, for a contact to the Communists. That was George Polk's last official and provable meeting with anyone. His body, with hands and feet bound, his eyes blindfolded, a bullet hole in the back of his neck, was found floating in the harbor of Salonika on the morning of May 16. According to the coroner's report the body had been in the water about seven days.

What happened between George Polk's departure from the British consulate on the morning of May 8 and the time the body was found on May 16 is obscured in the fog of an official Greek government "solution" to the crime that remains to this day uncorroborated and that has been repudiated by its author. It was accepted at the time by the American government and by General William J. ("Wild Bill") Donovan, acting as counsel for the Overseas Writers Special Committee, known as the Lippmann Committee. But that solution has since been challenged as a whitewash in two scholarly books, *The Salonika Bay Murder*, by Edmund Keeley of Princeton University, and *The Polk Conspiracy*, by Kati Marton, daughter of one distinguished journalist, Andrew Marton of the Associated Press, and wife of another, Peter Jennings of ABC News.

These two books have given me personal concern. I was a member of and secretary of the Overseas Writers Special Committee set up in Washington to investigate the murder of George Polk. So far as I know I am one of the only two members of that committee still alive, the other being James R. Reston of the *New York Times*. Both of us believe that the Greek government produced a flawed and improbable version of what happened, but we cannot accept that any member of the committee, and certainly not our chairman, Walter Lippmann, ever consciously participated in a whitewash or cover-up.

In April 1949, almost a year after the murder, there was a public trial in the civil court in Salonika. The key witness, Gregory Staktopoulos, whom George Polk had met on the day of his disappearance, was convicted, on his own testimony, of having been an accessory to the murder and given a life sentence—later commuted.

But what we on the committee did not know at the time, and what did not come out in the trial, was that during most of that year Staktopoulos was in the hands of the local Security police and probably (as he later stated) was given a carefully prepared "confession" that he was required to assert in court on pain of personal injury to himself and his mother. He later alleged that his confession was forced on him under torture.

One thing we did know is essential to the question of whether the U.S. government and the Lippmann Committee were party to a fraudulent solution to the crime. On June 10, a month after the murder, when General Donovan went to Greece as counsel and special investigator for the committee, he took along with him Lt. Col. James Kellis (U.S. Air Force), who had served in the OSS under Donovan during the war, working with the Greek partisans against the Germans, and who spoke Greek fluently. When Donovan came back to the States after his first trip to Athens, he left Kellis behind to continue the investigation. Without consultation with Donovan or notice to Donovan or to the committee, Kellis was recalled by the air force. Earnest Lindley, president of Overseas Writers, then discovered that the recall had been requested by the U.S. embassy in Athens after it was learned that Kellis believed that the murder might well have been committed by persons on the right wing of Greek politics, not necessarily by the Communists. This recall of Kellis without word to Donovan or to the committee broke an agreement the committee had with Secretary of State George Marshall that the committee would be kept informed of all communications about the Polk case from the embassy in Athens.

Today, from the reading of the available material on the subject done by the authors of the two books (including U.S. government files broken open by the Freedom of Information Act), it seems clear that the U.S. embassy in Athens joined with the Greek government in seeking not the true solution to the mystery of who killed George Polk, but rather a

"Communist" solution. The removal of Colonel Kellis from the scene at the request of the embassy is rationally explainable only as part of a deliberate effort to protect the Greek government from the possibility that the murderers may have come from some non-Communist Greek faction. The embassy, clearly, was determined to find a Communist solution to the crime.

The Greek government obliged. At the trial, Gregory Staktopoulos provided a lurid story of sitting at night with George in a café facing the bay waiting for a rowboat with a specific name to come for them. He and Polk boarded the boat, which took off with a single man for a crew, and made a stop down the beach, where two more persons boarded the boat. George was allegedly talked into allowing himself to be bound and blindfolded, then was shot from behind. Two of the boatmen were identified by Staktopoulos as Adam Mouzenides and Evangelos Vasvanas, both known as active members of the Greek Communist guerrilla movement. In this scenario Staktopoulos knew that he was a guide and interpreter for George Polk but had no advance knowledge that Polk would be killed. He was nevertheless convicted of being an accessory to the crime.

The trial held in open court in Salonika from April 12 to 21, 1949, was attended throughout by General Donovan and by two CBS correspondents, Winston Burdett and Alexander Kendrick. I and other members of the committee knew both of them. I shared an office at CBS News in Washington for over a year with Winston Burdett.

I and my colleagues on the committee trusted both Kendrick and Burdett to be honest and honorable reporters who would tell the story straight and truly. I knew that Burdett's personal inclinations were to the left. He subsequently confessed to having at one time been a member of the Communist party. Neither Burdett nor Kendrick would have been inclined to support a cover-up of the Greek government. Both considered that the trial had been fair and that the verdict was justified by the testimony. Neither at the time questioned the validity of the Staktopoulos version of the murder. Nor did General Donovan, who, on the basis of what he heard in court, was confident that an American jury would have come up with the same verdict of guilt in absentia for the two alleged Greek guerrillas and guilt as an accessory for Staktopoulos.

Back in Washington we members of the committee were unhappy. We trusted the American reporters present, but the recall of Colonel Kellis greatly troubled us. We waited for a promised report from General Donovan, which was long in coming. In March 1950, with the trial already over by nearly a year, the general was prodded by Eugene Meyer, owner of the *Washington Post* and a member of the Lippman Committee who had raised the funds for the investigation. General Donovan then handed all his notes and papers about the case to a young lawyer in his firm, Mary G. Jones, and told her to "make something out of it." Her work was finally finished in October of that year. It was inconclusive. Meanwhile Walter Lippmann had submitted the Staktopoulos confession to a Harvard Law School friend, E. M. Morgan. The opinion had come back that the story it told was "fantastic" and that as evidence the elements in it were "so inherently weak as to be practically worthless unless they are corroborated by other credible evidence."

After the Mary Jones draft arrived we on the committee had in hand all we were likely to get in the way of material. We were reluctant to write a report at all because the case was far from being resolved. The verdict of the Greek court, which placed the blame on two persons who could not be apprehended or tried in person (and one of whom may already have been dead), was less than totally convincing to our members. And there lingered in the minds of most of us the fact that the Greek government had more motives for doing harm to George Polk than did the Communists.

George had obtained information that the Greek foreign minister Constantine Tsaldaris had been diverting some American economic aid funds to his own personal use. George's general writing about Greece had been critical of the Greek government. His life had apparently been threatened. He was regarded at the American Embassy as being leftist, was sometimes called a Communist. I have never been able to think of any reason for the Communists to have wanted to kill George Polk.

We on the committee wrestled with the problem of writing our formal report on what remained an inconclusive investigation. We put it off as long as possible. When we could delay no longer we produced a report that was as inconclusive as the situation it described. We quoted General Donovan as saying that the trial had been "efficiently and honestly conducted," but we did not commit ourselves to that conclusion. We decided that the Greek government's investigation "was, after some hesitation and delay, pursued with vigor," but we also noted that the work of our own "independent investigator in Greece [Colonel Kellis] was not facilitated, that in fact [it] was frustrated by the Greek and American authorities." We committed ourselves to one statement probably few of us would accept today. The report said, "The Committee is satisfied that Staktopoulos and his mother received a fair trial." We were also "satisfied" that "Staktopoulos was in fact an accessory, that he was the 'trigger man' who led Polk into the trap where his murderers were waiting for him."

Walter Lippmann himself went further in a personal statement made at a testimonial dinner for General Donovan. He said he was satisfied that "one of the guilty men has been caught and that no innocent man has been made the scapegoat for a crime of which he was innocent." The committee was not willing to go that far.

Could the committee have done more than it did? Were we the dupes of a deliberate cover-up by our own government in collusion with the Greek government?

George Polk was undoubtedly a political victim of the cold war, which had begun in 1948. Undoubtedly, he was murdered by someone for a political purpose. Beyond that nothing is certain. Some people at the time suspected that the British had a hand in the murder. At the U.S. embassy in Athens it was considered a public relations imperative that the blame be pinned on the Communists. Any other explanation would disserve the American foreign policy purpose of supporting the Greek government.

Was our choice of General Donovan as our chief investigator a mistake? I cannot think of any other American who could have gone to Greece at that time wielding as much influence as he did. He had successfully organized and operated the OSS during the war. He was prominent in the discussions that led to the setting up of the CIA. He knew everyone in Washington and was highly regarded by just about everyone. He could bully and prod the Greek government better than anyone else who might have been sent there. In fact, the Greek investigation of the murder really began, and only reluctantly, after he reached Athens.

When we asked him to take the assignment we specified that he pursue any lead objectively, no matter where it pointed. He said he would, and I think that in the beginning he was as eager to pursue a lead pointing to the right as to the left. But halfway through his efforts in Greece itself he seems to have swung over to the official American government attitude of seeking only a left-wing solution. I asked a friend who served on his personal staff during his OSS days whether he was capable of having become mentally a part of a cover-up to protect the Greek government. Her reply was that he would do anything he believed to be truly in the national interest of the United States. Did the embassy make him its ally? It is certainly possible. As evidence: he acquiesced in the recall of Colonel Kellis, he bought the authenticity of the Staktopoulos story, and he never actually wrote his report on his investigation.

To sum up: I do not believe that any other independent investigation or investigator could have done more than was done. Both Greek and American governments would have blocked any effort that pointed to a non-Communist solution for the crime. In my own opinion it is remarkable that our final report, issued on May 21, 1951, was as restrained as it was. We did not buy the official Greek scenario. We regarded the story as unfinished and the murder of George Polk as unsolved. It remains unsolved to this day. It is not even certain that Gregory Staktopoulos led George Polk to his murderers, whether innocently or knowingly. The only basis for even that scenario is a repudiated confession. Any American who went to Greece at that time and dug for evidence pointing to the Greek political right might well have ended up blindfolded and bound hand and foot in a rowboat in Salonika Bay. The game was being played roughly in Greece in the civil war that erupted there at the end of World War II.

Where We Are and Why

From George Marshall's speech at Harvard on June 5, 1947, until the first year of George Bush's presidency, 1989, there was really only one great news story—the story of a new world being formed out of the convulsions of World Wars I and II.

I find it helpful in understanding that story to remember what the world was like when I was born in 1905. Britain was the greatest power on earth. Her empire covered roughly a fourth of the earth's habitable surface—much of Africa, much of China and Southeast Asia, India, Australia, Canada, and scores of small footholds and islands. But there were other empires, all European. France, Spain, Portugal, Belgium, and Germany possessed and ruled substantial empires.

Except for the United States and much of Latin America the world at the beginning of this century was largely a European world. Most of it was owned and ruled from Europe. The only independent country in Africa was Ethiopia. The only independent countries in Asia were Japan, Thailand, and Tibet.

If the Europeans had managed to work together they might have continued to rule most of the world. But they did not work together. Rivalry between Britain and France dominated history from the Middle Ages through the Napoleonic era on to 1870. Then a new rivalry between Britain and Germany took over. World Wars I and II should rather be called the first and second German wars. They grew out of the rising power of the new Germany that was united for the first time in the industrial age by Bismarck at Versailles at the climax of the War of 1870. In the true sense those two German wars were civil wars, wars fought inside what once had been the Roman Empire and what would become in our times the new Europe of the European Economic Community.

The age of discovery had led to the world into which I was born. Once the Europeans had learned how to build ships that could cross the open oceans they soon discovered all of the world and took over all of it. Then, in the first half of this century Europe tore itself apart in those two dreadful, bitter, bloody European civil wars. That ended in 1945 with a new beginning for all the nations.

Looking back from today's vantage point we can see that what has happened between the Marshall speech at Harvard in 1947 and the last full year of the Reagan presidency, 1988, was not only one single story, now finished, but also a story inevitable in its nature, although not necessarily inevitable in its outcome.

We journalists who covered the story tended usually to present it in the same terms commonly used by the politicians—as a great struggle between two rival ideological systems, that is, communism versus capitalism. But that had little to do with it. What we have called the cold war was an inevitable result of the shape of the world at the end of World War II. Its conclusion in the great "love feast" of 1988 between Ronald Reagan and Mikhail Gorbachev was, just as inevitably, a result of the massively different shape of the world of 1988.

Try thinking of it in the following terms.

On the first of September 1939, when Germany invaded Poland and triggered World War II, there were two newly powerful expansionist states in the world, Germany and its ally Japan.

Both had ambitions at the expense of what lay between them. Hitler wanted to control all of Europe and also much of Russia. In his thinking Europe included everything from the English Channel to the Ural Mountains. Japan wanted control of East Asia on the one side and the islands of the Pacific Ocean on the other. Western Europe and its offspring, the United States, lay between those two expanding powers on one side. Russia lay between them on the other. A wartime alliance between Russia and the Anglo-Americans was imposed by circumstances. They had common enemies. Whether they liked it or not they were joined together in a common effort to frustrate German and Japanese expansion.

But in 1945 what had been the great and expanding German and Japanese empires had become power deserts. Add that Britain and France were exhausted. Two countries only, the United States and the USSR, emerged from the struggle with enhanced military power. For the first time in history there was no mountain range of power separating them. They themselves were mountain ranges of power with nothing in between to challenge or restrain either. They looked at each other and both were dismayed.

They also saw, lying between them on both sides, the fragments of what had once been the parts of the older European empires.

Europe's nineteenth-century colonial empires were a by-product of economic conditions. They melded the factories of Europe with the raw materials and markets of the colonies. They were valid and useful for both factory and colony so long as Europe held a monopoly on industrial progress. By 1945 the monopoly was gone. The nineteenth-century empires were obsolete. They fell apart, leaving the landscape between Moscow and Washington littered with ex-colonial fragments struggling with economic inadequacy and, often, with political incompetence. This is what we came to call the Third World. Each of the surviving and newly "great powers"—the United States and the USSR—watched to see how much of this Third World the other would try to draw into its economic, political, and military orbit.

That was the condition that converted the United States and the USSR into rivals and competitors. That was the cause of the cold war.

We are at the end of it now, but not because Ronald Reagan built more new airplanes than Mikhail Gorbachev could afford. We are at the end of it because the conditions that brought it into existence no longer exist. Look now at what has come to fill those deserts of power of 1945. If Americans look west they no longer see Stalin grabbing large chunks of China or Leonid Brezhnev trying to woo the Philippines. They see instead in Japan the world's most advanced and successful economic power and a China united and outpacing Russia in economic development. East Asia is no longer a power desert. It is filled by two rising powers, which, if they learn to cooperate, could easily become an economic and political giant.

Then look the other way. Between Moscow and Washington on the other side is the new Western Europe of Jean Monnet's dreams. It is 1992. There are no longer any national barriers (at least in theory) to the free movement of people, goods, and money among the members of the European Economic Community. Western Europe is one vast common market—the first market of the world in value of gross product, second only to China in number of consumers.

Mikhail Gorbachev's greatness lay in his ability to recognize correctly this new shape of the world. The world of two superpowers that begat the cold war belongs now to history along with the nineteenth-century colonial empires. The Soviet state was briefly one of only two superpowers in the world. It may well be the weakest of five superpowers in the world that lies ahead. It can hardly afford to enter that world in a state of hostility with the other four.

By Leonid Brezhnev's day the Soviet state had succeeded in isolating itself from most others. It literally had no friends. It had three well-paid clients: Cuba, Vietnam, and Mongolia. It had a small scattering of underpaid clients: Angola, Mozambique, Ethiopia, Nicaragua, and Afghanistan. But a stagnating economy was undermining its ability to satisfy the needs of even those few.

Mr. Gorbachev could not only grasp this condition. He could also recognize the steps that would have to be taken to rescue his country from sliding down into becoming the weakest and most friendless in a five-power world. He had to liquidate the expansionism that had frightened and alienated so many. And he had to grope his way out of economic stagnation. To do that he would need easy and relatively friendly relations with the most technically advanced parts of the world—Western Europe, North America, and Japan.

He started doing all those things a reasonable man, recognizing the shape of today's world, would know that he would have to do. He pulled out of Angola and Mozambique. He cut so far back on aid to Nicaragua that Daniel Ortega had to reopen relations with Washington. He pulled his troops out of Afghanistan and pushed the Vietnamese to start withdrawing their troops from Cambodia. Finally, and most important, he pulled back out of Europe. The Berlin Wall came down. The center of Europe was set free.

In short, Mikhail Gorbachev took his country out of the power expansion business. He did it because he was intelligent enough to realize that doing it is essential to the long-term welfare of his country.

And then there is the United States of America. What has it learned from the experiences of this remarkable century that lies behind us now? At the beginning of the century it was a regional power of the second rank. Today it stands revealed by the Gulf War as the only true superpower on the face of the earth. Only the United States could have projected to the far side of the world the military power that was sent to the Arabian peninsula in 1991, where it ejected a substantial and well-armed regional power, Iraq, from a local conquest, Kuwait. It was a brilliant achievement in power projection comparable in quality of performance to Douglas MacArthur's Inchon landing in 1950, to Israel's six-day war in 1967, and to Britain's recapture of the Falkland Islands in 1982. All four operations go down in military history as almost flawless exercises of the military art. But the scale was different. In terms of the amount of manpower, weaponry, and distances involved the American deployment to Arabia in 1991 was far larger—and halfway around the world. It was the action of a true superpower. Not even the Soviet Union at its peak could have done the same. In its decline it could not even overcome the guerrillas of Afghanistan next door. At the end of the century the United States is unique. Its physical power and its ability to use that physical power anywhere in the world has no equal. For anything comparable one must go back to Britain at the peak of the Victorian Empire.

But the century has retaught an old lesson. Power of this sort is transitory. It is an accident of history that the United States has achieved this pinnacle of military power at a time when its economic base is in relative decline. The American economy is still the richest in the world, but at the moment it is stationary while some others are growing. The fastest growing now is China. The fastest growing ten years from now may well be the European Community. Professor Paul Kennedy of Yale University has freshly explained to us in his *Rise and Fall of the Great Powers* an old truth, that military power is a by-product of economic health and strength. The military power the United States displayed in Arabia in 1991 was earned in the surge of the America economy from 1945 to the beginning of the Reagan administration in 1981. We were the world's greatest creditor from 1945 to 1980. We have been turned since into the world's biggest debtor.

No one can look ahead today and foresee with clarity what the world will be like fifty years from now any more than in 1900 one could foresee 1950 or 1990. The future relations of Japan and China are one of the uncertainties, perhaps the biggest of all. The new Europe is still in its birth pangs. It may produce the leading power of the next century. It may fall apart. How much future does the Soviet Union have?

My own guess, and it is only a guess, is that the rising economic giants will be Western Europe and China. Whether the United States can regain enough economic momentum to keep up with them will depend much on whether the next American generation can improve the quality of life in America, meaning a more prosperous, healthier, and safer environment for its people. In the twentieth century the United States mastered German, Japanese, and then Soviet military expansion. Can the United States in the twenty-first century master its own slums, its waste, and its crime?

I had several reasons for bowing out of daily journalism on the last day of December 1988. One of them was that I had written the end of the story of the cold war. It was finished. The world that caused it was gone. A new world lay ahead. Already the top stories in the news at the turn of the year were about the terms of trade between the United States and Japan and between the United States and the new Europe. Our last "cold warrior" president was heading for the setting sun. It seemed appropriate also to step aside and leave the chronicling of the world ahead to the next generation of those young enough to see it through. It may well be a long story.

Letter: Franklin D. Roosevelt to Myron Taylor

THE WHITE HOUSE
Washington
April 26 1938

My dear Mr. Taylor:

As you know, I have requested certain other governments to cooperate with this Government in the constitution of an International Committee for the purpose of facilitating the immigration of political refugees from Germany and Austria.

I have hoped that prompt and effective action by this Committee might relieve the distressing situation which has arisen as the result of the persecution of so many thousands of individuals in those two countries. I am glad to say that all of the American republics and Great Britain, France, Norway, Sweden, Denmark, the Netherlands, Holland, and Switzerland, have cordially agreed to cooperate in this endeavor.

As I see the problem, the task of the International Committee would be primarily to meet the emergency which has arisen, through the coordination of efforts on the part of the several governments involved in the humanitarian endeavor, and through the expenditure of funds received from private sources within the respective nations represented on the Committee to expedite and facilitate the immigration of refugees to those countries willing to receive them within the provisions of their existing legislation. The proper objectives of the International Committee would be to undertake the formulation of long range plans for the solution in years to come of the problem represented in those European countries where there exists excess populations.

I have designated an American Committee to cooperate with the International Committee, and this American Committee, I hope, will act as the intermediary between the International Committee and the many private organizations and individuals within the United States who are willing to extend effective assistance to these political refugees. I presume that many of the other countries represented on the International Committee will take similar action.

It has seemed to me that you could represent this Government admirably as the American member of the International Committee, and I hope very much that you will be willing to serve as the official representative of the United States on that body.

The representative of this Government will have the honorary rank of Ambassador Extraordinary and Plenipotentiary, and, in view of the fact that this Government has taken the initiative in suggesting the creation of the International Committee, it is probable that the other members of the Committee will select the United States representative as the chairman of that body. I can further assure you that the Government will give you the technical assistance that you may find necessary.

I feel that your acceptance of this position would do much to insure the successful achievement of the objectives which I had in mind when I sanctioned the creation of the International Committee, and in the furtherance of which I believe public opinion in this country is deeply interested.

Believe me,

Yours very sincerely,
(Sd) Franklin D. Roosevelt

Telegram: Cordell Hull to Myron Taylor

Department of State
Washington
January 14, 1939

AMEMBASSY

LONDON (ENGLAND)

STRICTLY CONFIDENTIAL PERSONAL FOR MYRON TAYLOR.

The President has asked me to transmit the following message of guidance from him to you:

QUOTE You may recall that my letter to you of June 14, 1938, expressed the view that the continuing Intergovernmental Committee should consider, as part of its long-range program, the possibilities of providing for the settlement in suitable areas of persons forced to emigrate from countries other than Germany because of their religious beliefs or racial origins.

QUOTE I fully appreciate the reasons which led the British and French Governments to oppose any development of that idea at Evian. Any action which might encourage other nations of Eastern Europe to apply pressure upon minority groups would not only be most undesirable in itself but might also jeopardize the specific efforts of the Committee to solve the German refugee problem. No one could be more anxious than I to avoid such a development. Were a suitable area available for the settlement of great numbers of people, however, the situation would be entirely different.

QUOTE The fact must be faced that there exists in Central and Eastern Europe a racial and religious group of some seven million persons for whom the economic and social future is exceedingly dark. While the Intergovernmental Committee has wisely treated the German refugee problem as being one of involuntary emigration regardless of race, creed or political belief, it must be frankly recognized that the larger Eastern

European problem is basically a Jewish problem. Acute as the German problem is, it is, I fear, only a precursor of what may be expected if the larger problem is not met before it reaches an acute stage, and indications are rapidly increasing that such a stage may be reached in the near future. The increasing seriousness of the problem may shortly make the political difficulties involved in finding a solution appear trivial in comparison.

QUOTE I do not believe that the migration of seven million persons from their present homes and their resettlement in other parts of the world is either possible or essential to a solution of the problem. I do believe that the organized emigration from Eastern Europe over a period of years of young persons at the age at which they enter actively into economic competition, and at which they may be expected to marry, is not beyond the bounds of possibility. The resultant decrease in economic pressure, the actual removal over a period of years of a very substantial number of persons, the decrease in the birthrate and the natural operation of the death rate among the remaining older portion of the population should reduce the problem to negligible proportions.

QUOTE It is estimated that such organized emigration would require the movement of perhaps 150,000 persons a year over a period of years. Such a movement of young persons of employable and marriageable age could not take place by means of infiltration, even if the legislation of the receiving countries permitted, without the danger of creating new anti-Semitism. The efforts of the Intergovernmental Committee to develop opportunities for mass settlement indicate the extreme difficulties of finding such opportunities of a nature remotely adequate to meet the need.

QUOTE I am convinced that the solution of the problem in Germany and throughout Eastern Europe requires the creation of a new Jewish homeland capable of absorbing substantially unlimited Jewish immigration. Even if the political difficulties could be overcome, it is doubtful whether Palestine could absorb and maintain the necessary influx of population, and consideration has accordingly been given to other possible parts of the world.

QUOTE It goes without saying that any part of the world in which the creation of such a homeland would be politically possible would be to a greater or lesser extent marginal in the economic sense. Many proposals have been made for large-scale colonization in areas such as Lower California, Madagascar, or the Guianas, but the possibilities of settlement in these areas do not appear sufficient to warrant the belief that the creation of a new Jewish homeland in any of them would be practicable.

QUOTE Of the less developed areas of the world, Africa appears to offer the greatest hope of future development and the satisfactory maintenance of a greatly increased population. Of the areas in Africa suitable for large-scale white colonization, Angola appears to offer by far the most favorable physical, climatic and economic opportunities.

QUOTE You may recall that creation of a Jewish homeland in Angola was actively considered in 1912 and 1913 and that a Jewish Coloniza-tion Bill concerning Angola was passed unanimously by the Portuguese Chamber of Deputies in 1912. The fact that nothing further came of the project is attributable to various causes, including lack of sufficient orga-nization and the outbreak of the World War, but it does not appear that any question as to the suitability of the area was involved.

QUOTE I believe that the actual problem of Jewish refugees from Ger-many and the threatened problem of involuntary Jewish emigration from other European countries requires an early and determined effort to cre-ate a supplemental homeland for that people. I should appreciate your opinion, after you have discussed the matter in the strictest confidence with Lord Winterton and the Prime Minister, as to the practicability of creating it in Angola along the following lines:

QUOTE Dr. Salazar has on various occasions stated that Portugal would never consider the transfer, by sale or otherwise, of any part of its colo-nial empire to any other Power. By the creation of a Jewish homeland in Angola, however, it would not become a part of any other colonial empire but rather an autonomous and perhaps eventually independent State. Portugal would not become the victim of the imperialism of any other Power but could, if it desired, make an immeasurable contribution to the cause of humanity and of European stability and peace.

QUOTE Portugal would naturally be entitled to just compensation for the area, which might take the form of a substantial initial payment by such Powers as might wish to contribute to this cause and additional annual payments over a period of years from the revenues of the new State. Portugal would retain sovereignty over the area until that period had elapsed. The revenue which Portugal would receive from such an undertaking would far exceed any revenue which it has yet received from Angola or which it might expect to receive at the present rate of develop-ment. The Portuguese Government could, in making a magnificent con-tribution to human welfare and world tranquillity, assure the increased revenue so sorely needed for the advancement of the people of Portugal and the development of their fatherland. Creation of a new Jewish homeland in Angola would undoubtedly increase both the prosperity of the present inhabitants of the colony and its trade with Portugal.

QUOTE The successful carrying out of such an undertaking would make Dr. Salazar one of the greatest figures in the history of his country and of our times.

QUOTE Naturally such an undertaking would require the most careful preparation and detailed planning. I have merely outlined my ideas to you in order that you may discuss them with Prime Minister Chamberlain and, if you and he share my views, with Dr. Salazar. Should you deem it advisable to discuss the matter with Dr. Salazar at this time, it occurs to me that you might proceed from England to Italy by boat after the forthcoming meeting of the Intergovernmental Committee, stopping off in Lisbon for the purpose.

QUOTE I cannot emphasize too strongly the importance which I attach to the creation of a supplemental Jewish homeland as a step essential to the solution of the Jewish problem or my belief that Angola offers the most favorable facilities for its creation.

UNQUOTE

Hull

Telegram: Robert Thomson Pell
to Cordell Hull

London
April 28, 1939

Secretary of State,
Washington
From Pell

One. I returned to London this morning after conferring in Berlin with Wohlthat, who wished to canvass the situation thoroughly because he has been invited to dine with Chancellor Hitler on Saturday and report on his conversations with the Intergovernmental Committee.

Two. On that occasion he will submit to the Chancellor the draft decrees setting up the central Jewish organization envisaged in point 7 of the "confidential memorandum" agreed upon with Mr. Rublee, and the draft decrees establishing the International trust. These decrees have been approved by all the Ministries and it is understood that if the Chancellor gives his approval, those setting up the central organization will be put into effect next week, while those setting up the trust will be held temporarily in abeyance until some definite action has been taken with regard to the outside private corporation.

Three. Wohlthat allowed me to read in strict confidence the decrees setting up the central organization. They are very complete. They give the Jews, as defined in point one of the "confidential memorandum" a definite legal status in Germany. They provide for the education of Jewish children and the practice of the Mosaic faith under the protection of the law. They provide machinery moreover for the re-training for purposes of emigration of 1000 young men and women at a time, with state aid. In short when the decrees are put into effect and if they are lived up to, the Jews will be given a wholly new standing in the Reich and Wohlthat gave me the most solemn assurances that Goering intends to see that the decrees are strictly enforced.

Four. Wohlthat was bitterly disappointed that I did not have something concrete to report with regard to the private corporation. I told him of the generally believed assurances of progress which I had received from Mr. Taylor, but he said that general assurances were of little value to him. He and Goering were placed in a most awkward position vis a vis the Chancellor. They had been saying since February that something was about to happen, and nothing concrete had happened, meanwhile those whose desire it was to destroy Jewish property in Germany had had their way. The total value of the property was decreasing daily, and those who scoffed at Goering's plans for solving the Jewish problems were beginning to say "I told you so." He hated to go to the Chancellor on Saturday with nothing concrete to report. I said that a very strenuous effort was being made to organize the corporation. Of that he could be absolutely assured. Frankly, a great deal of resistance had had to be overcome in the beginning. The point had now been reached however, I was convinced, where the necessary action would be taken without much further delay. Wohlthat said that in that event he would report that I had given definite assurances that positive action was being taken by private persons with regard to the corporation and that I would have something concrete to report shortly.

Five. It had been arranged that I should hand Wohlthat a letter, the text of which had been approved by Rothschild and Bearstead as well as by Winterton and Emerson, formally proposing Bruins as the third or foreign trustee and putting various questions with regard to his status and remuneration. I handed this letter to Wohlthat and suggested that it might be helpful to him in his conversation with the Chancellor as an indication that serious action was contemplated with regard to financing on the outside. Wohlthat agreed that the letter would be helpful and said that a reply would be made as soon as possible.

Six. Wohlthat then touched on various questions which had arisen in our recent conversations. With regard to the departure of ships from German ports carrying emigrants without visaes for receiving countries, he said that the Ministry of Communications had issued the most formal instructions opposing this practice and providing serious penalties for any one, shipowner or master or travel agent, who should be found guilty of aiding and abetting irregular departure. With regard to the position of Jews in the protectorates he said that the policy of the German Government, with which Von Neurath was in accord, was to discourage measures which would induce a competitive emigration of Jews. It was the intention of the German Government to give precedence to the Rublee plan. Regarding those persons who had permission to enter certain countries, notably the United Kingdom, but who had not been allowed to leave Germany, he said that if I would send him a list he would personally see to it that these cases were acted upon without further delay.

With regard to the point which I raised that German propaganda of an anti-Semitic character was hampering our efforts to place settlers in some countries, he said that he had obtained the most positive assurances from the Minister of Propaganda that if it were indicated by the Intergovernmental Committee that a country was disposed to receive Jewish settlers in substantial numbers stringent orders would be given to the effect that propaganda, if any existed, should cease.

Seven. In conclusion I extended in behalf of Winterton the invitation, which was approved by the British Foreign Office, to Wohlthat to come to London. We discussed the manner of his coming, and he suggested that he might make use of the Whaling Conference which would hold a meeting during the first week in June. He would attend as the German delegate and I might arrange a dinner where I could present him to Winterton, Emerson and others connected with the work of the Intergovernmental Committee. In any event the invitation would be of great value in his report to the Chancellor and he was exceedingly grateful for it.

Telegram: Robert Thomson Pell to Cordell Hull

London
May 18, 1939

Secretary of State,
Washington
Confidential from Pell

Winterton held a meeting this morning which Emerson, I and others attended with leaders of the Jewish community in Germany who said that they had been sent to London by the Gestapo. The burden of their message was that unless the Intergovernmental Committee took immediate steps to find openings, either in places of refuge or settlement, for substantial numbers of involuntary emigrants, and unless "world Jewry" set up the private corporation, the German authorities would return to the shock tactics which were so successful in ridding Germany of Jews in the past. The group from Berlin brought with them a document laying down how many Jews each member of the Intergovernmental Committee should take annually over a period of three years and begged Winterton to accept as the Committee's this or a similar plan and to place it in the hands of the German authorities at once if a further brutal attack on the Jewish community in Germany were to be prevented.

Winterton replied that certainly the British Government, and he was sure, the Committee, did not propose to have the German police dictate what it was and was not to do. The Committee had shown great liberality and patience in dealing with the German authorities. It was doing everything in its power to find places of refuge and settlement for refugees from Germany and he had reason to believe that the interested financial people who were setting up the private corporation were doing everything to arrange for financing this emigration. The Committee could not be asked to do the impossible. (END SECTION ONE)

250

(SECTION TWO)

There was a limit to the absorption of immigrants, whatever their race or religion, beyond which it was dangerous to go and it should be understood by the German authorities that the outside governments would not exceed this limit. The result of the shock tactics adopted by the German authorities in the past had been to render the Committee's task extremely difficult. A repetition of these tactics would have the result of making the Committee's task impossible. Doors everywhere would be firmly closed to this enforced emigration and no money would be forthcoming under the shadow of a threat.

Winterton then reminded the delegation that the German authorities had indicated an intention of doing a great many things such as retraining intending emigrants, setting up a central Jewish organization in Germany and so on and had done none of them. Many of the Governments participating in the Committee were restless. Despite this, however, he was not prepared as yet to doubt the good faith of the German authorities with whom we were dealing and was ready to proceed in this matter pari passu.

Israel who spoke for the Berlin group replied that there could be no doubt of the sincerity of Goering and Wohlthat in this matter but they were fighting a losing battle. He said that when Chancellor Hitler received Wohlthat recently to hear his report on the progress of the conversations the Chancellor let it be understood that he was not impressed and refused to allow Wohlthat to go ahead with the publication of his decrees until the Committee should have made a better showing.

The delegation was obviously distressed by the reception accorded it by Winterton but was somewhat consoled by the fact that Winterton asked Emerson and me to examine with them their plan. This we shall do tomorrow morning although we have made it plain that the United States is in no position to commit the participating governments to any plan of future action. (END MESSAGE)

Balfour Declaration

Foreign Office
November 2nd. 1917

Dear Lord Rothschild:

I have much pleasure in conveying to you, on behalf of His Majesty's Government, the following declaration of sympathy with Jewish Zionist aspirations which has been submitted to, and approved by, the Cabinet:

His Majesty's Government view with favor the establishment in Palestine of a national home for the Jewish people, and will use their best endeavors to facilitate the achievement of this object, it being clearly understood that nothing shall be done which may prejudice the civil and religious rights of existing non-Jewish communities in Palestine, or the rights and political status enjoyed by Jews in any other country.

I should be grateful if you would bring this declaration to the knowledge of the Zionist Federation.

Yours,
Arthur James Balfour

United Nations Security Council Resolution 242

22 November 1967

The Security Council,

Expressing its continuing concern with the grave situation in the Middle East,

Emphasizing the inadmissibility of the acquisition of territory by war and the need to work for a just and lasting peace in which every State in the area can live in security,

Emphasizing further that all Member States in their acceptance of the Charter of the United Nations have undertaken a commitment to act in accordance with Article 2 of the Charter,

1. *Affirms* that the fulfillment of Charter principles requires the establishment of a just and lasting peace in the Middle East which should include the application of both the following principles:

(i) Withdrawal of Israeli armed forces from territories occupied in the recent conflict;

(ii) Termination of all claims or states of belligerency and respect for and acknowledgement of the sovereignty, territorial integrity and political independence of every State in the area and their right to live in peace within secure and recognized boundaries free from threats or acts of force;

2. *Affirms further* the necessity

(a) For guaranteeing freedom of navigation through international waterways in the area;

(b) For achieving a just settlement of the refugee problem;

(c) For guaranteeing the territorial inviolability and political independence of every State in the area, through measures including the establishment of demilitarized zones;

3. *Requests* the Secretary General to designate a Special Representa-

tive to proceed to the Middle East to establish and maintain contacts with the States concerned in order to promote agreement and assist with efforts to achieve a peaceful and accepted settlement in accordance with the provisions and principles in this resolution;

4. *Requests* the Secretary General to report to the Security Council on the progress of the efforts of the Special Representative as soon as possible.

Adopted unanimously at the 1382nd meeting

Index

Blount, Anthony, 6, 62
Boehmer, Karl, 45
Boettiger, John, 18
Bohlen, Chip (Charles E.), 148, 150
Bonus marchers, 12–13
Borah, William, 18
Bradley, Omar, 111, 122, 156–57, 159
Brereton, Lewis H., 93–94
Brett, George H., 87–88
Brezhnev, Leonid, 236, 237
Britain: as great power (nineteenth
    century and early twentieth), xiv,
    xv, 234, 238; and steel production,
    xv; and Japanese invasion of
    Manchuria, 11, 21; and Hitler's
    peace plans, 37, 50–52, 58; and
    early World War II quiet, 46;
    Battle of Britain, 49, 52–54; U.S.
    aid to, 66, 68–70; JCH's affinity
    for, 68–69; and cross-Channel
    invasion, 106, 108; U.S. feelings
    toward, 114, 181–82; postwar
    conditions in, 131; end of Greece
    and Turkey aid from, 133, 135, 136;
    Tito aided by, 149, 153; and
    Communist China, 164; and Suez
    crisis, 174, 177–82; and Korean
    War, 182; and Indian Army, 198–
    99; and Palestine problem, 208,
    209; Falkland Islands recaptured
    by, 237
Broadcasting: from Berlin, 43–44;
    JCH in, 217–19, 220–26; and
    advent of TV, 219; influence of,
    219–20; and Halls of Congress,
    220–21; development of, 223;
    Yevtushenko interview, 224; and
    Huntley's conflict of interest, 225
Broz, Josip. See Tito
Buchenwald, 122. See also
    Concentration camps and
    death camps
Bulgaria: purge trial in, 153
Burdett, Winston, 230
Burgess, Guy, 6, 61–62

Burgholtzer, Frank, 219
Bush, George: and 1980
    campaign, 220
Butler, Smedley D., 114

Caccia, Sir Harold, 180–81, 183–84
Cambridge University: JCH at, x,
    3, 4–6
Campbell, Charles, 116–17
Camp David accords, 210, 214
Canaletto paintings: and
    reconstruction of Warsaw, 146
Carter, Jimmy, 214
Cavalry: and bonus marchers, 12, 13
Censorship: and Nazi government,
    41–42; at Pearl Harbor, 75; and
    stories from New Zealand, 83–85;
    and MacArthur-vs.-Australians
    debate, 99; and Washington
    press, 117
Chamberlain, Neville, ix, 27, 33, 37
Change: in twentieth century, xiii
Charge of the Light Brigade, 1
Chiang, Mme. (Mei-Ling
    Soong), 166
Chiang Kai-shek, 155–56, 164, 165,
    166, 170, 183
China: Japanese invasion of, 21, 22;
    Communist takeover of, 155–56,
    164, 183; and Soviet Union, 156,
    161, 162, 164, 168–69, 171, 172–73,
    190, 196–200; in Korean War, 157–
    63; U.S. policy toward, 164–66,
    167–68, 169–70; U.S. attachment
    to, 165–66; and Indochina
    conflict, 167; and Vietnam, 171;
    and Eastern Europe, 190, 200; and
    UN partition of Palestine, 209;
    growth of, 236, 238
China Lobby, 162, 166, 169–70
Chou En-lai, 159, 167, 178, 190, 200
Christian Science Monitor: JCH as
    reporter for, ix–x, 6–7, 8–9, 64,
    120, 218
Churchill, Winston: Hitler

excoriates, 50; and Atlantic Charter, 66; and strategy, 102, 106, 111, 118; and de Gaulle, 118; "iron curtain" speech of, 141; retirement of as prime minister, 177, 179; on U.S.-Britain relations, 181; funeral of, 193

Ciano, Count Galeazzo, 35

Civil War, U.S.: and Truman on staff organization, 110–11; opposition to, 112, 113–14

Clark, John, 185

Clark, Mark, 120

Clark, William, 184–86

Clayton, Will, 136

Clem, Rhoman E., 125

Cold war, 174, 182–83, 235; Noel and Herta Field in, 60–61; and iron curtain, 139, 144, 152–53; beginning of, 141; and Third World, 236; end of, 239

Colonial empires, 236

Cominform (Communist Information Bureau), 148, 155

Communism: repudiation of, 15, 143; and Noel and Herta Field, 60–61; and Guy Burgess, 61–62; and Lady X, 62; Soviets' spreading of, 139; in Czechoslovakia, 139, 147; in Yugoslavia, 143, 148–50, 153; and Poland, 146; "seamless cloak" of, 148, 153, 165, 168; roll-back of, 152–53; in Soviet-China alliance, 156; 1950s expansionism of, 183; Polish editor on, 196

Concentration camps and death camps, 42–43, 122–23, 204

Conservatism: Pickthorn on, 5–6

Coolidge, Harold James, 4

Coral Sea, battle of, 100, 101, 104

Corey, Ed, 151

Coulson, John, 174–75

Crimean War, 1–2

Cuba: as Soviet client, 169, 213, 237; and UN partition of Palestine, 209

Cuban missile crisis, 161, 201

Curtain Isn't Iron, The (Harsch), x, 152–53, 155

Curtin, John, 98, 100, 102

Czechoslovakia: Jews under Hitler in, 27; and communism, 139, 147; postwar condition of, 142–43; Communist takeover in, 146–47, 152, 155; purge trial in, 153

Dachau, 123. *See also* Concentration camps and death camps

Daladier, Edouard, 27

Darlan, Jean, 118

Death camps. *See* Concentration camps and death camps

Deir Yassin massacre, 209

Deland, Paul, 8, 64

Denmark: German invasion of, 47–48; German surrender in, 127

Desert Rats, 91

Deuel, Wally, 38, 56, 59

Deutschland (pocket battleship), 46

Dewey, Thomas E., 208, 219

Dido (British cruiser), 82

Diem, Ngo Dinh, 176

Dien Bien Phu, 167, 176

Doenitz, Karl, 126, 129–30

Dole, Robert: and 1988 campaign, 220

Domino theory, 172

Donovan, William J. ("Wild Bill"), 228, 229, 230–31, 232–33

Drake, Waldo, 72, 77, 78, 79–80

Dulles, Allan, 60, 63

Dulles, John Foster, 137–38, 167

Dutch East Indies: JCH in, 85, 87–90, 92, 96–97; independence movement in, 175–76, 177

Earhart, Amelia, 8

Early, Steve, 18

Galbraith, John Kenneth, 145
Garner, John, 13–14
Gaspee (British revenue cutter), 1
Gaulle, Charles de, 58, 118–19, 179
Geneva conference (Vietnam War),
176–77
George VI (king of England), 110
Georgetown, 19–20
Germany: in early twentieth
century, xiv; and steel
production, xv, 20; reunification
of, 2, 3; post–World War II
division of, 3; and Versailles
treaty, 20–21; Jews forced out of,
24–32; attitude toward Nazis in,
40, 41; concentration camps in,
42–43; early in World War II, 47,
58; Nazi "euthanasia" in, 59–60,
117; postwar contrasts of, 123;
postwar conditions in, 140–41;
Berlin airlift, 151–52; *The Rise and
Fall of the Third Reich* on, 223; and
World Wars, 234; expansionism
of, 235. *See also* Berlin; Hitler,
Adolf
Ghormley, Robert L., 104
Giraud, Henri H., 118–19
Goebbels, Joseph, 49
Goering, Hermann, 49–50
Goldberg, Arthur, 211
Gomulka, Wladyslaw, 153–54, 198
Gorbachev, Mikhail, 197, 235,
236–37
Gorday, Michael, 224
Gore-Booth, Sir Paul, 194
Gotwald, Klement, 147
Gould, Jack, 224
Graf Spee (pocket battleship), 46
Gratke, Charles, 34, 38, 57, 175–76
Great Depression, 8, 10; and
reporting jobs, 6; and media role,
11; and bonus march, 12–13; and
public works projects, 13, 14;
revolutionary conditions in, 14
Great Leap Forward, 198

Great-power states: in early
twentieth century, xiv
Greece: and Truman Doctrine, 132–
36, 140, 156; Soviet pressure on,
134, 183; and UN partition of
Palestine, 209; and George Polk
affair, 227–33
Greer (U.S. destroyer), 70
Grouse shooting: by JCH, 184–86
Gruson, Sidney, 141
Guadalcanal: American landings on,
104, 112
Guingand, Francis De, 127
Gulf War: and Arab-Israel peace
efforts, 211; and U.S. as
superpower, 237–38

Halsey, William ("Bull"), 78, 101, 111
Harcourt, Lord William, 175, 180,
183–84
Harsch, Anne (wife), 19, 64; at Pearl
Harbor, ix, 71–74; and Italy trip,
34, 35; on return voyage, 77; and
Lippmann visit, 188; visiting son
at school, 190; on Lippmann
collaboration, 195; in Sian, 196
Harsch, Jonathan (son), 65, 77,
189, 225
Harsch, Joseph C., ix–xi; and
Christian Science Monitor, ix–x,
6–7, 8–9, 64, 120, 218; childhood
memories, xiii–xiv, 1, 68–69; at
Cambridge, x, 3, 4–6; at
Williams, x, 3–4; on
intergovernmental refugee
committee, 24, 26, 202–3, 204;
Patterns of Conquest written, 64–65;
grouse shooting, 184–86; and
Protestant Succession, 226
JOURNALISTIC ASSIGNMENTS AND
STORIES: London Naval
Conference, ix, 20, 21, 23, 60; in
London (beginning of World
War II), ix, 33–34; in Berlin, ix,
39–45, 53, 54–56, 57, 58–59, 62–63;

Harsch, Joseph C. (*continued*)
at Pearl Harbor attack, ix–x, 71–
77; in Rome, 35–38; journeying in
Far Pacific, 78–91, 92, 96–97,
100–101; as MacArthur
messenger, 102–4; at World War II
end, 120–22, 124–25, 127–30; at
death camps, 122–23; in Eastern
Europe, 140, 141–44, 145–52, 190;
in London (postwar), 183–84,
187–95, 223–24; covering Arab-
Israeli conflict, 214–15; in
broadcasting, 217–19, 220–26;
end of daily journalism for, 239
Harsch, Paul (son), 189, 190
Harsch, William (son), 64–65, 71,
77, 189–90
Hartigan, John, 44, 69
Hasset, Bill, 18
Hearst, William Randolph, 14
Henderson, Loy, 206
Herzl, Theodor, 203
Hiss, Alger, 137
Hiss, Donald, 137
History: JCH's interest in, 1
Hitler, Adolf, 22; and Versailles
treaty, ix, 22; and German
grievances, 20–21; anti-Semitism
of, 24; peace overtures from, 37,
50–52; lack of popular confidence
in, 42; and continuation of war,
46–47, 58; at Reichstag triumph,
49–50; as orator, 52–53; and peace
possibilities, 58; hostile acts
against U.S. forbidden by, 65;
suicide of, 126
Hitler-Stalin pact, 36–37
Hobson, Valerie, 191
Ho Chi Minh, 167, 170, 171
Holocaust: and Jewish emigration
(pre–World War II), 25–32; and
concentration camps, 42–43; and
Wannsee conference, 43;
beginning of, 117; and Jewish

homeland problem, 204–5,
206, 216
Homma, Masaharu, 93
Hoover, Herbert: and Japan's
invasion of Manchuria, ix; and
endless prosperity, 6; and Great
Depression, 9; press conference
with, 10; and Wilmot Lewis, 11;
and 1932 election, 13; and Great
Depression, 14–15; at end of term,
16; report to on World War II, 44;
on conditions in postwar Europe,
134; and Fortress America
policy, 162
Hopkins, Harold B., 207
Howe, Quincy, 114, 115
Hull, Cordell, 243, 247, 250
Hungary: postwar condition of, 143;
under Communist control, 147–
48; purge trial in, 153; and
China, 190
Huntley, Chet, 224–25
Huss, Pierre, 45
Hussein, Saddam, 214, 218
Hutchins, Robert, 114

Ibn Saud (king of Saudi Arabia), 207
Ideology, 172; as false account, 235
Inchon landing, 157, 158, 161, 237
Indochina War of France, 167, 170–
71, 176–77. *See also*
Vietnam War
Industrial power, xiv–xv
Intergovernmental Committee on
Political Refugees, 28–30, 203–4,
241–44
Inverchapel, Lord, 133
Iran: Soviet pressure on, 183
Iron curtain, 139, 152–53; variety of
impacts of, 144
Islam: communism compared with,
139; and Israel-Arab relations,
201–2
Isolationism, 69, 114. *See also*

America First Committee;
Fortress America policy
Israel: population density of, 28; as
nuclear power, 218
Israel-Arab relations, 201; and Suez
crisis, 174, 177–81; and Jerusalem,
201–2, 212; wars and conquests,
209–10; and refugees, 210; and
Camp David accords, 210, 214;
and UN Resolution 242, 210–12,
246–47; and PLO, 211; and dream
of three-part community, 212–13;
and U.S. subsidization of Israel,
213; and Saddam Hussein's offer,
214; and Kiryat Arba settlement,
215; students' stories of, 215–16;
German treatment of Jews
compared to, 216
AND ESTABLISHMENT OF ISRAEL: and
1939 White Paper, 203, 205;
and Zionism, 203–4, 207; and
Holocaust, 204–5, 216; and
Balfour Declaration, 205; Jewish
immigration efforts, 205–6;
terrorism, 206; U.S. and British
positions on, 206–8; and UN
partition of Palestine, 208–9, 212;
state of Israel proclaimed, 209
Italy: Mussolini's plans for, 22; and
World War II beginning, 35–38, 46

Japan, 23; Manchuria conquered by,
ix, 10, 11, 21–23; and London
Naval Conference, ix, 20, 21, 23;
rise of in twentieth century, xiv;
as independent, xiv, 234; and steel
production, xv; "reversal of
alliances" by, 21, 23; U.S.
occupation of, 157; expansionism
of, 235; economic development
of, 236. *See also* World War II
Java: JCH in, 85, 87–90, 92, 96–97
Java Sea, battle of, 90, 99
Jennings, Peter, 228

Jerusalem, 201–2, 212
Jews: Nazis force out of Germany,
24–32; as enemies of Nazis, 42.
See also Holocaust; Israel;
Israel-Arab relations
Johnson, Hugh, 114
Johnson, Lyndon: and Vietnam
War, 23, 167, 177
Jones, Mary G., 231
Journalism: career in, 2. *See also*
Broadcasting; Press
Jovanovitch, Arso, 149
Joyce, William (Lord Haw-Haw), 44
Judd, Walter, 162, 166

Keeler, Christine, 191
Keeley, Edmund, 228
Kellis, James, 229–30, 231, 233
Kellogg, Frank B., 9
Kendrick, Alexander, 230
Kennan, George, 64, 148, 158, 200
Kennedy, John F., 14, 225, 226
Kennedy, Joseph P., 14, 34, 44, 69,
114, 162
Kennedy, Paul, 238
Kesselring, Albert, 125
Khrushchev, Nikita, 154, 171, 197,
198, 199
Kimmel, Husband E., x, 72–73, 119
King, Ernest J., 96, 101, 104, 105–6,
108–9, 111, 116
Kintner, Bob, 225
Kirchway, Freda, 221
Kirk, Alan, 33, 34, 50, 56, 65
Klang (Malayan ship), 89–90
Knickerbocker, Herbert Renfrew
("Red"), 78–82, 83–86, 87–89,
92, 99
Korean War, xiii, 156–63, 171; and
memory of Manchukuo Incident,
23; numbers killed in, 170; lessons
of, 171–72; and NATO, 182;
anxiety produced by, 183
Kostov, Traicho, 153

Roosevelt, Anna, 16, 18
Roosevelt, Eleanor, 17
Roosevelt, Franklin Delano: election of, 13, 15; at Warm Springs before inauguration, 16–18; and navy buildup, 20; and refugee problem, 26, 30, 203, 241–42; re-election of (1940), 55–56, 66; and buildup to World War II, 66, 70; and grand strategy, 111; and McCormick alliance, 115–16; and de Gaulle, 118; death of, 120–21; and Palestine issue, 207
Roosevelt, Theodore, Jr., 64
Rosenberg, Alfred, 127
Rothschild, Lord, 29, 31, 245
Royal Oak sinking, 46
Rublee, George, 26, 27, 29
Runstedt, Karl Gerd von, 124
Rusk, Dean: and Vietnam War, 23
Russia: in early twentieth century, xiv; British containment of, 21. *See also* Soviet Union

Sadat, Anwar, 214
St. Louis (German liner), 31
Salazar, Antonio, 30, 243–44
Salt, Dame Barbara, 193
Salvation Army: in Great Depression, 14
Samoa, JCH on, 80–81, 84
San Bernardino Straits, 104
Sarnoff, David, 189, 191–92, 223
Sarnoff, Mrs., 192
Saunders, Douglas, 116
Sayre, Francis B., 96
Schacht, Hjalmar, 27
Schoenbrun, David, 187
Shamir, Yitzhak, 211
Sharp, William F., 97
Shirer, William L., 41, 43, 56, 59, 217, 221–23
Shultz, Sigrid, 59
Sian, China: JCH visits, 196–97
Simon, Sir John, 10

Singapore: Japanese conquest of, 85, 88
Slansky, Rudolf, 153
Smith, Bromley, 218
Smith, Howard K., 189
Socialism: and JCH, 6; Pickthorn on, 5–6
Somersby, Kay, 121
Soong, Mei-Ling (Mme. Chiang), 166
Soviet Union: German invasion of, x, 55, 71, 112; as dominant between wars, xiv; and steel production, xv; U.S. recognition of, 18; as German supplier in World War II, 46–47; German preparations to invade, 51, 54–55; U.S. aid to, 66; and war against Japan, 110; and cross-Channel invasion, 118; and Yugoslavs, 123–24; postwar expansionism of, 134, 135, 139, 156, 237; communism repudiated in, 143; nuclear weapon developed by, 155, 183; and China, 156, 161, 162, 164, 168–69, 171, 172–73, 190, 196–200; and Korean War, 171; and Nasser, 178; and Suez crisis, 180; decline in power of, 199; at World War II end, 235; in world ahead, 236–37; and Afghan guerrillas, 238
Spanish civil war, 22
Speer, Albert, 129
Spens, Sir Will, 4
Sperber, A. M., 221
Staktopoulos, Gregory, 228, 229, 230, 232, 233
Stalin, Joseph: Hitler-Stalin pact, 36–37; as Hitler's supplier, 46–47; and German invasion of Soviet Union, 55; and Eastern Europe, 61; and Marshall Plan, 136; "guns not butter" speech of, 141; and Soviet-China alliance, 156. *See also* Soviet Union